The Other African Americans

The Other African Americans

Contemporary African and Caribbean Immigrants in the United States

Edited by
Yoku Shaw-Taylor and Steven A. Tuch

ROWMAN & LITTLEFIELD PUBLISHERS, INC.
Lanham • Boulder • New York • Toronto • Plymouth, UK

ROWMAN & LITTLEFIELD PUBLISHERS, INC.

Published in the United States of America
by Rowman & Littlefield Publishers, Inc.
A wholly owned subsidiary of The Rowman & Littlefield
Publishing Group, Inc.
4501 Forbes Boulevard, Suite 200, Lanham, Maryland 20706
www.rowmanlittlefield.com

Estover Road
Plymouth PL6 7PY
United Kingdom

British Library Cataloguing in Publication Information Available

Library of Congress Cataloging-in-Publication Data:

The other African Americans : contemporary African and Caribbean
immigrants in the United States / edited by Yoku Shaw-Taylor and Steven A.
Tuch.
    p. cm.
Includes bibliographical references and index.
ISBN-13: 978-0-7425-4087-3 (cloth : alk. paper)
ISBN-10: 0-7425-4087-1 (cloth : alk. paper)
ISBN-13: 978-0-7425-4088-0 (pbk. : alk. paper)
ISBN-10: 0-7425-4088-X (pbk. : alk. paper)
  1. Africans—United States—Social conditions. 2. Africans—United
States—Ethnic identity. 3. West Indian Americans—Social conditions. 4.
West Indian Americans—Ethnic identity. 5. African Americans—Social
conditions. 6. African Americans—Ethnic identity. 7. Immigrants—United
States—Social conditions. 8. Immigrants—United States—Ethnic identity.
9. United States—Race relations. 10. United States—Ethnic relations. I.
Shaw-Taylor, Yoku. II. Tuch, Steven A., 1949–
  E184.A24O84 2007
  305.896'073—dc22   2007003788

Printed in the United States of America

∞™ The paper used in this publication meets the minimum requirements of
American National Standard for Information Sciences—Permanence of
Paper for Printed Library Materials, ANSI/NISO Z39.48-1992.

Contents

Acknowledgments

The quality of an edited volume reflects, first and foremost, the quality of its contributing authors. We are deeply grateful to the scholars who contributed their work to this volume. We thank The George Washington University department of sociology and Bette J. Brinkerhoff for financing the preparation of the index, and Lorraine McCall for insights that improved the manuscript. We are grateful to our families—Elaine, Anaya, and Egjayba Shaw-Taylor and Sandra Hanson—for their support during the many hours we devoted to this project.

Donated by Spartans.4.Spartans (S.4.S)

S.4.S is a student organization that solicits for textbooks donations and makes them available to students through the MSU Library over subsequent semesters.

Get involved by:

- *Donating a textbook*
- *Joining the volunteer team*
- *Spreading the word – tell a friend!*

Contact us
Email:
spartans.4.spartans2017@gmail.com
Facebook: *Spartans4Spartans*
Tel: *+1 (517) 899 1261*

CHAPTER 1

The Intersection of Assimilation, Race, Presentation of Self, and Transnationalism in America

Yoku Shaw-Taylor

This volume is an inquiry into the similarities and differences between native African-American families (native black Americans), immigrant Caribbean families of African descent (Caribbean black Americans) and black African families (African black Americans), who have migrated to the United States in greater numbers since 1965. The studies in this volume look beyond the master status (Hughes 1945) of race or "blackness" in the United States and examine ethnic or intraracial characteristics among these black groups. The idea of ethnicity is not an obscure one; it signifies a sense of kinship, group solidarity, and shared culture that yields a common identity for a community of people (cf. Hutchinson and Smith 1996), while race definitions link physical features to the assumed superior or inferior cultural attributes of a social group (Feagin and Feagin 1999). In the United States, the concurrent focus on intraracial relations, inspired by growing migration patterns in the past twenty years, captures an enduring interest in examining so-called ethnic immigrant blacks in America. In his 1939 book *The Negro Immigrant,* Ira Reid observed that "the Negro group in the United States is not a distinct ethnic group which has maintained its original racial characteristics and social customs. Contacts with other racial and cultural groups have resulted in an increasing blend of diverse bloods [*sic*] and modification of customs. The background for such a study as this is furnished by one of the most universal American stereotypes 'all Negroes'" (25). Reid's book is the first comprehensive account of black immigration to the United States. Although his study revealed that the West Indies was significantly the highest supplier of immigrant blacks to the United States, he did not set out to study only West Indian blacks in the United States. And, whereas intraracial differences among blacks have not been as imperative as interracial relationships and racism between whites and blacks in U.S. society, increasing migration from the Caribbean and Africa since 1960s has brought intraracial relations into sharper study.

The short and obvious answer to the emergent questions about differences is that native African Americans, or black Americans, are descendents of black Africans brought to North America in the 1600s through the 1800s, who have become native to the United States. Black Caribbean immigrants are, in the main, non-Hispanic people who report their race as black and their ancestry or country of origin as the black islands of the Caribbean. Black Caribbean immigrant families are also descendents of Africans who were brought to the Caribbean Islands (or West Indies) in the 1600s through the 1800s.[1] Within the United States, black Hispanics from the Caribbean, by definition, fall within the overlap between racial identity and Spanish cultural affiliation compared with Caribbean black Americans whose cultural affiliation is Anglophonic. Although small in numbers and proportions, black Hispanics represent another obvious marker of intraracial variation in culture (or historical cultural domination) as these groups converge in the United States. Among people identifying themselves as Hispanic in the 2000 census, 2 percent (or approximately 710,400) were black or African American (see Grieco and Cassidy 2001).

Contemporary black African immigrants generally come from sub-Saharan Africa; this group excludes descendants of Europeans who settled in the southern part of the continent and Arabs who inhabit the northernmost section of the continent near the Mediterranean Sea. Sub-Saharan Africa includes all countries south of the Sahara desert, which separates the North from the rest of the continent. This includes thirty-two countries extending from the Indian Ocean in the east to the Atlantic Ocean in the west, including the islands of Cape Verde, the Seychelles, and Madagascar. Black Caribbean immigrants come from both the larger islands, known as the Greater Antilles, in the northern Caribbean Sea and the smaller islands, or Lesser Antilles, in the east of the Caribbean; these include Hispaniola or the Dominican Republic and Haiti, Jamaica, Trinidad and Tobago, Grenada, Barbados, Saint Lucia, Saint Vincent, Martinique, Dominica, Saint Christopher (Saint Kitts), Nevis, Saint Martin, Antigua, Anguilla, and Guadeloupe. Guyana and Suriname, on the northeastern coast of South America, are also represented among Caribbean immigrants. The Caribbean islands extend from the coast of Florida to the coast of South America, and most of them are English speaking, a characteristic they share with several sub-Saharan African countries. In America, while black Americans are found in all states, the majority of them live in twenty states (and the District of Columbia), including Alabama, Arkansas, California, Delaware, Florida, Georgia, Illinois, Louisiana, Maryland, Michigan, Mississippi, New Jersey, New York, North Carolina, Ohio, Pennsylvania, South Carolina, Tennessee, Texas, and Virginia. Most blacks also live in metropolitan areas (McKinnon 2001).

Native black Americans, Caribbean black Americans, and African black Americans share the legacy of external and internal colonial domination by the English and other European countries (cf. Blauner 1969), the legacy of the transatlantic trade in slavery, as well as the contestations of racial status in the United States. At the same time, among immigrant groups, particularly within the first-generation, there is considerable variation in linguistic, ethnic, and national identity, which may challenge any implied homogeneity based on the generalized "black" label imposed on all people showing traces of African descent in our American racial taxonomy.

CULTURE VERSUS STRUCTURE

The research agenda entailed bridging the ideas and thinking about the structure of migration of black Caribbean and African families to the United States and the historiography of their settlement in the United States, as well as that of native black Americans. The research agenda also entailed bridging ideas about the development and construction of ethnic identities and black existential thought—that is, how has the economic and cultural domination of blacks by whites in the past three hundred years or so uniquely shaped the existential experiences of Caribbean blacks, African blacks, and native black Americans (cf.

Okpewho, Davies, and Mazrui 2001; Appiah 1992; Mudimbe 1988; Gordon 2000)? Most importantly, the goal is to answer the following related questions: Beyond the ascribed status of race, to what extent are observable and perceived differences based on cultural factors? Do structural variables, such as selectivity of immigration and immigrant networks of support during settlement, explain variations among these groups? Can we identify an empirical intersection of culture and structure in terms of earnings and labor market involvement?

In her important research on Caribbean immigrants in America, Mary C. Waters (1999) has elaborated on the mutual stereotyping of Caribbean immigrants and native black Americans (cf. Reid 1939; Bryce-Laporte 1972; Foner 1987; Kasinitz 1992) and notes that what might be perceived as cultural differences in terms of work ethic, attitudes about education, and values may actually be structural effects based on the selectivity of immigration. Black immigrants who self-select to migrate may be characterized by higher levels of motivation to succeed (cf. Chiswick 1978, 1979; Butcher 1994), and when they settle in America, immigrant associations serve as social support systems (cf. Attah-Poku 1996). At the same time, discriminatory acts by the dominant group may suggest to Caribbean immigrants (and black immigrants in general, for that matter) that they are favored over native blacks. These preferences are captured by employers' recruitment practices based on a hierarchy of acceptable racial, gender, or other perceived traits that place employees in queues or ranking order (cf. Thurow 1968, 1975; Hodge 1973; Reskin and Roos 1990).

The stereotypical idea is that Caribbean black Americans, especially, are a model minority, that Caribbean Americans possess distinct attitudes and traditional values in relation to work and are therefore able to succeed in America despite the structural barriers of racial prejudice and discrimination (cf. Reid 1939; Glazer and Moynihan 1964; Sowell 1978, 1981). These notions, which black immigrants also hold as part of globalized stereotypes of native black Americans (Rodriguez 1995; Smith and Feagin 1995; Feagin and Feagin 1999), may reinforce a certain "otherness" for black immigrants.

In his careful study of the social mobility of Caribbean blacks, Winston James (2002) provides a sweeping discussion of the culture-versus-structure argument, and his conclusions undermine the so-called cultural superiority thesis as espoused by Thomas Sowell and others; James notes that Caribbean immigrants to America since the late 1890s and early 1900s have possessed, on average, more human capital (literacy, education, and occupational skills) on arrival. Particularly before 1965, "immigration to United States was the most selective of all Caribbean immigration streams" (James 2002, 226). Rubén Rumbaut (1997) observes that since the mid-1960s, the United States has admitted "over 2 million engineers, scientists, university professors, physicians, nurses and other professionals and executives" (20), that the proportion of highly educated professionals admitted was higher than the percentage of these professionals among the native-born population, and that the educational attainment of these immigrants generally surpasses the average educational status of the native-born American population. It may be improvident, therefore, to draw conclusions about cultural differences in reference to work ethic or values without a careful consideration of structural effects.

Indeed, the notion that native black Americans do not value education and work as highly as other groups is simply false. When Jennifer Hochschild (1995) analyzed data from the U.S. Department of Education, she concluded, "African Americans are no more likely to drop out of school than whites, are more likely to choose an academic than a vocational curriculum, and are more likely to choose a four-year than a two-year college" (160). Native black American attitudes about work do not vary significantly from the mainstream; Hochschild (1995) observes that "the level of wages below which poor blacks will not accept a job is almost as low as immigrants. . . . [J]obless young black men are much more willing than comparable white men to accept unskilled jobs at low wages" (161). Many poor blacks work now, and accumulated data on poverty and employment indicate that, given the chance, most would. These values of education and work are not relative to any one particular ethnic or racial group; they are universal cultural values that all communities hold in response to broadly similar societal problems (cf. Hess, Markson, and Stein 1992, 45). They are basic to all cultures based on universal needs. Ulf Hannerz (1992) writes instructively about "commonsense" processes in every culture that allow for communities to develop and survive; such commonsense processes of development and survival are cultural practices not unique to any one community.

In a pioneering article in 1972, Roy Bryce-Laporte, writing about black immigrants, anticipated the complexity of current intraracial relations when he contemplated the extent to which an ideology of "togetherness" can be forged in the face of "genuine individual, cultural or even finer ideological variation among blacks" (53). In a recent text, Parrillo (2000) observed that "although many non-blacks use negroid racial features as the basis of group classification, much cultural diversity exists among blacks in the United States. . . . [C]ultural differences make West Indian black immigrants unlike native-born blacks . . . [and] recent black immigrants from Africa are culturally distinct . . . [and] although many native-born U.S. blacks call themselves African Americans, a wide gulf separates them from the more recent African immigrants" (389). We do not know if the "wide" gulf Parrillo writes about is exaggerated, but the growing diversity and mutual stereotyping among the black population is not, and Darryl Fears (2002) documents this in his article in the *Washington Post* about the black foreign-born population in America.

How do cultural perceptions of immigrant blacks as model minorities, therefore, affect intraracial relationships? And, at what point during the assimilation and acculturation process do Caribbean blacks and African blacks either become overwhelmed by race relations or overcome race relations and racial casting, as native blacks have experienced, in pursuing their economic and social aspirations in American society?

BEFORE AND AFTER 1965

The increasing migration of Caribbean blacks to the United States since 1965 and of black Africans since the late 1970s and 1980s has engendered a growing discourse and literature in sociology on the contemporary experiences of these groups within America. Notably, the breadth of understanding and examination of black Caribbean experiences, identities, and expectations in the United States (cf., inter alia, Palmer 1990, 1995; Vickerman 1994, 1999; Waters 1990, 1996, 1999; Kasinitz 1992; Foner 1985, 1987, 2000; Hintzen 2001; Levine 1987; Sutton and Chaney 1987; Sutton 1992) contrasts with the invisibility of black African immigrants in the United States, who have immigrated in fewer numbers and whose settlement and residence in the United States is perhaps bounded by geographic distance. However, this cloak of invisibility is gradually beginning to lift (cf. Obiakor and Grant 2002; Arthur 2000; April Gordon 1998; Takougang 1995; Takyi 2002; Kposowa 2002; Apraku 1991; Dodoo 1997; Dodoo and Takyi 2002 Djamba 1999; Kamya 1997; Nwadiora 1996).

The significance of 1965 is that new immigration laws were enacted that changed U.S. immigration policy. For the first time, the ethnically restrictive immigration laws of the United States based on national origins were replaced by a quota system that established the basic structure of today's immigration law; at the same time, these immigration laws and policies encouraged naturalization and provided a preference for relatives of U.S. citizens over relatives of permanent residents. The Hart-Celler Immigration Act abolished the national-origins quota system (originally established in 1921 and modified in 1952) and established family reunification as the cornerstone of U.S. immigration policy. Under the new law, immediate relatives of immigrants (i.e., spouses, minor children, and parents of U.S. citizens over the age of twenty-one) were not counted as quota immigrants and were not counted as part of either the hemispheric or country ceiling. The new immigration reforms also removed country limits for Caribbean Island nations as they are part of the Western Hemisphere; Caribbean Island nations could also take advantage of 120,000 immigrant quota allowed to all countries in the hemisphere. Although in 1976 the law was amended to impose a limit of twenty thousand immigrants for nations in the hemisphere, the 1965 Hart-Celler Act had the effect of increasing immigration from the Caribbean Islands to the United States. The connection between the Hart-Cellar Act and civil rights legislation was no accident as previous immigration laws (in 1921, 1924, 1929, and 1952) were seen as clearly ethnically discriminatory or racist (Auerbach 1955; Bernard 1969; Keely 1980; Weeks 1986). In the previous fifty years, immigration laws restricted the immigration of non-European people. The U.S. Congress passed the first act in U.S. history imposing a limit on immigrants in 1921, which was amended in 1924 and 1929 to establish the national-origins quota system. The quota system assigned an immigrant quota of 3 percent from the country of birth of foreign-born persons resident in the United States. This meant, of course, that the countries of Europe were favored. Robert Warren (1980, 3) writes that the national-origins quota system assured that most of the immigrants after 1925 would be from Europe. In 1952, more restrictive immigration legislation (McCarran-Walter Act) was passed that retained the national-origins quota system and added a system of preferences based on occupation (Keely 1980).

The momentum of the civil rights movement and civil rights legislation gave impetus to the 1965 Hart-Cellar Act. The changes to immigration law were made in consonance with the trend toward eliminating legal racism in the United States as the civil rights movement gained traction.

After the 1965 immigration act, which was fully implemented in 1968, immigration from the Caribbean Islands surged (cf. Kasinitz 1992; Palmer 1995). Subsequent immigration reforms in 1986 and 1990 enabled contemporary immigration of blacks to America.

The 1986 Immigration Reform and Control Act (IRCA) and the Immigration Act of 1990 (which took full effect in 1993) also provided significant changes that have led to the increase of black immigration, especially from Africa and the Caribbean. IRCA provided amnesty to undocumented immigrants in America (cf. Bean, Edmonston, and Passel 1990), and the 1990 Act wrought major changes, including the introduction of the diversity visa program and increases in employment visas. The diversity program involved a "lottery" system for underrepresented countries in the immigration flow to America. These visas were developed to increase diversity in America and contained minimal eligibility requirements. The increase in technical and managerial professional immigrants from Africa was due, according to Arun Lobo (2001), to this diversity program because it provided quick passage for these Africans, who would not qualify for visas otherwise. This visa program has become one of the key ways for immigrant families from Africa to come to America. The diversity program has indeed yielded a strange scenario of developmental role reversals as a significant proportion of visa program immigrants (44–47 percent from Africa) are professional, managerial, and technical professionals who leave their countries of origin, where their services are most needed (especially those of physicians, nurses, and other health professionals), to come to America. The increase in allotments under this program was specifically designed to attract more professional immigrants, and this has been the effect with the flow from Africa. Of the African immigrants who came to America between 1990 and 1998, 28 percent were admitted under this visa scheme (Lobo 2001), and African presence will most likely increase because these immigrants are able to bring in their families (and extended families). Comparatively, the immigration from Africa is still proportionately small, and quite apart from the related impact on African countries, who are, for instance, subsidizing the economy of America through the export of professionals (Takyi 2002; Kposowa 2002), these immigrant flows from Africa to America hold unexamined questions in terms of the tug and the price of assimilation in America.

Between West Indian or Caribbean blacks and native black Americans, there has been a long history of continuous interaction extending back before 1965. During the colonial period and from the late 1700s to 1900s, Caribbean slaves were brought to South Carolina and New York; according to Philip Morgan (1998), 15 to 20 percent of slaves in South Carolina came from the Caribbean during the eighteenth century. The presence of Caribbean blacks in New York also dates back to the mid-1700s, at which time the majority of slaves imported to New York came from Jamaica, followed by Africa (Burrows and Wallace 1999). In the mid-1800s, there was a small, but growing, population of free Caribbean blacks in New England, and the population of black immigrants increased during this period (Horton 1993). The immigration of enslaved and free Haitians to Louisiana in the early 1800s after the Haitian revolution (and after the Louisiana Purchase in 1803) was notable for its impact on the Battle of New Orleans in 1814 (cf. Pamphile 2001). By the end of the eighteenth century, the majority of slaves in New York were from the Caribbean (Hodges 1999), and the importation of slaves from the Caribbean to North America surpassed that of slaves directly from Africa. From the early to mid-1900s, the restrictive immigration legislations of 1921, 1924, and 1929, as well as the Great Depression, curbed immigration flows from the Caribbean, but the migration to America from the Caribbean at this time was distinct because these Caribbean immigrants were comparatively literate, skilled professionals or white-collar workers (James 2002). The familiar ideas of the push-pull theory including economic dislocation and opportunity, do not fully account for the unremitting, if uneven, Caribbean immigration to America; these two geographic spheres were close, and the communication and transportation developments that took place in the 1900s (cf. Reimers 1985) facilitated greater contact between Caribbean blacks and native black Americans.

The propinquity of the Caribbean to North America fostered ties between the two spaces after the dreadful period of slavery, but the same cannot be said for ties between Africa and America or the Caribbean and Africa after the end of the slave trade. After the end of the trade in the 1870s, the voluntary migration of Africans to America was almost nonexistent, except from the Cape Verde Islands off the coast of Senegal. Marilyn Halter (1993) writes that between 1860 and 1940, about twenty thousand black immigrants from Cape Verde made their way to Massachusetts, which was by far the largest proportion of voluntary immigration from sub-Saharan Africa during the period. It is perhaps not surprising that voluntary immigration from sub-Saharan Africa was next to nonexistent immediately after the slave trade; sub-Saharan Africa was still reeling from the effects of the transatlantic trade. S. Daget (1989), writing in the *General History of Africa*, noted that the political and class structures of some of the African societies were overturned by the trade, and the trade also "bled the states that encouraged and subsidized it, . . . killed tens of thousands of whites and hundreds of thousands of blacks . . . [and] prevented the diversification of trade on the African coast" (64–65). At the same time, the emergence of the literate and educated black elite in West and South Africa and the agitation of some of the nascent nation-states for self-rule (e.g., the Fante Confederation, which drew up a constitution in 1874) rendered this tumultuous, immediate postslavery period a time that was not amenable to voluntary migration even if the immigration policies of America had allowed it (cf. Adu Boahen 1989). Walter Williams (1980) observes that in the late 1800s, the very few Africans who migrated to the United States after the abolition of slavery were mostly students who came to attend historically black colleges and universities, such as Lincoln, Fisk, Livingstone College (North Carolina), Central Tennessee College, Morris Brown College (Georgia), and Wilberforce. Williams catalogues sixty-eight Africans who came to the United States during this period to study, including J. E. K. Aggrey from Ghana, who became prominent in Pan-African thought and later influenced Kwame Nkrumah. Most of these Africans were sponsored by American missionaries with the aim of training black missionaries for Africa. These few Africans provided the first contacts between Africans and their freed kinfolk after slavery, and their interactions provided the first cultural encounters that linked these groups in their racial identity as blacks. "With no large African intelligentsia to establish substantial intercontinental communications . . . with no immigration from Africa, there were few opportunities for black people in the United States to have first-hand contacts with Africans" (Williams 1980, 228).

Clearly, whereas the recent black immigrants from Africa may be aptly termed *new African Americans* (Millman 1997, 172) or *new Americans* (Barone 2001), the same term cannot be applied to Caribbean immigrants because of their extensive migration patterns dating before 1965.

According to historical data from the *2003 Statistical Yearbook of the Immigration and Naturalization Service*, from 1891 to 1970, voluntary migration from Africa totaled 74,610, which is approximately 0.3 percent of overall immigration to America during the period, an insignificant pattern of movement. From 1971 to 2003, immigration from Africa totaled 805,564, approximately 3.3 percent of overall immigration to America; this was after the 1965 Hart-Celler Immigration Act took effect. These immigration numbers from Africa include flows from the Arab North and not just sub-Saharan Africa. Caribbean immigration (including Cuba) accounted for approximately 3.4 percent (997,468) of all immigration to America from 1891 to 1970 and 11.9 percent (2,936,697) of immigration to American from 1971 to 2003. Among black Caribbean immigrants, Jamaicans and Haitians dominate; among black African immigrants, there are more Nigerians, Ethiopians, and Ghanaians than immigrants from other black African countries. (Also, very small proportions of refugees are admitted to the United States; for instance, from 1990 to 2000, the proportion of African and Caribbean individuals admitted as refugees to the United States was less than 0.3 percent and 0.1 percent, respectively, of the total number of arriving refugees).

The experiences of immigrant blacks in America were affected by the great migrations of black Americans in the twentieth century from

1910 to 1940 and from 1940 to 1970, which greatly transformed black Americans into a largely urban population that lived outside the South. Over 1 million blacks left the South between 1910 and 1940 (cf. Marks 1989), and between 1940 and 1970, another 1.5 million were estimated to have moved North or West. Overall, approximately six million blacks left the South for northern or western States in the five decades following World War I. By 1970, the proportion of blacks in the South had declined from 90 percent to 53 percent due to outmigrations. These migrations were the greatest internal migration in American history, spurred by an unremitting racial divide between whites and blacks in the South, where a caste system had replaced slavery. Marks (1989) writes, in reference to the first wave of internal migration, that "the Great Migration represents a 'watershed' in the experience of blacks in the United States because it was the first mass movement out of the South, the beginning of significant industrial employment and the initial exercising of the rights of citizenship" (2).

Notably, the current proportions of black immigrants among the black American population are small; according to census data and immigration counts, there are 1.5 million blacks from the Caribbean and a little over six hundred thousand Africans from sub-Saharan Africa, representing approximately 4 percent and 2 percent, respectively, of the overall black population. This shows that, overwhelmingly, the vast majority of the black American population remains native to America (which, of course, includes generations of Caribbean families who have become natives since migrating here in the early 1900s). Regardless of their numbers, however, contemporary black immigrants, like other immigrants, meet head-on the force of assimilation in America.

ASSIMILATION IN AMERICA

Assimilation ideas and concepts have, since the early twentieth century, attempted to capture the nature of immigrant incorporation into, and adaptation to, American society. Assimilation ideas are also constant themes in the normative ideal that the immigrants will become American and embrace the generalized value system (Parsons 1982) or cultural philosophy of this country. Descriptively, assimilation ideas also depict a process of immigrant survival, success, and presentation of self (definition of self) in America. The relationship between assimilation and ethnic identification is a dynamic one because "today's ethnics are immigrants of the past and vice versa . . . [and] present immigrants are already forging tomorrow's ethnic identities" (Fernández Kelly and Schauffler 1996, 31). However, early ideas and concepts about assimilation were, for the most part, based on the immigrant flows from Europe, or what is now called the "old" immigration in comparison to the "new" immigration from Africa, Asia, and Latin America since 1965 (Bryce-Laporte 1980; Glazer 1992; Rumbaut and Portes 2001; Suárez-Orozco and Suárez-Orozco 2001; Bean and Stevens 2003; Alba and Nee 2003). The new immigration is also happening within a complex American milieu unlike that of the previous era; in the post–civil rights era, ideas of race, ethnicity, economic opportunity, and equality intersect in many different ways, making assimilation a more contingent prospect. In their *Introduction to the Science of Sociology* (1921), Robert Park and Ernest Burgess made a distinction between accommodation and assimilation, which they defined as "a process of interpenetration and fusion in which persons and groups acquire the memories, sentiments, and attitudes of other persons or groups, and by sharing their experience and history are incorporated with them in a common cultural life" (735). This process of fusion comes after social organization of relations among groups has been developed to "prevent or reduce conflict, to control competition, and to maintain a basis of security" (735).

In other writings, Park (1928) noted that the process of migration can be marginalizing because the migrant is "striving to live in two diverse cultural groups" (881). In *Race and Culture,* Park (1950) explicated his ideas about the race relations cycle, involving the processes of "contacts, competition, accommodation and eventual assimilation" (150). Whereas there may be racial barriers and constraints in the process of assimilation, the process of eventual assimilation is "progressive and irreversible" (151). The phase of initial competition to gain advantage among races leads to stable relationships based on accommodation among them, and in this process, group barriers gradually decline (cf. Alba and Nee 1997, 2003).

In 1945, W. Lloyd Warner and Leo Srole contributed to the discourse on assimilation with their book *The Social Systems of American Ethnic*

Groups, in which they set forth the factors that inhibit or enhance the assimilation of ethnic groups. They maintained that assimilation was moderated by the ascribed status of race or ethnicity, proposing that "when the combined cultural and biological traits are highly divergent from those of the host society the subordination of the group will be very great, their subsystem strong, the period of assimilation long, and the processes slow and usually painful" (Warner and Srole 1945, 286). Their emphasis on ethnicity and ascribed status as an important predictor of the level of assimilation and residential and occupational mobility was a direct statement and acknowledgment of the premium placed on Anglo conformity; their ranking of ethnic groups based on similarity or cultural acceptability to Anglo-Saxons corresponded to the assimilation period during which these groups become fully incorporated into American society (cf. Alba and Nee 2003, 3–4). Of note, too, in the assimilation discourse are the works of Child (1943) and Wirth (1956), who posited that native cultural traits, ethnic enclaves, or subcultures become sources of social and economic disadvantage to immigrants.

These early ideas and concepts about assimilation have stressed the tug of America's culture, a kind of one-sided process compelling immigrants to unlearn their ethnicity, and the ultimate absorption of immigrants into the American society dictated by "Eurocentric hegemony." In 1964, Milton Gordon expounded on these early themes of assimilation in his book *Assimilation in American Life*. Importantly, Gordon reviewed prior definitions of assimilation and acculturation (amalgamation, integration) and noted the overlap and ambiguities in the various conceptualizations of these terms. His presentation of a typology of assimilation pathways that tracks the process of adaptation for immigrants is therefore a detailed and informed evaluation of the nature of assimilation. Gordon's work was instructive because he proposed a unified framework of assimilation in his typology. In this framework, cultural or behavioral assimilation or acculturation is the first stage,[2] which involves the adoption of the cultural patterns of the host society. The other stages of the assimilation process involve structural assimilation, which entails entry of immigrants into the organizations, clubs, and cliques of the host society; marital assimilation, which involves large-scale intermarriage or amalgamation; and identificational assimilation, which requires the development of identities linked to the host society. During the stage of attitude receptional assimilation, immigrants experience an absence of prejudice and stereotyping, and when behavior receptional assimilation occurs, there is absence of discrimination. Civic assimilation, the final stage in this process, is when there is an absence of value or power conflict (Gordon 1964, 71). Gordon also proposed the three competing ideas of assimilation as Anglo-conformity, the melting pot, and cultural pluralism. Gordon argued that acculturation does not inevitably lead to the other stages and that structural assimilation is the "keystone of the arch of assimilation" (81), whereas Anglo-conformity is the "most prevalent ideology of assimilation in America throughout the nation's history" (89). Absorption into the core society is the outcome of these processes, with the concomitant disappearance of distinct ethnic characteristics or values. The trajectory of assimilation, as noted in 1965 by Vladimir Nahirny and Joshua Fishman (1996), was such that by the third-generation, immigrants' sense of their own ethnicity is on the wane: "the erosion of ethnicity and ethnic identity experienced by most (but not all) American ethnic groups takes place in the course of three generations. . . . Ethnic heritage, including the ethnic mother tongue, usually ceases to play any viable role in the life of the third generation" (266).

Antipathies and reactions to Park's ideas and Gordon's framework demonstrate the potency of these contributions. Reactions to these ideas about the processes of acculturation or structural assimilation extended the discourse at the same time that the new immigration law of 1965 was yielding new social realities that confirmed or undermined aspects of these themes. The work of Tamotsu Shibutani and Kian Kwan (1965), for instance, extended Park's idea of the race relations cycle by examining the process of ethnic stratification globally (Alba and Nee 1997). Extensions of Gordon's ideas have included the explication of the significance of secondary structural assimilation or integration into formal organizations, as distinct from primary structural assimilation or informal organizations, such as cliques and clubs (Burkey 1978; Hunt and Walker 1974; cf. Feagin and Feagin 1999, 38). This exegesis argues that the process of secondary structural assimilation or integration involves the deconstruction of ethnicity as a barrier to social mobility. Revisions to these early concepts and ideas have not radically altered the core ideas defining assimilation as they still stress the decline in ethnic identification. For instance, in their recent review of assimilation ideas, Richard Alba and Victor Nee (2003) reiterate the significance of the assimilation process in America and define it as "the decline of an ethnic distinction and its corollary cultural and social differences. Individuals' ethnic origins become less and less relevant in relation to the members of another ethnic group" (11; cf. Yinger 1981).

However, it is the work of Andrew Greeley (1976), based on data collected by the National Opinion Research Center at the University of Chicago and early ideas about cultural pluralism (or the existential claim to one's heritage), that directly challenged the idea of assimilation. Greeley's arguments about cultural heterogeneity among Americans were based on variations among white immigrant groups in terms of nationality (cultural pluralism) and religion (denominational pluralism). The progression toward homogeneity was based on assumptions that assimilation was irresistible. Arguing against the tide of assimilation, Greeley (1976) wrote, "The influences of the common school, the mass media, common political and social norms, and ethnic and religious intermarriage work toward the elimination of diversity in a society. Basic beliefs, socialization styles, personality characteristics, political participation, social attitudes, expectations of intimate role opposites, all tend toward a similarity that is differentiated only by social class. Social class is generally assumed to be a 'rational' basis for differentiation as opposed to differentiation based on religion and national origin, which are 'irrational.' Race was formerly an irrational focus for differentiation but is now rational" (293). Greeley proposed the alternate concept of ethnogenesis to describe the idea that "ethnic groups come into being in the United States and have a 'natural history'" (297). Greeley's contribution is significant because it provides a reference for current studies on multiculturalism, cultural diversity, and the historiography of groups as they settle in America. These ideas underscore the interactive nature of acculturation and the persistence of ethnicity, which the early ideas of assimilation do not account for. The need to study the unique heritage of ethnic groups and their processes of settlement in America, "free of the dogmatic assumption that their destiny is obliteration" (297), is as important as studying the processes that lead to structural assimilation. Despite Greeley's concept of ethnogenesis and its significance for studying groups in their own right, the pressures of assimilation within the American milieu remain palpable; this is because assimilation "has involved groups with very different characteristics at the time of immigration and varied histories in the United States, [suggesting] that the forces promoting it have been, and perhaps still are, deeply embedded in American society" (Alba and Nee 1997, 842).

In their masterful review of the "canon" of assimilation theories, Alba and Nee (1997) reinforce the significance of assimilation concepts and their enduring relevance to new immigration trends, noting that as a "state-imposed normative program aimed at eradicating minority cultures, assimilation has been justifiably repudiated. But as a social process that occurs spontaneously and often unintendedly in the course of interaction between majority and minority groups, assimilation remains a key concept for the study of intergroup relations (827)." The work of Alba and Nee (1997, 2003) captures key strains of thinking influenced by the early concepts of Park, Warner and Srole, and Gordon. They review the concepts of straight-line assimilation, which assume that assimilation is a generational progression of stages of adaptation, and antipathies to these concepts, which argue that ethnicity can be recreated (Lieberson 1973; Glazer and Moynihan 1964; Yancey, Ericksen, and Juliani 1976); they also review reconceptualizations of acculturation to capture the dynamic exchange between the cultures of ethnic immigrants and the core society that may facilitate or obstruct assimilation. As the argument goes, assimilation will facilitate status attainment and eventually endow minority ethnic immigrants with attributes such as education, occupation, and income that will resemble those of majority groups (cf. Neidert and Farley 1985).

The shift in focus from the "old" European migrations to the "new" migrations from Africa, Asia, and Latin America has nevertheless yielded anomalies in the reading of assimilation concepts (Zhou 1997). Notably, the processes of assimilation as expounded in the "canon," or early, ideas may vary and not take a "straight-line" trajectory due to the fact that the new immigration involves ethnic groups who are phenotypically different and tend to concentrate in urban areas. As such, the processes of incorporation may involve not a progression of social or residential mobility but diminution in social attainment, and acculturation will not go hand in hand with structural assimilation. Herbert Gans

(1992, 173–74), for instance, argues that the second-generation of the new ethnic immigrants may actually experience a decline in social status due to lack of educational successes and the effects of a changing economy; he writes that the "pathology and crime of today's urban poor is associated with second-generation decline on the part of young blacks and Hispanics whose parents came to the cities a generation or longer ago and who are unable or unwilling to work in immigrant jobs but are excluded, for skill or other reasons, from better jobs" (174).

Alejandro Portes and Min Zhou (1993) review the literature on post-1965 immigration and offer informed variations on new assimilation trends as they affect the second-generation. Their idea of "segmented assimilation" describes how today's immigrants encounter different social contexts that make it difficult for them to follow the path of advancement of earlier immigrants in America: these social contexts are color (race), location (urban areas, inner cities), and the unavailability of "mobility ladders." The effect of color is obviously the problematic of prejudice and stigma that may be attached to "blackness," for instance (cf. American Sociological Association 2003). The concentration of the new immigrants in cities (as opposed to sub- or ex-urban areas) means that these immigrants are unable to escape the vulnerability of growing up in areas where income levels are comparatively low and exposure to marginalized native youths is high. Second-generation immigrant youths may become socialized in these subcultures, and this increases their social distance from other groups who are not economically and socially disadvantaged. The phenomenon of ethnic concentration or ethnic enclaves (Portes and Manning 1986; Portes 1989), which has facilitated upward mobility for immigrants, does not hold the same advantages for black immigrants and their second-generation progeny in inner-city neighborhoods. At the same time, the new economy, with its emphasis on specialized training, may make it more difficult to advance, so that "assimilation may not be into mainstream values and expectations but into the adversarial stance of impoverished groups confined to the bottom of the new economic hourglass" (Portes and Zhou 1993, 85).

A consistent fact in the readings on the variations and revisions in assimilation ideas is that black immigrants must also confront the structure of racialized social systems in America, which provide rules for judging attributes of blacks and justify the practice of racism based on racial ideas (Bonilla-Silva 1996). Zhou (1997), for instance, writes about the intersection between socioeconomic class and "color" for immigrant blacks and discusses the "obvious effect of race, implying a severe class handicap associated with skin colors" (988). Zhou maintains that "racial status influences the social adaptation of immigrant children in ways closely connected to family socioeconomic status" (988). In his review of the research directions and propositions that reacted to the core assumptions of assimilation, Charles Hirschman (1983) argued that the intersection of ethnicity and socioeconomic differentiation within the assimilationist framework has changed, observing that whereas "ethnicity is now a symbol of cultural and political differentiation . . . for some minorities, especially blacks and Puerto Ricans, most of the barriers to achievement are still in place" (415).

In a conclusive reckoning, the process of assimilation, of becoming American through social and cultural routines or acculturation, does not constitute a kind of "cultural suicide" (Millman 1997, 172). In contemporary America, typically, this assimilation process is an interactive one (DeWind and Kasinitz 1997), wherein reaffirmation of ethnicity or cultural identity becomes part of the process of social incorporation into America (cf. Portes and Rumbaut 1996). But this interactive process is not a simple one for black immigrants, especially those from Africa. For these black immigrants, who are coming relatively late into America's complex, and sometimes not so nuanced, interracial (white versus black) and intraracial (native American black versus Caribbean black) social relations dynamic, the process of transition to Americanness also involves quickly coming to terms with managing and presenting the ethnic self in reaction to the master status of race. Indeed, it may be said that becoming race conscious, or "racialized," is a part of the process of assimilation for black immigrants in America. In his arguments for the structure of the racial state, Eduardo Bonilla-Silva (1996, 475) notes that racialized social systems are not based merely on racial ideas but on relative autonomous practices that pervade social encounters and reinforce a certain "rational" basis for the different interests and behaviors of different races.

At the same time, the ethos of assimilation, of becoming American, of an ecumenical America with a universal culture (Patterson 1994) that transcends historically racialized structures and multicultural anxieties and imparts a new ethnicity in its wake, is a powerful one. The evolution of Orlando Patterson's (1994) ecumenical America "is a complex process of selection and universalization of particular cultural forms and styles generating its great cultural innovations" (115). Anyhow, for black immigrants who are not used to presenting self strictly in terms of their phenotype, becoming American also means becoming aware of the racial basis of self in this society.

THE PRESENTATION OF THE ETHNIC SELF

The comparative literature on settlement experiences in America unveils the salience of ethnic identity, or the presentation of self (Goffman 1959), in an American society where the master status (Hughes 1945) of race can be blind to the diversity among blacks. In his original work on the dilemmas of status ascriptions in American society, Everett Hughes (1945) illustrated the power of the ascribed social position that defined black Americans: "membership in the Negro race, as defined in American mores and/or law, may be called a master status-determining trait. It tends to overpower, in most crucial situations, any other characteristics which might run counter to it" (357). Thus, regardless of the professional or social standing or occupation of the black American, "the dilemma, for those whites who meet such a person, is that of having to choose whether to treat him as a Negro or as a member of his profession" (357). Ellis Cose (1992, 210), in his review of the evolution of the American ethos, observes that when the first Congress of the United States limited naturalization to only so-called whites, they set the tone for the fixation on, and the centrality of race, racial purity, and identity in the politics and populating of America. American racial thinking, rigid in its designation of "blackness," and ascription of racial status fabricates a certain level of racial consciousness for all who cross its shores. Reid (1939), in his seminal work on black immigration remarked that "Africans, black, is the cover-all term employed by the Bureau of Immigration and Naturalization to cloak with racial identification all persons of Negro extraction admitted to or departing from the United States" (24). And, the historical dynamic of racial identity in

America means that there is more flexibility in choosing ethnic or racial identity for white descendants of Europeans than for descendants of Africans, who are confined to being labeled as "black" (cf. Kasinitz 1992, 5). The study of ethnic identities among black Americans is therefore an examination of each person's ethnic presentation of self against the master determining trait, or status, of race, the imposition of racial identity (Feagin 2001), and the superstructure of racial attitudes about black Americans (cf. Tuch and Martin 1997). An overarching theme, then, is the extent to which the master status of race, or "blackness," and its historical baggage define ethnic identity and affect presentation of self in America.

Blacks in America and the Caribbean shared the historical experience of the plantation slavery system and the social construction of blackness in the 1800s just as slavery was ending. But among Caribbean blacks, native black Americans, and African blacks, sociodemography yielded different ideas about "blackness" after slavery.

The historical legacy of slavery in America and the Caribbean created a heightened sense of racial consciousness that blacks in Africa were generally unfamiliar with. Peter Ekeh (1999), for instance, notes, "In black America, there is an absence of ethnic consciousness; instead, there is an exaggerated form of race consciousness that includes other African Americans and indeed blacks everywhere in shared sentiments. That is to say, whereas Africans on the African continent lack conception of race in their behaviors, African Americans' folkways are suffused in race consciousness. Interactions between Africans and African Americans have sometimes been brittle because of these differing patterns of primordial consciousness" (89). Kwame Appiah (1992) writes, "What race meant to the new Africans affectively, was not on the whole, what it meant to educated blacks in the New World. For many African Americans, raised in a segregated American society and exposed to the crudest forms of discrimination, social intercourse with white people was painful and uneasy" (6). Few of the many Africans, on the other hand, "seem to have been committed to ideas of racial separation or to doctrines of racial hatred. Since they came from cultures where black people were in the majority and where lives continued to be largely controlled by indigenous moral and cognitive conceptions, they had no reason to believe they were inferior" (6).

Race consciousness also involves a certain attention to shades of blackness and skin tone (Russell, Wilson, and Hall 1992), a recognition among blacks, especially in the Caribbean and the United States, of the color of being or complexions ranging from very light to dark brown that become part of the self (i.e., self-esteem and perception of attractiveness) (Hill 2002). This notion of colorism, or the social stigmatization of dark skin and physical traits associated with African ancestry, especially for women (cf. Thompson and Keith 2001; Hill 2000), is a corollary of race consciousness. In parts of the Caribbean (e.g., Haiti and Dominican Republic), this recognition is preserved in the labels attached to gradations of skin color.

European colonial domination in Africa and the concomitant slave trade yielded cultural philosophies based on different existential experiences for black Americans, Caribbean blacks, and African blacks; the divide was palpable. At the turn of the twentieth century, the idea of race and its social construction held different meanings for these groups. For native black Americans, suffering under the yoke of a racist social structure in America and struggling to hold white America accountable to its ideals of equality, the perception of Africa was determined by the Euro-American cultural philosophy of racial superiority. If anything, the idea of Africa, for black Americans, provided some kind of "subconscious psychological surety" (Okpewho 2001, xv) that allowed them to summon values of humanity from their folklore and lives as slaves and ex-slaves, values these black Americans found completely lacking in the wicked system of American racism and segregation. It is no accident that blacks in America and the Caribbean were the first to begin articulating the consciousness of racial identity. The presence of "Africanisms," or African cultural traits, may have been moderated by the propinquity of the dominant culture (cf. Herskovits 1958), but "Africanness" was perhaps an onerous heritage, and the surety it gave to black Americans was mixed. Stripped of their culture and devalued as human beings, the ex-slaves in America and the Caribbean in the early to mid-1800s used the prism of Christianity and received Western thinking to explicate their "blackness," or the idea of Africa. This process yielded a certain level of estrangement or marginalization for these thinkers in a world that completely devalued their black race. Christianity, after all, was used as justification to enslave the "pagan" indigenes of Africa, and the generalized idea of Africa in Europe was one of "inferior" cultures (cf. Harris 1992, 113). Alexander Crummell (1819–1898), the black American, Episcopalian priest, and, later, citizen of Liberia who, together with Edward Blyden, is credited with laying the foundation for the idea of Pan-Africanism and African nationalism, did not entirely hold the Negro race in high esteem.

In *The Souls of Black People*, W. E. B. DuBois (1903) writes about Crummell's despair and his labor to rescue his black race, whose "fatal weaknesses were the dearth of strong moral character and unbending righteousness" (180). Phyllis Wheatley (1753–1784), the poet who was transported from Senegal and became native to America, articulated the angst of racial consciousness in her poem "On Being Brought from Africa to America," which describes a certain ambivalence and shame, born of her Christian schooling in America, for her place of birth. The story is told of Philip Quaque, the African (born of Fantes in Cape Coast, Gold Coast, now Ghana) who spent some twelve years in England in the 1750s to become an Anglican minister. Upon returning to Cape Coast, he had completely forgotten his Fante language and was so estranged and marginalized by his Africanness that he declared the culture of his people to be "detestable." Elliott Skinner (1999) reckons that "Quaque had been psycho-culturally estranged by the hegemonic paradigm of his day and denigrated himself and his culture" (30).

Edward Blyden (1832–1912), a black Caribbean, who later became a citizen of the nations of free black people in Liberia and Sierra Leone, was an early Pan-Africanist, but he believed in the "civilizing mission" of the Europeans and could not transcend the racist thinking that suggested that blacks were inferior to whites. Appiah (1992; cf. Lynch 1967, 80) surmises that in the mid to late 1800s, Crummell and Blyden, arguably the key progenitors and thinkers of Pan-Africanist, black ethnocentric ideas, and the black personality, "inherited a set of conceptual blinders that made them unable to see virtue in Africa, even though they needed Africa, above all else, as a source of validation. Since they conceived of the African in racial terms, their low opinion of Africa was not easily distinguished from a low opinion of the Negro" (5). Such was the burden of being black. Within the framework of Christianity and received Western wisdom and thinking, the identity of "blackness" was problematic. Native American blacks, Caribbean blacks, and African blacks all shared a powerful cultural "imperative" based on the ideology of racism—which defined and still defines the social space of "blackness."

Among these three groups, however, the obvious differences in historical experiences regarding racial identity and the master status of race have engendered distinct forms of ethnic or racial consciousness and identities among them. At the same time, although native black Americans, Caribbean blacks, and African blacks may indeed be multi-ethnic or multiracial and descended from many peoples, their experience of race is the history of African people in America. (Among the black American population, approximately 5 percent, or 1.8 million, reported another race in addition to black in 2000 according to the U.S. Census Bureau; these include black Hispanics [see McKinnon 2001]). And even though individuals in these black groups may choose ethnic identities to suit group cultural attributes (such as black American or African American for native-born Americans or Haitian American, Jamaican American, or Nigerian American for recent immigrants), their presentation of self is bounded by the master status of their race.

In Africa, the legacy of Blyden and Crummell yielded a certain ideal of self, conceptualized as "negritude." Aimé Césaire (cf. Davis 1997) and Léopold S. Senghor (cf. Hymans 1971; Valliant 1990) were to promote this spirit of racial identity based on a restatement of an African worldview, or "racial psyche." It was also a vision of restoring and glorifying the attributes of that distinct worldview. The idea of negritude was meant to be antithetical, in a dialectic sort of way, to the notion of white racial superiority. And, in many respects, negritude became a powerful paradigm, or program, that attenuated African marginality, or the marginality of "blackness." Yet, Wole Soyinka (1976) has argued that negritude did not help the African or those of African descent: "Negritude trapped itself in what was primarily a defensive role, even though its accents were strident, its syntax hyperbolic and its strategy aggressive. It accepted one of the most commonplace blasphemies of racism, that the black man has nothing between his ears, and proceeded to subvert the power of poetry to glorify this fabricated justification of European cultural domination" (129). The idea of Africa as a milieu of ritual, myth, and drama derives from a metaphysical community of Africa south of the Sahara that does not need to be reconstructed, according to Soyinka. The endogeny of Africa, or even the sociocultural idea of Africa, assumed a certain spiritual solidarity among the ethnic nations south of the Sahara generated by centuries of social, symbolic, and substantive interaction through commerce and politics, long before the white men landed on the shores of the western, eastern, and southern coasts. Whether or not this solidarity is a recent invention, and whether or not negritude was a useful devise (Mudimbe 1988), these ideas were later to inform Afrocentric ideas (Asante 1987, 1988; cf. Gilroy 1993; Wright 2004), as well as Nkrumah's Pan-Africanist program and other movements, which relied on the core notions of a proto–Pan Africanism and claimed ancient Egypt as a definitive African civilization[3] (cf. Diop 1987, 1992).

The role of the African consciousness movement was perhaps a transitory one, which was grounded in that endogeny of Africa and its sociohistorical traditions—an antithetical moment in the racial dialectic that was to culminate in a cause for liberation. At the time of independence, the African thinkers and leaders were equipped with an ideology and a consciousness that was going to emancipate blacks. The attempt to redeem "blackness" was informed by a shared cultural history and a shared history of colonialism. The black or African world was spiritually and culturally homogenous. This monolithic black community may have been mythic, but it became a symbolic and reliable point of reference. Whether or not this black or African world was a product of the racial discourse, and whether or not the African identity was a "product of a European gaze," the fact is that the idea of Africa, or Africa itself, became a powerful theme for the redemption of blackness (cf. Fanon 1968, 1970).

In the Caribbean and the United States, the endogeny and awareness of an African identity was characterized by a certain ambivalence toward Africa; Eurocentric normative values were dominant at the same time that a syncretic evolution of the reconfigured "black" culture was underway. DuBois (1903, 5) wrote perceptively about this when he described the native black American's "double consciousness" and attempts to define self in America. Maureen Warner-Lewis (1999) observes that, in the Caribbean, "blackness" was embedded in an ethnic community "that resisted reciprocity and symbiosis with the African historical and cultural connections" (20)—this, even though Caribbean thinking about blackness had been prominent in the Pan-African project, especially in the work of people like George Padmore, Marcus Garvey, and C. L. R. James, for instance.

When Haiti declared its independence from France on January 1, 1804, it became the most powerful symbol of the redeemed black person because it represented the world's first emancipation of black slaves (cf. Pamphile 2001). Although Haitian independence may have been a Pyrrhic victory (Stepick 1987), ushering in a period of economic disintegration for the country, the idea of the first black republic in the Western Hemisphere was a powerful one. In America, the native black American quest for freedom and self-determination found validation in the heritage of the free black nation in Haiti—Leon Pamphile (2001) writes that "by overcoming the contradictions of the American Revolution and extending freedom to all, the Haitian Revolution created a new vista for African Americans . . . and fulfilled man's universal aspiration to be free by including people of African descent" (11). The establishment of the free nations of Liberia and Sierra Leone were important events in the redemptive process, and later, the independence of the black nations in sub-Saharan Africa and the Caribbean in the late 1950s and 1960s served to intensify the restorative program. The choice of identity (of being black) and the presentation of self need not be onerous, the script goes. But, the basis of self for blacks was an array and layering of identities within larger black ethnic communities attempting to reconfigure and redetermine "blackness" based on existential experiences of historical legacies in the Caribbean, Africa, and, finally, the United States. In America, the strands of Black Nationalism and black consciousness culminated in a manifesto of ideas and actions that promoted "self-love, self-defense, and self-determination, [which viewed] white supremacy as the definitive systemic constraint on black cultural, political, and economic development" (Gates and West 1996, 73).

The choice of ethnicity (cf. Waters 1990, 1999; Hintzen 2001) in the American milieu is therefore made within the broad context of adopting social identities suffused with historical baggage, which becomes, perhaps, one of the most important ascriptive designations for the native black American and the black immigrant. For some native black Americans, self-identification of mixed heritage, or layered pedigree (American Indian ancestry for example), becomes part of the presentation of self (cf. Frazier 1957). For all blacks, race or ethnicity is not, and does not, become merely symbolic or expressive (Gans 1979); it is also instrumental. The significance of race may have declined in the economic sector and been replaced by economic class differentiation (Wilson 1980), but in interactive episodes that take place in public places or "regions in the community freely accessible to members of that community" (Goffman 1963b, 9), the master status of race continues to be significant. The cumulative effects of lived experiences of discrimination (or the perception of it) and of racial hostility in social encounters at restaurants, hotels, motels, and other public places, as well as the outlook on life these experiences foster, mean that ethnicity for blacks, whether immigrant or native to America, is instrumental (Feagin 1991; Feagin and Sikes 1994); it affects everyday lived experiences in particular sites. There is a continuing process of cultivating self-image and affirming group worth.

In his expansive, influential, and original contributions to the study of the self in society, Erving Goffman provides ideas about how the adoption of social identities becomes part of the public order in society. In 1959, Goffman noted in his microstudies that, in general, we are all, as human beings, interested in presenting ourselves based on the conception of ourselves, and we seek the same from others (their attitudes, socioeconomic status) as we attempt to define the social situations in which we find ourselves. This is important because we are interested in calling forth certain desired responses based on the presentation of ourselves. Every definition of the situation and our collective representations of self enable us to cohesively express ourselves. The presentation of self is most significant in the interaction process where the dialogue is negotiated between one's attempt at presenting a certain self (a proud black person) and the disruptive identification framework that traps one's self (e.g., master status of race). Goffman (1959) suggests that "life may not be much of a gamble, but interaction is" (243). The presentation of self trapped in the master status of race and the negotiation of self based on a choice of ethnicity (e.g., Caribbean American, West Indian, Nigerian American) is a dynamic that, for most blacks, must be an unremitting process of defining and negotiating social situations in America. "Since the reality that the individual is concerned with is unperceivable at the moment [in the social interaction], appearances must be relied upon in its stead. And paradoxically, the more the individual is concerned with the reality that is not available to perception, the more must he concentrate his attention on appearances" (249). For blacks, however, reliance on appearances means that they are trapped in the social identity that needs to be negotiated because it is anchored in the host society's negative ideas about the black person.

Bonnie Leadbeater and Niobe Way (1996) catalogued the processes of immigrant self presentation among urban girls, and Waters (1999), in her extensive studies of Caribbean blacks, has noted that upon arrival in America, "the immigrant must decide how he or she self-identifies," and the people in the host society must decide how "they will categorize or identify the immigrant. The social identities the immigrants adopt or are assigned can have enormous consequences for individuals" (44). These processes, based on the microinteractions of daily life, feed the structures of stratification and domination in society. Randall Collins (1990, 72) notes, for instance, that the patterns of antagonism and domination (racism), on one hand, and the patterns of group solidarity (e.g., race), on the other, are based on the interactive rituals that motivate groups differently; the motivation to present one's self in a particular encounter will reinforce the racialized structure of domination and stereotype while creating a sense of solidarity among groups about their "otherness." In Africa, structures of domination and stratification were not tied to race or color, and in the Caribbean, the evolution of social hierarchies gradually discounted the significance of race because of the black majority. In the United States, however, these systems of domination and stratification were fully racialized.

Milton Vickerman (1999, 126) writes, for instance, about West Indian black immigrants encountering racism in America and constructing a common identity with native African Americans based on blackness. Goffman (1971, 238) noted that these social encounters or interactions might involve "dissociated vigilance" for individuals who may constantly monitor their social surroundings for disruptions. Special attentiveness is required in presenting one's self and in defining social situations where one cannot fully control or take for granted the ascriptions attached to him- or herself. This realization of the need for attentiveness in social situations demonstrates that there is always a level of alertness as we present ourselves as blacks when we are among members of the dominant group. This does not mean that blacks are at liberty to choose any identity they want—their racial options are limited and distinctly defined, and the ethnic labels they choose are secondary to their racial marker (cf. Waters 1999, 47). The production of racial or ethnic identity is done, therefore, in consideration of the advantages or disadvantages of being "other" (than merely "black") in defining the social situation.

In *Stigma: Notes on the Management of Spoiled Identity*, Goffman (1963a) writes that blackness, or race, "equally contaminates all members of a family" (4), and the presentation of an identity of the self is perilous when there are outward blemishes and features that undermine other attributes and claims we may have on the social encounter. Goffman's ideas about spoiled identity help us understand how structures of domination and stratification become manifest in the interaction order, how blacks may pay a price for interactional existence by presenting spoiled identities. The spoiled identity of self is particularly problematic in the face-to-face domain of interactions (Goffman 1983) because the stigma associated with blackness permits discrimination (cf. Bonilla-Silva 1996). As Goffman (1963a) argues, the stigma theory explains assumed imperfections and allows imputation, without hesitancy, of undesired attributes. While Goffman's influential ideas about the self display, in sharp relief, the burden of maintaining black identities in the United States, where a rigid racial caste system was once operational, the production of black ethnicity in contemporary times has been influenced by the changing normative superstructure of race relations in this country.

In a sense, the production and presentation of self is never a settled social phenomenon, and at the situational level, encounters may reflect a changing normative structure. There is an unremitting process of change in cultural definitions of identities, and for blacks, this has been a long process of coming to terms with the social construction of race and the black self (cf. Omi and Winant 1986; Omi 2001; Lee 1993). Thus, protestations of race status in the social encounter become what Goffman (1961) calls "role distance," or a process where blacks actively attempt to separate themselves from their putative stereotyped disposition in a racialized society or to refute their "virtual" blackness as they define themselves in the social encounter. In presentation of the black self, the choice and maintenance of personal identity become a social narrative of the options, costs, and opportunity of racial status in the United States. At the same time, among native blacks in the United States, differences in complexion have been part of the social construction of identities and have historically created "the aristocracy of color among black people" (Blackwell 1975, 282). These distinctions, forged by variations in complexion, created the first lines of class stratification among native black Americans (cf. Frazier 1957, 20; Herskovits 1958, 134; Landry 1987, 23; Hughes and Hertel 1990). The production and presentation of the black self in the United States becomes an experience in understanding the biography of identity.

During the 2004 senatorial campaign in Illinois, Alan Keyes, the Republic candidate, claimed that he was the "real" African American, not Barack Obama, the Democratic candidate, because Obama's father was African and his mother was white. The not-so-subtle suggestion was that native-born U.S. blacks with a cultural history of subordination in the United States had a greater claim to the label *African American* than other groups. John McWhorter (2004), a fellow at the Manhattan Institute, wrote in the *Los Angeles Times* about his preference for the term *black American* because he shares little in common with current immigrants from Africa: they speak English as a second language, their cuisine is nothing like Southern black cooking, their musical traditions are unlike jazz and ragtime, and their ways of dressing are different from those of native-born black Americans. Native-born black Americans, according to this thinking, must celebrate their triumphant historical heritage in the United States and not emphasize a legacy of bondage insinuated by the African prefix in a label depicting their ethnic identity.

Among African and Caribbean black Americans, identification of self as "other" may not be an option for third-and fourth-generation descendants of immigrants as they become culturally assimilated and shed their immigrant characteristics (cf. Gordon 1964; Hirschman 1983; Lieberson and Waters 1988). Yet, the adoption of an identity of "otherness" for the first- and second-generations may depend on the concurrent effects of assimilation and whether becoming American is facilitated or hindered by cultural or economic resources, or both, within the receiving communities (Portes and Zhou 1993; Portes and Rumbaut 2001). "Otherness" may as well be more profound to the extent that immigrant families, regardless of the recency of migration, sustain multiple relations between their place of origin or birth and their place of residence in the United States. This process of trans- nationalism (Basch, Glick Schiller and Blanc 1994; Levitt and Waters 2002), whether instrumental or expressive (Gans 1979), becomes part of the process of self-identification.

THE TRANSNATIONAL PERSPECTIVE

The process of transnationalism and the extension of family and social networks beyond just the United States is part of the transformative process for black immigrants; Kofi Apraku (1991) and John Arthur (2000), for instance, report that the majority of black African immi- grants in their respective surveys indicated that they had plans of re- turning and resettling in Africa. Vickerman (2002) writes about the de- velopment of transnational consciousness among second-generation Caribbean immigrants through contact with their parents' birthplaces and maintenance of family and social relations in these countries. This process of transnational migration, or forging and maintaining "multi- stranded social relations that link together societies of origin and set- tlement" (Basch, Glick Schiller and Blanc 1994, 7), is an involved one. The connections developed across cultures "enable individuals to sus- tain multiple identities and loyalties and create new cultural products" (Levitt and Waters 2002, 6). And perhaps for black immigrants, the likelihood of maintaining such multiple identities and loyalties may be heightened because of race and racial discrimination (Apraku 1991; Kasinitz 1992; Waters 1999; Arthur 2000; Foner 2000). The study of transnational migration, which focuses on the reorganization of immi- grants' lives and the emergent social, economic, and political outcomes in both the countries of origin and settlement, is distinguished from state or governmental activities relating to citizenship rights and from global nonstate or nongovernmental organizations and corporations that involve transnational or international economic relations or social movements (Levitt, DeWind, and Vertovec 2003; Levitt and Waters 2002, 7–8; cf. Kearney 1995, 548).

Transnational migration is a process that immigrants have under- taken in one form or another since the turn of the twentieth century;

these activities have involved sending remittances and maintaining social links with kin, for instance (cf. Glick Schiller 1999). As an emergent contemporary process, it is concurrent with the general pattern of
global linkages across nations and has become an important aspect of
current black immigrant experiences in the American milieu; it is a
process facilitated and sustained by modern technology, such as cheap
airline tickets, the Internet, cell phones, faxes, and videotapes (cf.
Foner 2000). Analysis of survey data from the New Immigrant Study
supports the contemporary pattern of transnationalism. Douglas
Massey and Nolan Malone (2002, 499) reveal that the majority of contemporary immigrants have had at least five to eight years of experience living in the United States by the time they become legal residents
and have taken extensive trips to and from their places of birth before
and after legalization in a kind of "circular migration" pattern.

Whereas racial consciousness, the perils of presentation of self, and
the process of assimilation into a racialized American society become
part of the overall black American narrative, regardless of black immigrant origins or American nativity, transnational experiences are not
meaningful to native black Americans. Assimilation into American society introduces blacks to a heightened racial consciousness; settlement
experiences are shaped by mutual stereotyping among blacks and
among the so-called races as they pursue opportunity in America; and
for blacks, the development and the presentation of the self kindle attitudes about multilayered identities at the same time that these identities
unwrap a shared African heritage. However, the idea of "social, economic and political connectedness across national borders and cultures" (Levitt and Waters 2002, 6) for native black Americans cannot
be enabling because any connectedness to a country of origin is fictive.
Among blacks in America, the children of the small proportion of
immigrants from the Caribbean and Africa (and arguably from elsewhere) may show a tendency to preserve a certain cross-cultural link
based on the origin of their parents, grandparents, or great grandparents, and even Euro-Americans who consider themselves now native to
this land may be able to trace cultural and ethnic links and lines of pedigree. For native black Americans, though, it does not make sense to talk
about the existence of transnational connections beyond the acceptance
of African heritage and the maintenance and sustenance of a certain affirmation of race (cf. Afrocentrism; Asante 1987, 1988).

Intraracial comparisons seem to stop at the doorstep of transnationalism—or do they? For native black Americans, the celebration of their existential experiences and triumphs in America (e.g., Black History Month), the liberating ideology of religion, and the creation of black American traditions (Kwanza) became part of the unique cultural identities that define them as American. The general ambivalence toward Africa may also be matched by a certain distrust of America. For native black Americans, constructions of cultural or ethnic connectedness cannot cross national borders or span the country of origin and country of settlement; the separation happened too long ago to attempt this. For black immigrants from the Caribbean, living transnationally in America is defined by connection to kinship in their countries of origin or their ethnic or national territory. Caribbean immigrants become transmigrants as they maintain economic, social, or political links with their homes of origin. For black African immigrants, living transnationally is defined by connection to kinship in their nations of origin, as well as their ethnic group (cf. Ekeh 1999). For Caribbean immigrants, the emergence of pidgin, patios, and Creole in their home countries also defines their ethnicity and culture beyond the mere existence of their national territory or country of origin; without original African languages, the creation and emergence of "creolized" languages, developed in the societies of the new world but of "old" world origins, became part of national cultures and identities in the Caribbean (Taylor 1971). Philip Kasinitz (1992, 3) observes that the term *Afro Creole Caribbean* is also used to refer to immigrants from the Caribbean based exactly on the intersection of Old World and New World. In the English-speaking Caribbean or West Indies, pidgin English developed as a dialect based on standard English, and Creole evolved into a so-called regular language based on French with its own distinctive sound, grammar, and vocabulary in Haiti. Forms of pidgin, patios, or Creole English exist in West Africa as well.

Kinship ties for most native black Americans do not cut across transnational borders, and the English dialect, Ebonics, created by black Americans has been associated with the working class and eschewed by middle-class blacks[4] (Rickford 1997); the evolution of the native black middle class involved education to "speak English correctly and thus avoid the ungrammatical speech and dialect of the Negro masses" (Frazier 1957, 77). When compared to those of black immigrants, the constructions of family and social networks for native black Americans have evolved along nonlinguistic and nonterritorial (cross-national) lines. Since the 1970s, the primarily return migrations of native black Americans to the South have served as a way to maintain kinship ties and social networks. Migration to the South from the Northeast, Midwest, and West represents a reversal of the exodus of blacks from the South during the great migrations in the early and mid-1900s. Migration southward is, for some black Americans, a way of maintaining transregional and intergenerational connectedness to their homeplaces—places where they were born and grew up, places that have become centers of familial history and where family, extended family, and friends live. These "homeplaces in the South offer alternatives to northern urban centers for working and raising a family and relatives and friends provide economic assistance, child care and moral support" (Cromartie and Stack 1989, 302). During the late 1960s and early 1970s, an estimated 171,176 blacks migrated to the South, and between 1975 and 1985, another 438,760 blacks migrated to the South (McHugh 1987; cf. Farley and Allen 1987, 117).

During the 1990s, migration to the South increased markedly from the Northeast, Midwest, and West; between 1990 and 1996, an estimated 368,800 native black Americans of all ages and education levels migrated to the South, settling in Texas, Georgia, Florida, Virginia, and North Carolina (Frey 1998). The pattern has continued through to the new millennium as an estimated 680,131 blacks migrated to the South between 1995 and 2000 (Frey 2000). William Frey reports that the migration to the South between 1995 and 2000 has completed the "full-scale long-term reversal" of the black exodus in the early to mid-1900s, and the overall reverse migration has demonstrated that blacks are more likely than whites to select destinations in the South (Frey 2000, 3–6). While the rates of migrations are smaller compared to the great migrations in the early and mid-1900s, these patterns reveal an overall net gain in the number of blacks migrating to, and living in, the South. These migrations have coincided with the dismantling of Jim Crow laws, the gradual improvement in interracial relations, and the economic resurgence in the South; at the same time, migration to the South follows similar settlement patterns recorded during the great migrations to the North, as black families settle predominantly in urban and nonurban areas where their kin live and work. The large numbers of Southern-born black Americans who live outside the region and the strong ties to the South still maintained by blacks in the West and North suggest that the patterns of migration to the South will continue within well-defined channels that tie native black Americans in the West and North to specific destinations in the South. Carol Stack (1996) notes that the migration back to the South is not purely based on financial considerations: "the resolve to return home is not primarily an economic decision but rather a powerful blend of motives" (xv).

The construction and maintenance of kinship ties and extended social networks across regions in America distinguish native black Americans from immigrant blacks. But the maintenance of such kinship and familial ties and connections does not extend beyond America. Transnational migration and for black immigrants in America extends familial and social ties to land and language groups outside America. These distinctions, based on how familial and social relations are linked among blacks in America, demonstrate that even with the absence of any connection to ethnic group or national territory outside America or any connection to an ethnic language other than American English, native black Americans construct familial ties and extend social networks all across America.

The singular consciousness of race as a form of primordial identity for all blacks in America may engender greater transmigrant activities among black immigrants in America in the form of sustaining links with the Caribbean or Africa, and for native black Americans, the return migration to the South is part of a transformative process that sustains their social networks within America.

STRUCTURE AND CONTENT OF THE BOOK

To place this study in context, I have attempted to outline core themes that run through the literature on these groups. We attempt to bridge, in this book, these sets of literature and, thereby, develop a greater understanding of how these groups are constructing black America.

In chapter 2, John Logan provides a description of these groups to set the background for knowing their relative sizes, their social and economic characteristics, and where they live. The profiles Logan presents are nonstatic, so we can undoubtedly expect that the census counts will change. Among the highlights of Logan's profiles is the fact that the immigration of Caribbean and African blacks is growing. But there is a degree of social distance in terms of residential patterns among these groups, especially in the metropolitan areas. Logan's chapter responds to the basic descriptive and definitional questions about these groups and summarizes what is known demographically about blacks in America.

Lewis Gordon's chapter leads us through his stream of thinking on the subject of racial-ethnic consciousness as he responds to the episteme of race and ethnicity in America in chapter 3. His approach is epistemological, but the theme of the chapter is an enduring sociological one; it has to do with the heterogeneous nature of contemporary identities in America—the creolized black community in America. This has been described by Patterson (1994) as "cosmopolitan creolization" that yields new cultural forms based on Afro-Caribbean, Haitian, Afro-Latin, African American, and Anglo-American influences. However, within this ecumenical black community, the configurations of identity and self constitute a dynamic that has not resolved.

To the social and demographic descriptions provided by Logan, Gordon adds an overview of the cultural history of racial and ethnic identity. Together, these two chapters provide the background for discussing the groups under study. Chapters 4 to 9 provide analysis of group experiences, as well as group similarities and differences.

Harriett Pipes McAdoo, Sinead Younge, and Solomon Getahun identify gaps in the research on marriage and socialization, especially for the heterogeneous African immigrant group in chapter 4. They note the centrality of religion in Caribbean and native black families and the pressure felt by the children of Caribbean immigrants to maintain a certain ethnic or cultural identity in America. The review by McAdoo, Younge, and Getahun reveals that among native black Americans and Caribbean families, marriage prospects are strained.

The study of family characteristics of these groups is challenged, first, by the lack of primary data and, second, by family patterns that are being formed through the blending of family structures and values in America yet to be studied.

The review of earnings, wealth, and social capital in chapter 5 by Yoku Shaw-Taylor and Steven Tuch reveals gaps in intraracial data on wealth and traces a history of research studies on earnings differentials among the three groups, which was perhaps spurred by the contention of a Caribbean advantage in work ethic. The preponderance of results, according to this review, discounts this advantage. While noting how social capital facilitates the differential maintenance of resources, Shaw-Taylor and Tuch's review is challenged by the unavailability of data on the economic behavior of native black Americans compared with Caribbean black Americans and African black Americans.

Yanick St. Jean extracts data from her larger study to compare black American and Haitian American Catholics. St. Jean's original analysis in chapter 6 sifts through attributes of ethnicity and language preferences for these two groups. For both black and Haitian Americans, familiarity with their culture is imperative for a priest to be accepted. For both groups within the Catholic faith, there seems to be an absence of race consciousness in their preference for priests. Faith may indeed transcend race or color as St. Jean's data seem to suggest, but between these two groups, faith may not necessarily hide ethnic or cultural distinctions.

Ana Liberato and Joe Feagin depict the tension between the racial taxonomy in America and self-identification for first- and second-generation Dominican Americans in chapter 7. Dominican Americans constitute a remarkable case study of a people whose social construction of identity is based on a heterogeneous, or mixed, heritage that clearly deemphasizes "blackness" or their African origins. The accounts of the respondents in the study focus on the management of identities. For these Hispanic blacks, their accents and Hispanic cultural heritage became markers of "otherness" in social interactions, separating them from native black Americans or African Americans.

As did Yanick St. Jean in chapter 6, Regine Jackson in chapter 8 extracts data from her larger study of social distancing among blacks in Boston to show how native and immigrant blacks (Haitian Americans) are removing and shifting ethnic boundaries through intermarriage. Jackson's analysis directly contradicts the tableau of intraracial tension (depicted by social scientists and journalists alike) and demonstrates that these couplings recreate black ethnic identities in America.

Hugo Kamya focuses on the stress of immigration in chapter 9 and examines how acculturation processes may affect the mental health of African immigrants. Kamya's review of African immigrants' means of coping is not based on original data and does not include a comparison group, but it highlights historical and contemporary writings on the adjustments to immigration. As Kamya suggests, primary data on African immigrants will enhance our knowledge of how African immigrants, from a range of contexts, respond to adaptation and acculturation pressures.

In the appendix, we present selected data from the first ever survey of immigrant experiences in America collected in 2003–2004. These bivariate categorical data for African and Caribbean immigrants add to the ideas, questions, and suggestions presented in this volume for future research.

A NOTE ON TERMINOLOGY

Several terms are used to describe the groups under study in this volume. In this chapter, I have referred to African Americans as native black Americans to distinguish them from contemporary immigrants from the Caribbean and Africa, who are referred to, respectively, as Caribbean black Americans and African black Americans. This nomenclature emphasizes the fact that, except for return migrants, these immigrants become immigrants no more once they enter the United States and embark upon a path toward eventual incorporation into their communities of residence and work.

The traditional and familiar terms used for people tracing their ancestry to the Caribbean include *Caribbean blacks*, *Caribbean immigrants*, or *Afro-Caribbean peoples*. Contemporary immigrants tracing their ancestry to Africa have been referred to as *African immigrants*, *Africans*, or *African blacks*. These terms project immigrants as perpetual newcomers to America by focusing only on their places of origin. In comparison to these terms, the terms used in this chapter attach the "American" suffix in order to underscore the new status of these immigrants as Americans. The terms used in this chapter therefore encompass both first-generation immigrants and subsequent generations, who, on the trajectory of assimilation or incorporation, are indeed more American than the first-generation. If there is an assimilation bias in my representation of the social reality of incorporation in American society, it is perhaps because there is.

NOTES

1. Ivan Van Sertima has argued in his book *They Came before Columbus* (1977) about the presence of Africans in America before Columbus. His series of books on African presence extends to Europe and Asia.

2. Herbert Gans (1997) has revisited the concepts of assimilation and acculturation and argues that acculturation (or adoption of culture) is a distinct and faster process than assimilation (or movement into nonethnic equivalents of immigrants' formal and informal social organizations).

3. Cheikh Diop (1992) notes that "Egyptian antiquity is to African culture what Graeco-Roman antiquity is to Western culture" (49).

4. For an excellent review of the issues and views on Ebonics, see John R. Rickford's commentary "Suite for Ebony and Phonics" in *Discover* magazine, December 1997.

REFERENCES

Alba, Richard, and Victor Nee. 1997. "Rethinking Assimilation Theory for a New Era of Immigration." *International Migration Review* 31, no. 4 (winter): 826–74.

——. 2003. *Remaking the American Mainstream: Assimilation and Contemporary Immigration.* Cambridge, MA: Harvard University Press.

American Sociological Association. 2003. *The Importance of Collecting Data and Doing Social and Scientific Research on Race.* Washington DC: American Sociological Association.

Appiah, Kwame A. 1992. *In My Father's House: Africa in the Philosophy of Culture.* New York: Oxford University Press.

Apraku, Kofi. 1991. *African Emigres in the United States: A Missing Link in Africa's Social and Economic Development.* New York: Praeger.

Arthur, John A. 2000. *Invisible Sojourners: African Immigrant Diaspora in the United States.* Westport, CT: Praeger.

Asante, Molefi K. 1987. *The Afrocentric Idea.* Philadelphia: Temple University Press.

——. 1988. *Afrocentricity.* Trenton, NJ: Africa World Press.

Attah-Poku, Agyemang. 1996. *The Socio-Cultural Adjustment Question: The Role of Ghanaian Immigrant Associations in America.* Brookfield, VT: Ashgate Publishers.

Auerbach, Frank L. 1955. *Immigration Laws of the United States.* Indianapolis: Bobbs-Merrill Company.

Barone, Michael. 2001. *The New Americans: How the Melting Pot Can Work Again.* Washington DC: Regnery Publishing.

Basch, Linda, Nina Glick Schiller, and Cristina S. Blanc. 1994. *Nations Unbound: Transnational Projects, Postcolonial Predicaments and Deterritorialized Nation-States.* Langhorne, PA: Gordon and Breach Science Publishers.

Bean, Frank D., Barry Edmonston, and Jeffery S. Passel, eds. 1990. *Undocumented Migration to the United States: IRCA and the Experience of the 1980s.* Lanham, MD: Rand Corporation and Urban Institute.

Bean, Frank D., and Gillian Stevens. 2003. *America's Newcomers and the Dynamics of Diversity.* New York: Russell Sage Foundation.

Bernard, William S., ed. 1969. *American Immigration Policy: A Reappraisal.* Port Washington, NY: Kennikat Press.

Blackwell, James E. 1975. *The Black Community: Diversity and Unity.* New York: Dodd, Mean, and Company.

Blauner, Robert. 1969. "Internal Colonialism and Ghetto Revolt." *Social Problems* 16, no. 4 (spring): 393–408.

Boahen, Adu A. 1989. "New Trends and Processes in Africa in the Nineteenth Century." In *Africa in the Nineteenth Century until the 1880s.* Vol. 6 of *UNESCO General History of Africa*, ed. J. F. Ade Ajayi, 40–63. Berkeley and London: University of California Press and Heinemann Books.

Bonilla-Silva, Eduardo. 1996. "Rethinking Racism: Toward a Structural Interpretation." *American Sociological Review* 62 (June): 465–80.

Bryce-Laporte, Roy S. 1972. "Black Immigrants: The Experience of Invisibility and Inequality." *Journal of Black Studies* 3, no. 1 (September): 29–56.

———, ed. 1980. *Sourcebook on the New Immigration: Implications for the United States and the International Community.* New Brunswick, NJ: Transaction Books.

Burkey, Richard M. 1978. *Ethnic and Racial Groups: The Dynamics of Dominance.* Menlo Park, CA: Cummings.

Burrows, Edwin G., and Mike Wallace. 1999. *Gotham: A History of New York to 1898.* New York: Oxford University Press.

Butcher, Kristin F. 1994. "Black Immigrants in the United States: A Comparison with Native Blacks and Other Immigrants." *Industrial and Labor Relations Review* 47, no. 2 (January): 265–84.

Child, Irvin L. 1943. *Italian or American? The Second Generation in Conflict.* New Haven, CT: Yale University Press.

Chiswick, Barry R. 1978. "The Effect of Americanization on the Earnings of Foreign-born Men." *Journal of Political Economy* 86, no. 5 (October): 897–921.

———. 1979. "The Economic Progress of Immigrants: Some Apparently Universal Patterns." In *Contemporary Economic Problems 1979*, ed. William Fellner, 359–99. Washington DC: American Enterprise Institute.

Collins, Randall. 1990. "Conflict Theory and the Advance of Macro-Historical Sociology." In *Frontiers of Social Theory: The New Synthesis*, ed. George Ritzer, 68–87. New York: Columbia University Press.

Cose, Ellis. 1992. *A Nation of Strangers: Prejudice, Politics and the Populating of America.* New York: William Morrow and Company.

Cromartie, John, and Carol B. Stack. 1989. "Reinterpretation of Black Return and Nonreturn Migration to the South 1975–1980." *Geographical Review* 79, no. 3 (July): 297–310.

Daget, S. 1989. "The Abolition of the Slave Trade." In *Africa in the Nineteenth Century until the 1880s.* Vol. 6 of *UNESCO General History of Africa*, ed. J. F. Ade Ajayi, 64–89. Berkeley and London: University of California Press and Heinemann Books.

Davis, Gregson. 1997. *Aimé Césaire.* Cambridge: Cambridge University Press.

DeWind, Josh, and Philip Kasinitz. 1997. "Everything Old Is New Again? Processes and Theories of Immigrant Incorporation." *International Migration Review* 31, no. 4 (winter): 1096–1111.

Diop, Cheikh A. 1987. *Precolonial Black Africa*, trans. Harold Salemson. Trenton, NJ, and Westport, CT: Africa World Press and Lawrence Hill and Company.

———. 1992. "Origin of the Ancient Egyptians." In *Ancient Africa*. Vol. 2 of *UNESCO General
History of Africa*, ed. G. Mokhtar, 27–57. Berkeley and London: University of California Press
and Heinemann Books.

Djamba, Yanyi K. 1999. "African Immigrants in the United States: A Socio-Demographic Profile
in Comparison to Native Blacks." *Journal of Asian and African Studies* 34, no. 2 (210–15).

Dodoo, F. Nii-Amoo. 1997. "Assimilation Differences among Africans in America." *Social Forces*
76, no. 2 (December): 527–46.

Dodoo, F. Nii-Amoo, and Baffour K. Takyi. 2002. "Africans in the Diaspora: Black-White Earnings
Differences among America's Africans." *Ethnic and Racial Studies* 25, no. 6 (November): 913–41.

DuBois, W. E. B. 1903 (reprint 1996). *The Souls of Black Folk*. New York: Penguin.

Ekeh, Peter P. 1999. "Kinship and State in African and African American Histories." In *The
African Diaspora: African Origins and New World Identities*, ed. Isidore Okpewho, Carole
Boyce Davies, and Ali A. Mazrui, 89–114. Bloomington: Indiana University Press.

Fanon, Franz. 1968. *Black Skin, White Masks*. New York: Grove Press.

———. 1970. *The Wretched of the Earth*. Middlesex, UK: Penguin Books.

Farley, Reynolds, and Walter R. Allen. 1987. *The Color Line and the Quality of Life in America*.
A Census Monograph Series. New York: Russell Sage Foundation.

Feagin, Joe R. 1991. "The Continuing Significance of Race: Antiblack Discrimination in Public
Places." *American Sociological Review* 56 (February): 101–16.

———. 2001. *Racist America: Roots, Current Realities and Future Reparations*. New York: Routledge.

Feagin, Joe R., and Clairece B. Feagin. 1999. *Racial and Ethnic Relations*. 6th ed. Upper Saddle
River, NJ: Prentice Hall.

Feagin, Joe R., and Melvin P. Sikes. 1994. *Living with Racism: The Black Middle-Class Experience*. Boston: Beacon Press.

Fears, Darryl. 2002. "A Diverse—and Divided—Black Community." *Washington Post*, February
14, A1.

Fernández Kelly, Patricia M., and Richard Schauffler. 1996. "Divided Fates: Immigrant Children
and the New Assimilation." In *The New Second Generation*, ed. Alejandro Portes, 30–53. New
York: Russell Sage Foundation.

Foner, Nancy. 1985. "Race and Color: Jamaican Migrants in London and New York." *International Migration Review* 19: 708–22.

———, ed. 1987. *New Immigrants in New York*. New York: Columbia University Press.

———. 2000. *From Ellis Island to JFK: New York's Two Great Waves of Immigration*. New Haven
and New York: Yale University Press and Russell Sage Foundation.

Frazier, Franklin L. 1957. *Black Bourgeoisie*. New York: Free Press.

Frey, William H. 1998. "Black Migration to the South Reaches Record Highs in 1990s." *Population Today* 26, no. 2 (February): 1–3.

———. 2000. *The New Great Migration: Black Americans' Return to the South, 1965–2000*. Living Cities Census Series. Washington DC: Brookings Institution.

Gans, Herbert J. 1979. "Symbolic Ethnicity: The Future of Ethnic Groups and Cultures in America." *Ethnic and Racial Studies* 2, no. 1: 1–20.

———. 1992. "Second-Generation Decline: Scenarios for the Economic and Ethnic Futures of the
Post-1965 Immigrants." *Ethnic and Racial Studies* 15, no. 2: 173–92.

———. 1997. "Toward a Reconciliation of 'Assimilation' and 'Pluralism': The Interplay of Acculturation and Ethnic Retention." *International Migration Review* 31, no. 4 (winter): 875–92.

Gates, Henry L., Jr., and Cornel West. 1996. *The Future of the Race*. New York: Vintage Books.

Gilroy, Paul. 1993. *The Black Atlantic: Modernity and Double Consciousness*. Cambridge: Harvard University Press.

Glazer, Nathan. 1992. "The New Immigration and the American City." In *Immigrants in Two Democracies: French and American Experience*, ed. Donald L. Horowitz and Gérard Noiriel, 268–91. New York: New York University Press.

Glazer, Nathan, and Daniel P. Moynihan. 1964. *Beyond the Melting Pot: The Negroes, Puerto Ricans, Jews, Italians and Irish of New York City*. Cambridge: MIT Press.

Glick Schiller, Nina. 1999. "Transmigrants and Nation-States: Something Old and Something New in the U.S. Immigrant Experience." In *The Handbook of International Migration: The American Experience*, ed. Charles Hirschman, Philip Kasinitz, and Josh DeWind, 95–119. New York: Russell Sage Foundation.

Goffman, Erving. 1959. *The Presentation of Self in Everyday Life*. New York: Doubleday.

——. 1961. *Encounters: Two Studies in the Sociology of Interaction*. Indianapolis: Bobbs-Merrill Company.

——. 1963a. *Stigma: Notes on the Management of Spoiled Identity*. Englewood Cliffs, NJ: Prentice Hall.

——. 1963b. *Behavior in Public Places: Notes on the Social Organization of Gatherings*. New York: Free Press.

——. 1971. *Relations in Public: Microstudies of the Public Order*. New York: Basic Books.

——. 1983. "The Interaction Order: American Sociological Association, 1982 Presidential Address." *American Sociological Review* 48 (February): 1–17.

Gordon, April. 1998. "The New Diaspora: African Immigration to the United States." *Journal of Third World Studies* 15, no. 1: 79–103.

Gordon, Lewis R. 2000. *Existentia Africana: Understanding Africana Existential Thought*. New York: Routledge.

Gordon, Milton M. 1964. *Assimilation in American Life: The Role of Race, Religion and National Origins*. New York: Oxford University Press.

Greeley, Andrew M. 1976. *Ethnicity in the United States: A Preliminary Reconnaissance*. New York: John Wiley and Sons.

Grieco, Elizabeth M., and Rachel C. Cassidy. 2001. *U.S. Census Bureau. Census Brief. Overview of Race and Hispanic Origin 2000*. Washington DC: Government Printing Office.

Halter, Marilyn. 1993. *Between Race and Ethnicity: Cape Verdean American Immigrants*. Urbana: University of Illinois Press.

Hannerz, Ulf. 1992. *Cultural Complexity: Studies in the Organization of Meaning*. New York: Columbia University Press.

Harris, J. E. 1992. "The African Diaspora in the Old and New Worlds." In *Africa from the Sixteenth to the Eighteenth Century*. Vol. 5 of *UNESCO General History of Africa*, ed. B. A. Ogot, 113–36. Berkeley and London: University of California Press and Heinemann Books.

Herskovits, Melville J. 1958. *The Myth of the Negro Past*. Boston: Beacon.

Hess, Beth B., Elizabeth W. Markson, and Peter J. Stein. 1992. *Sociology*. New York: Macmillan.

Hill, Mark E. 2000. "Color Differences in the Socioeconomic State of African American Men: Results of a Longitudinal Study." *Social Forces* 78, no. 4 (June): 1437–60.

——. 2002. "Skin Color and the Perception of Attractiveness among African Americans: Does Gender Make a Difference?" *Social Psychology Quarterly* 65, no. 1 (March): 77–91.

Hintzen, Percy C. 2001. *West Indian in the West: Self-Representations in an Immigrant Community*. New York: New York University Press.

Hirschman, Charles. 1983. "America's Melting Pot Reconsidered." *Annual Review of Sociology* 9: 397–423.

Hochschild, Jennifer. 1995. *Facing Up to the American Dream: Race, Class and the Soul of the Nation.* Princeton, NJ: Princeton University Press.

Hodge, Robert W. 1973. "Toward a Theory of Racial Differences in Employment." *Social Forces* 52, no. 1 (September): 16–31.

Hodges, Graham R. 1999. *Root and Branch: African Americans in New York and East Jersey, 1613–1863.* Chapel Hill: University of North Carolina Press.

Horton, James O. 1993. *Free People of Color: Inside the African American Community.* Washington DC: Smithsonian Institution Press.

Hughes, Everett C. 1945. "Dilemmas and Contradictions of Status." *American Journal of Sociology* 50: 353–59.

Hughes, Michael, and Bradley R. Hertel. 1990. "The Significance of Color Remains: A Study of Life Chances, Mate Selection, and Ethnic Consciousness among Black Americans." *Social Forces* 68, no. 4 (June): 1105–20.

Hunt, Chester, and Lewis Walker. 1974. *Ethnic Dynamics.* Homewood, IL: Dorsey Publishers.

Hutchinson, John, and Anthony D. Smith, eds. 1996. *Ethnicity.* Oxford: Oxford University Press.

Hymans, Jacques L. 1971. *Léopold Sédar Senghor: An Intellectual Biography.* Edinburgh: Edinburgh University Press.

James, Winston. 2002. "Explaining Afro-Caribbean Social Mobility in the United States: Beyond the Sowell Thesis." *Comparative Studies in Society and History* 44, no. 2: 218–62.

Kamya, Hugo A. 1997. "African Immigrants in the United States: The Challenge for Research and Practice." *Social Work* 42, no. 2 (March): 154–65.

Kasinitz, Philip. 1992. *Caribbean New York: Black Immigrants and the Politics of Race.* Ithaca, NY: Cornell University Press.

Kearney, Michael. 1995. "The Local and the Global: The Anthropology of Globalization and Transnationalism." *Annual Review of Anthropology* 24: 547–65.

Keely, Charles B. 1980. "Immigration Policy and the New Immigrants." In *Sourcebook on the New Immigration*, ed. Roy S. Bryce-Laporte, 15–26. New Brunswick, NJ: Transaction Books.

Kposowa, Augustine. 2002. "Human Capital and the Performance of African Immigrants in the U.S. Labor Market." *Western Journal of Black Studies* 26, no. 3 (fall): 175–83.

Landry, Bart. 1987. *The New Black Middle Class.* Berkeley: University of California Press.

Leadbeater, Bonnie, J. R., and Niobe Way, eds. 1996. *Urban Adolescent Girls: Resisting Stereotypes, Creating Identities.* New York: New York University Press.

Lee, Sharon M. 1993. "Racial Classifications in the U.S. Census: 1890–1990." *Ethnic and Racial Studies* 16, no. 1 (January): 75–94.

Levine, Barry B. 1987. *The Caribbean Exodus.* New York: Praeger.

Levitt, Peggy, Josh DeWind, and Steven Vertovec. 2003. "International Perspectives on Transnational Migration: An Introduction." *International Migration Review* 37, no. 3 (fall): 565–75.

Levitt, Peggy, and Mary C. Waters, eds. 2002. *The Changing Face of Home: The Transnational Lives of the Second Generation.* New York: Russell Sage Foundation.

Lieberson, Stanley. 1973. "Generational Differences among Blacks in the North." *American Journal of Sociology* 79: 550–65.

Lieberson, Stanley, and Mary C. Waters. 1988. *From Many Strands: Ethnic and Racial Groups in Contemporary America.* New York: Russell Sage Foundation.

Lobo, Arun P. 2001. "U.S. "Diversity Visas Are Attracting Africa's Best and Brightest." *Population Today* 29, no. 5: 1–4.

Lynch, Hollis R. 1967. *Edward Wilmot Blyden: Pan-Negro Patriot, 1832–1912*. London: Oxford University Press.

Marks, Carole. 1989. *Farewell, We're Good and Gone: The Great Black Migration*. Bloomington: Indiana University Press.

Massey, Douglas S., and Nolan Malone. 2002. "Pathways to Legal Immigration." *Population Research and Policy Review* 77, no. 6 (December): 473–504.

McHugh, Kevin E. 1987. "Black Migration Reversal in the United States." *Geographical Review* 77, no. 2 (April): 171–82.

McKinnon, Jesse. 2001. *U.S. Census Bureau. Census Brief. The Black Population: 2000*. Washington DC: Government Printing Office.

McWhorter, John H. 2004. "Why I'm Black, Not African American." *Los Angeles Times*, September 8, B11.

Millman, Joel. 1997. *The Other Americans: How Immigrants Renew Our Country, Our Economy and Our Values*. New York: Viking, Penguin Group.

Mintz, Sidney W. 1971. "The Caribbean as a Socio-Cultural Area." In *Peoples and Cultures of the Caribbean*, ed. Michael M. Horowitz, 17–46. Garden City, NY: Natural History Press.

Morgan, Philip. 1998. *Slave Counterpoint: Black Culture in the Eighteenth-Century Chesapeake and Lowcountry*. Chapel Hill: University of North Carolina Press.

Mudimbe, V. Y. 1988. *The Invention of Africa: Gnosis, Philosophy and the Order of Knowledge*. Bloomington: Indiana University Press.

Nahirny, Vladimir C., and Joshua A. Fishman. [1965] 1996. "American Immigrant Groups: Ethnic Identification and the Problem of Generations." In *The Theories of Ethnicity: A Classical Reader*, ed. Werner Sollors. New York: New York University Press.

Neidart, Lisa J., and Reynolds Farley. 1985. "Assimilation in the United States: An Analysis of Ethnic and Generation Differences in Status and Achievement." *American Sociological Review* 50, no. 6 (December): 840–50.

Nwadiora, Emeka. 1996. "Therapy with African Families." *Western Journal of Black Studies* 20, no. 3: 117–24.

Obiakor, Festus E., and Patrick A. Grant, eds. 2002. *Foreign-Born African Americans: Silenced Voices in the Discourse on Race*. New York: Nova Science Publishers.

Okpewho, Isidore. 1999. Introduction to *The African Diaspora: African Origins and New World Identities*, ed. Isidore Okpewho, Carole Boyce Davies, and Ali A. Mazrui, xi–xxvii. Bloomington: Indiana University Press.

Okpewho, Isidore, Carole Boyce Davies, and Ali A. Mazrui, eds. 1999. *The African Diaspora: African Origins and New World Identities*. Bloomington: Indiana University Press.

Omi, Michael A. 2001. "The Changing Meaning of Race." In *America Becoming: Racial Trends and Their Consequences*, Vol. 1, ed. Neil Smelser, William Julius Wilson, and Faith Mitchell, 243–63. Washington DC: National Academy Press.

Omi, Michael A., and Howard Winant. 1986. *Racial Formation in the United States: From the 1960s to the 1980s*. New York: Routledge.

Palmer, Ransford W., ed. 1990. *In Search of a Better Life: Perspectives on Migration from the Caribbean*. New York: Praeger.

———. 1995. *Pilgrims from the Sun: West Indian Immigration to America*. New York: Twayne Publishers.

Pamphile, Leon D. 2001. *Haitians and African Americans: A Heritage of Tragedy and Hope*. Gainesville: University Press of Florida.

Park, Robert E. 1928. "Human Migration and the Marginal Man." *American Journal of Sociology* 33, no. 6: 881–93.

——. 1950. *Race and Culture*. Glencoe, IL: Free Press.

Park, Robert E., and Ernest W. Burgess. 1921. *Introduction to the Science of Sociology*. Chicago: University of Chicago Press.

Parrillo, Vincent N. 2000. *Strangers to These Shores: Race and Ethnic Relations in the United States*. 6th ed. Boston: Allyn and Bacon.

Parsons, Talcott. 1982. *On Institutions and Social Evolution: Selected Writings*, ed. Leon H. Mayhew. Chicago: University of Chicago Press.

Patterson, Orlando. 1994. "Ecumenical America: Global Culture and the American Cosmos." *World Policy Journal* 11, no. 2 (summer): 103–17.

Portes, Alejandro. 1989. "The Enclave and the Entrants: Patterns of Ethnic Enterprise in Miami before and after Mariel." *American Sociological Review* 54, no. 6: 929–49.

Portes, Alejandro, and Robert D. Manning. 1986. "The Immigrant Enclave Theory and Empirical Examples." In *Competitive Ethnic Relations*, ed. Joane Nagel and Susan Olzak, 47–68. Orlando, FL: Academic Press.

Portes, Alejandro, and Rubén Rumbaut. 1996. *Immigrant America: A Portrait*. Berkeley: University of California Press.

——, eds. 2001. *Ethnicities: Children of Immigrants in America*. Berkeley: University of California Press.

Portes, Alejandro, and Min Zhou. 1993. "The New Second Generation: Segmented Assimilation and Its Variants." *Annals of the American Academy of Political and Social Science* 530 (November): 74–96.

Reid, Ira De A. 1939. *The Negro Immigrant: His Background, Characteristics and Social Adjustments, 1899–1937*. New York: Columbia University Press.

Reimers, David M. 1985. *Still the Golden Door: The Third World Comes to America*. New York: Columbia University Press.

Reskin, Barbara, and Patricia Roos, eds. 1990. *Job Queues, Gender Queues*. Philadelphia: Temple University Press.

Rickford, John R. 1997. "Commentary: Suite for Ebony and Phonics." *Discover* 18, no. 12 (December): 82–87.

Rodriguez, Néster P. 1995. "The Real 'New World Order': The Globalization of Racial and Ethnic Relations in the Late Twentieth Century." In *The Bubbling Cauldron: Race, Ethnicity and the Urban Crisis*, ed. Michael P. Smith and Joe R. Feagin, 211–25. Minneapolis: University of Minnesota Press.

Rumbaut, Rubén G. 1997. "Ties that Bind: Immigration and Immigrant Families in the United States." In *Immigration and the Family: Research and Policy on U.S. Immigrants*, ed. A. Booth, A. C. Crouter, and N. Landale, 3–46. Mahwah, NJ: Lawrence Erlbaum Associates,

Rumbaut, Rubén G., and Alejandro Portes, eds. 2001. *Ethnicities: Children of Immigrants in America*. Berkeley and New York: University of California Press and Russell Sage Foundation.

Russell, Kathy, Midge Wilson, and Ronald Hall. 1992. *The Color Complex: The Politics of Skin Color among African Americans*. New York: Anchor Books.

Shibutani, Tamotsu, and Kian M. Kwan. 1965. *Ethnic Stratification: A Comparative Approach*. New York: Macmillan.

Skinner, Elliott P. 1999. "The Restoration of African Identity for a New Millennium." In *The African Diaspora: African Origins and New World Identities*, ed. Isidore Okpewho, Carole Boyce Davies, and Ali A. Mazrui, 28–48. Bloomington: Indiana University Press.

Smith, Michael P., and Joe R. Feagin, eds. 1995. *The Bubbling Cauldron: Race, Ethnicity and the Urban Crisis*. Minneapolis: University of Minnesota Press.

Sowell, Thomas. 1978. "Three Black Histories." In *American Ethnic Groups*, ed. Thomas Sowell and Lynn D. Collins, 37–64. Washington DC: Urban Institute.

———. 1981. *Ethnic America*. New York: Basic Books.

Soyinka, Wole. 1976. *Myth, Literature and the African World*. Cambridge: Cambridge University Press.

Stack, Carol. 1996. *Call to Home: African Americans Reclaim the Rural South*. New York: Basic Books.

Stepick, Alex. 1987. "The Haitian Exodus: Flight from Terror and Poverty." In *The Caribbean Exodus*, ed. Barry B. Levine, 131–52. New York: Praeger.

Suárez-Orozco, Carola, and Marcelo Suárez-Orozco. 2001. *Children of Immigration*. Cambridge: Harvard University Press.

Sutton, Constance. 1992. "Transnational Identities and Cultures: Caribbean Immigrants in the United States." In *Immigration and Ethnicity*, ed. Michael D'Innocenzo and Josef P. Sirefman. Westport, CT: Greenwood Press.

Sutton, Constance, and Elsa M. Chaney, eds. 1987. *Caribbean Life in New York City: Sociocultural Dimensions*. New York: Center for Migration Studies.

Takougang, Joseph. 1995. "Recent African Immigrants to the United States: A Historical Perspective." *Western Journal of Black Studies* 19, no. 1: 50–57.

Takyi, Baffour K. 2002. "The Making of the Second Diaspora: On the Recent African Immigrant Community in the United States of America." *Western Journal of Black Studies* 26, no. 1: 32–43.

Taylor, Douglas. 1971. "New Languages for Old in the West Indies." In *Peoples and Cultures of the Caribbean*, ed. Michael M. Horowitz, 77–92. Garden City, NY: Natural History Press.

Thompson, Maxine S., and Verna M. Keith. 2001. "The Blacker the Berry: Gender, Skin Tone, Self Esteem, and Self-Efficacy." *Gender and Society* 15, no. 3 (June): 336–57.

Thurow, Lester. 1968. *Income and Opportunity*. Washington DC: Brookings Institution.

———. 1975. *Generating Inequality: Mechanisms of Distribution in the U.S. Economy*. New York: Basic Books.

Tuch, Steven A., and Jack K. Martin, eds. 1997. *Racial Attitudes in the 1990s: Continuity and Change*. Westport, CT: Praeger.

U.S. Immigration and Naturalization Service. 2003. *2003 Statistical Yearbook of the Immigration and Naturalization Service*. Washington DC: Government Printing Office.

Valliant, Janet G. 1990. *Black, French and African: A Life of Léopold Sédar Senghor*. Cambridge: Harvard University Press.

Van Sertima, Ivan. 1977. *They Came before Columbus: The African Presence in Ancient America*. New York: Random House.

Vickerman, Milton. 1999. *Crosscurrents: West Indian Immigrants and Race*. New York: Oxford University Press.

———. 2002. "Second-Generation West Indian Transnationalism." In *The Changing Face of Home: The Transnational Lives of the Second Generation*, ed. Peggy Levitt and Mary C. Waters, 341–66. New York: Russell Sage Foundation.

Warner, W. Lloyd, and Leo Srole. 1945. *The Social Systems of American Ethnic Groups*. New Haven, CT: Yale University Press.

Warner-Lewis, Maureen. 1999. "Cultural Reconfigurations in the African Caribbean." In *The African Diaspora: African Origins and New World Identities*, ed. Isidore Okpewho, Carole Boyce Davies, and Ali A. Mazrui, 19–27. Bloomington: Indiana University Press.

Warren, Robert. 1980. "Volume and Composition of United States Immigration and Emigration." In *Sourcebook on the New Immigration*, ed. R. S. Bryce-Laporte, 1–14. New Brunswick, NJ: Transaction Books.

Waters, Mary C. 1990. *Ethnic Options: Choosing Identities in America*. Berkeley: University of California Press.

———. 1996. "The Intersection of Gender, Race and Ethnicity in Identity Development of Caribbean American Teens." In *Urban Adolescent Girls: Resisting Stereotypes, Creating Identities*, ed. Bonnie Leadbeater and Niobe Way, 65-84. New York: New York University Press.

———. 1999. *Black Identities: West Indian Immigrant Dreams and American Realities*. New York and Cambridge: Russell Sage Foundation and Harvard University Press.

Weeks, John R. 1986. *Population: An Introduction to Concepts and Issues*. 3rd ed. Belmont, CA: Wadsworth Publishing.

Williams, Walter L. 1980. "Ethnic Relations of African Students in the United States with Black Americans, 1870-1900." *Journal of Negro History* 65, no. 3 (summer): 228-49.

Wilson, William J. 1980. *The Declining Significance of Race: Blacks and Changing American Institutions*. 2nd ed. Chicago: University of Chicago Press.

Wirth, Louis. 1956. *The Ghetto*. Chicago: University of Chicago Press.

Wright, Michelle M. 2004. *Becoming Black: Creating Identity in the African Diaspora*. Durham, NC: Duke University Press.

Yancey, William L., Eugene P. Ericksen, and Richard Juliani. 1976. "Emergent Ethnicity: A Review and Reformulation." *American Sociological Review* 41, no. 3 (June): 391-403.

Yinger, J. Milton. 1981. "Toward a Theory of Assimilation and Dissimilation." *Ethnic and Racial Studies* 4: 249-64.

Zhou, Min. 1997. "Segmented Assimilation: Issues, Controversies, and Recent Research on the New Second Generation." *International Migration Review* 31, no. 4 (winter): 975–1008.

CHAPTER 2

Who Are the Other African Americans? Contemporary African and Caribbean Immigrants in the United States

John R. Logan

As quickly as the Hispanic and Asian populations in the United States have grown, there has been nearly equal growth among black Americans with recent roots in Africa and the Caribbean. The number of black Americans born in sub-Saharan Africa nearly tripled during the 1990s. The number identifying a Caribbean ancestry increased by over 60 percent. Census 2000 shows that Afro-Caribbeans in the United States number over 1.5 million—more than some more visible national-origin groups, such as Cubans and Koreans. Africans number over six hundred thousand. In some major metropolitan regions, these "new" black groups amount to 20 percent or more of the black population. And, nationally, nearly 25 percent of the growth of the black population between 1990 and 2000 was due to people arriving from Africa and the Caribbean.

This chapter summarizes what is known about these "new" black Americans: their numbers, social backgrounds, and residential locations in metropolitan areas. It makes the following key points:

- It is well known that the socioeconomic profile of non-Hispanic blacks is unfavorable compared to whites, and Asians. There is also striking variation within America's black population. The social and economic profile of Afro-Caribbeans and Africans is far above that of African Americans and even better than that of Hispanics.
- Afro-Caribbeans are heavily concentrated on the East Coast. Six out of ten live in the New York, Miami, and Ft. Lauderdale metropolitan regions. More than half are Haitian in Miami; Haitians are

well represented, but outnumbered by Jamaicans, in New York and Ft. Lauderdale.

- America's African population, on the other hand, is much more geographically dispersed. The largest numbers are in Washington, D.C., and New York. In both places, the majority are from West Africa, especially Ghana and Nigeria. East Africa, including Ethiopia and Somalia, is the other main region of origin.

- Like African Americans, Afro-Caribbeans and Africans are highly segregated from whites. But these black ethnic groups overlap only partly with one another in the neighborhoods in which they live. Segregation among black ethnic groups reflects important social differences among them.

- In the metropolitan areas where they live in largest numbers, Africans tend to live in neighborhoods with a higher median income and education level than African Americans and Afro-Caribbeans. In these metro areas, Afro-Caribbeans tend to live in neighborhoods with a higher percentage of homeowners than either African Americans or Africans.

COUNTING NONHISPANIC BLACKS IN AMERICA

The Census Bureau provides different ways of identifying these black populations, depending on the data source that is used.

For data on individuals, the 1990 5 percent Public Use Microdata Sample (1990 PUMS) data files and the Census 2000 1 percent Public Use Microdata Sample (2000 PUMS) make it possible to count the number of African Americans, Afro-Caribbeans, and Africans by combining information on their race, birth, and ancestry. Among non-Hispanic blacks, this study classifies those reporting their ancestry, country of birth, or both in the predominantly black islands of the Caribbean (including such places as Jamaica and Trinidad, but not Guyana) as "Afro-Caribbean." Whereas it is preferable to count immigrants from Guyana as "Afro-Caribbean," such information is not separately identifiable for all data sources. This study classifies people reporting their ancestry, country of birth, or both as a specific sub-Saharan African country as "African." It classifies the remainder of the black population, including those who report their ancestry as

"African" without a specific country reference and who were not born in Africa, as "African American."

The 1990 and 2000 censuses also provide aggregate data in STF4A (1990) and SF3 (2000) through which one can determine more precisely where members of these three black populations lived (in terms of metropolitan regions or even census tracts). Afro-Caribbeans are defined by ancestry in the predominantly black and non-Hispanic islands of the Caribbean (again including such places as Jamaica and Trinidad). However, the available tabulations force us to define "Africans" solely by country of birth (sub-Saharan African). This means that counts at the national level, from the 1990 and 2000 PUMS, include group members of all generations, but analyses at the metropolitan or tract level only include first-generation African immigrants. This implies a substantial underestimate of Africans in metro-specific tables. Based on national data, the "true" African population in each metro area, including immigrants and their descendants, might be 20 percent higher than our count. The African-American population may be slightly overestimated for this same reason.

These data are sample estimates (based on census returns from one of every six households), rather than population enumerations. At the national level, they provide a very close approximation of group characteristics. Also, after combining information from many census tracts to calculate metrolevel measures, error from sampling has only a small effect.

THE SIZE AND REGIONAL DISTRIBUTION OF THE BLACK POPULATION

Census 2000 counted over thirty-five million non-Hispanic blacks, as shown in table 2.1. This represents over 12 percent of the U.S. population. The non-Hispanic black population grew by over six million people, a growth rate of almost 21 percent, since the last decennial census. More than nine out of ten of these were African American (based on our classification of persons using 2000 PUMS), but the percentage of other black groups is growing rapidly (from 4 percent in 1990, based on 1990 PUMS data, to 6.1 percent in 2000).

Over 1.5 million blacks can now be classified as Afro-Caribbeans, and over 600,000 can be classified as African. The Afro-Caribbean

**Table 2.1.   Composition and Growth of the
Non-Hispanic Black Populations of the U.S., 1990–2000**

Group	Population 1990	Population 2000	Percentage of Black Population 1990	Percentage of Black Population 2000	Percentage of Total Population 1990	Percentage of Total Population 2000	Growth 1990-2000
African American	28,034,275	33,048,095	96.0	93.9	11.3	11.7	17.9
Afro-Caribbean	924,693	1,542,895	3.2	4.4	0.4	0.5	66.9
African	229,488	612,548	0.8	1.7	0.1	0.2	166.9
Non-Hispanic white	188,013,404	194,433,424			75.6	69.1	3.4
Non-Hispanic black	29,188,456	35,203,538			11.7	12.5	20.6
Hispanic	21,836,851	35,241,468			8.8	12.5	61.4
Asian	6,977,447	10,050,579			2.8	3.6	44.0
United States Total	248,709,873	281,421,906			100.0	100.0	13.2

population grew by more than 618,000 (almost 67 percent), and Africans grew by more than 383,000 (a growth rate of almost 167 percent, approaching a tripling of the African population). These two groups combined, despite being much smaller than the African-American population, contributed about 17 percent of the six-million-person increase in the non-Hispanic black population during the 1990s. Although not an often recognized part of the American ethnic mosaic, both of these groups are emerging as large and fast-growing populations. Afro-Caribbeans now outnumber and are growing faster than such well-established ethnic minorities as Cubans and Koreans.

Analysis of all 331 metropolitan regions reveals distinct residential patterns for African Americans, Afro-Caribbeans, and Africans. Consider the ten metropolitan regions with the largest representation of the latter two groups. These are listed in tables 2.2 and 2.3. New York, Boston, Washington, D.C., and Atlanta are the metros represented in both tables.

Like African Americans, who are present in large numbers in many metro areas, Africans are dispersed throughout the country. Only a quarter of Africans live in one of the ten largest metropolitan regions, and these metro areas are geographically dispersed. This dispersion, in combination with their smaller numbers, may help explain the "invisibility" of African immigrants in the United States (Arthur 2000). In contrast, Afro-Caribbeans are heavily concentrated in just a few metro areas, all on the East Coast. Six out of ten live in the New York, Miami, and Ft. Lauderdale metro areas; nearly six hundred thousand live in New York alone.

Table 2.2.   Metros with Largest Afro-Caribbean Population, 2000

Metro Area	Afro-Caribbean 1990	Afro-Caribbean 2000	Percentage of Black Total 1990	Percentage of Black Total 2000	Percentage of Metro Total 1990	Percentage of Metro Total 2000	Growth 1990-2000
New York, NY	403,198	566,770	20.3	25.7	4.7	6.1	40.6
Miami, FL	105,477	153,255	28.5	34.4	5.4	6.8	45.3
Fort Lauderdale, FL	55,197	150,476	29.6	43.4	4.4	9.3	172.6
Boston, MA–NH	40,825	62,950	20.6	25.6	1.3	1.8	54.2
Nassau–Suffolk, NY	32,210	60,412	17.7	25.5	1.2	2.2	87.6
Newark, NJ	29,818	55,345	7.3	12.1	1.6	2.7	85.6
West Palm Beach– Boca Raton, FL	20,441	49,402	19.8	30.3	2.4	4.4	141.7
Washington, D.C.– MD–VA–WV	32,440	48,900	3.1	3.7	0.8	1.0	50.7
Orlando, FL	14,872	42,531	10.4	18.4	1.2	2.6	186.0
Atlanta, GA	8,342	35,308	1.1	2.9	0.3	0.9	323.3

All of the top ten metro regions for Afro-Caribbean populations show growth rates of at least 40 percent since 1990, but four metro areas more than doubled the size of this population. Atlanta saw a four-fold increase in its Afro-Caribbean population, while Orlando nearly tripled its population of this group. With the exceptions of Washington, D.C., and Atlanta, the percentage of the non-Hispanic black population accounted for by Afro-Caribbeans in these top metropolitan regions is quite striking. For instance, over one-quarter of the non-Hispanic black population in the New York and Boston metro areas is Afro-Caribbean.

Table 2.3.   Metros with Largest African-born Population, 2000

Metro Area	African Born 1990	African Born 2000	Percentage of Black Total 1990	Percentage of Black Total 2000	Percentage of Metro Total 1990	Percentage of Metro Total 2000	Growth 1990-2000
Washington, D.C.– MD–VA–WV	32,248	80,281	3.0	6.1	0.8	1.6	148.9
New York, NY	31,532	73,851	1.6	3.4	0.4	0.8	134.2
Atlanta, GA	8,919	34,302	1.2	2.9	0.3	0.8	284.6
Minneapolis–St. Paul, MN–WI	3,788	27,592	4.3	15.4	0.1	0.9	628.4
Los Angeles–Long Beach, CA	16,826	25,829	1.8	2.7	0.2	0.3	53.5
Boston, MA–NH	11,989	24,231	6.0	9.8	0.4	0.7	102.1
Houston, TX	9,882	22,638	1.6	3.1	0.3	0.5	129.1
Chicago, IL	8,738	19,438	0.6	1.2	0.1	0.2	122.5
Dallas, TX	7,373	19,134	1.8	3.6	0.3	0.5	159.5
Philadelphia, PA–NJ	5,098	16,344	0.6	1.6	0.1	0.3	220.6

Jamaicans and Haitians are the two major sources of Afro-Caribbeans in all ten areas shown in table 2.2. A majority in Miami (61 percent), West Palm Beach (62 percent), and Boston (57 percent) and a near majority in Newark (49.8 percent) are of Haitian ancestry. Jamaicans are the larger group in Ft. Lauderdale (46 percent), New York (40 percent), Nassau-Suffolk (39 percent), Washington, D.C. (49 percent), and Atlanta (53 percent).

Washington, D.C., and New York have the largest African-born populations (80,281 and 73,851, respectively). The 1990–2000 growth rates exceed 100 percent in all the top metro areas for this population (save Los Angeles-Long Beach at 53.5 percent). Minneapolis–St. Paul saw a 628.4 percent increase in its African population, largely due to refugees from East Africa. In Minneapolis–St. Paul, Africans contribute over 15 percent of the non-Hispanic black population; in Boston, Africans account for nearly 10 percent of non-Hispanic blacks.

In the ten metro areas in table 2.3, most Africans were born in West Africa (mainly Nigeria and Ghana) or East Africa (Ethiopia or Somalia). East Africans are the larger source in Minneapolis (61 percent), and they approximately equal West Africans in Los Angeles-Long Beach (37 percent) and Dallas (40 percent). Elsewhere, West Africans predominate: Washington, D.C. (53 percent), New York (69 percent), Atlanta (48 percent), Boston (60 percent), Houston (61 percent), Chicago (58 percent), and Philadelphia (53 percent).

SOCIAL AND ECONOMIC CHARACTERISTICS OF AMERICA'S BLACK POPULATIONS

We know that the socioeconomic profile of non-Hispanic blacks does not compare favorably to those of whites and Asians. Table 2.4 offers a comparison based on the 1990 and 2000 PUMS. Less recognized is the diversity within the black population. African Americans have lower educational attainment and median household income and higher unemployment and impoverishment than Afro-Caribbeans and Africans. Afro-Caribbeans and Africans generally compare favorably to America's Hispanic population, while African Americans fare worse. There has been considerable debate about the source of these differences (see, especially, Sowell 1978 and a review of critiques of Sowell's conclusions by James 2002; see also chapter 5). Thomas Sowell

**Table 2.4.   Social and Economic Characteristics of
Non-Hispanic Black Populations in Comparison with Major U.S. Racial
and Ethnic Groups, 1990 and 2000**

Group	Population	Foreign Born (%)	Years of Education	Median Household Income ($)	Unemployed (%)	Below Poverty (%)
1990						
African American	28,034,275	1.8	11.7	29,251	12.5	32.8
Afro-Caribbean	924,693	72.4	12.1	42,927	9.4	17.8
African	229,488	72.1	14.3	35,041	8.5	24.7
Non-Hispanic white	188,013,404	3.9	12.9	47,481	4.7	11.3
Non-Hispanic black	29,188,456	4.7	11.7	29,850	12.3	32.3
Hispanic	21,836,851	42.7	10.2	35,041	9.9	27.0
Asian	6,977,447	67.5	13.1	54,508	5.0	15.9
2000						
African American	33,048,095	2.2	12.4	33,790	11.2	30.4
Afro-Caribbean	1,542,895	68.3	12.6	43,650	8.7	18.8
African	612,548	78.5	14.0	42,900	7.3	22.1
Non-Hispanic white	194,433,424	4.2	13.5	53,000	4.0	11.2
Non-Hispanic black	35,203,538	6.4	12.5	34,300	11.0	29.7
Hispanic	35,241,468	40.9	10.5	38,500	8.8	26.0
Asian	10,050,579	66.5	13.9	62,000	4.6	13.9

suggests that they are due to cultural gaps, where the thrift and work ethic of immigrants operate in favor of the newer black groups. Mary Waters (1999) reports that Afro-Caribbean immigrants tend to agree with this thesis and that they often seek to distance themselves from an African American identity; however, she also finds that employers favor Afro-Caribbean workers, in part because they are perceived to be more compliant and more willing to accept inferior wages and working conditions. Winston James (2002) argues that most differences in outcomes are due to immigrant selectivity (see also Takyi 2002a) and that black immigrants, like African Americans and unlike most other immigrant groups, are strongly affected by racial discrimination in the United States.

In sum, table 2.4 makes the following points:

- *Nativity:* Over two-thirds of the Afro-Caribbean and nearly 80 percent of the African population is foreign-born. The percentage of foreign born in these groups is higher than that of Asians. Not surprisingly, the percentage of foreign born among the group we define as African American is small.

- *Education:* Educational attainment of Africans (14.0 years) is higher than Afro-Caribbeans (12.6 years) or African Americans (12.4 years); indeed, it is higher even than that of whites and Asians.
- *Income:* Median household income of African Americans is lower than that of any other group in the table, lower even than that of Hispanics. Africans and Afro-Caribbeans have much higher median incomes (about $43,000), though these are still well below those of whites and Asians.
- *Unemployment and poverty:* Africans and Afro-Caribbeans also have the lowest rates of unemployment and impoverishment among blacks, comparing favorably to Hispanics. Their position is substantially worse than that of Asians and whites, but Africans' unemployment is not far from that of these two groups.

The social and economic profile of all three black groups generally improved during the 1990s, though the gain in median household income of Afro-Caribbeans was marginal, and the average educational attainment of Africans slipped. Gains for African Americans somewhat diminished their gap with other non-Hispanic black populations. Very substantial differences in the average socioeconomic standing of these groups remain, though it is unclear how these various characteristics are interrelated. Some studies have shown, for example, that among employed males, there are no differences among black groups in work intensity and motivation to work (Dodoo 1999). There are also additional differences among Africans with different national origins (Takyi 2002b; Kollehlon and Eule 2003).

RESIDENTIAL PATTERNS WITHIN METROPOLITAN REGIONS

Another way to evaluate and compare the experiences of these black populations is to look at the degree to which their neighborhoods are segregated from those of other groups and from one another. It was shown above that the socioeconomic conditions of Afro-Caribbeans and Africans are different from those of African Americans; are their residential surroundings also distinct?

This question can be studied through the summary files in which Afro-Caribbeans are identified by ancestry and Africans by country of birth. The 1990 and 2000 population censuses provide the counts necessary to calculate levels of group isolation (the percentage of same-group members in the census tract where the average group member lives); exposure to all non-Hispanic blacks and exposure to whites (defined as the percentage of non-Hispanic blacks and non-Hispanic whites, respectively, in the census tract where the average group member lives); and segregation (the Index of Dissimilarity) from non-Hispanic whites and other black groups (the scores show the percentage of a given group that would have to move to another tract in order for the two groups to be equally distributed). These are indicators of the extent to which a group has developed its own residential enclaves in metropolitan areas. These figures have been calculated by computing levels of isolation, exposure, and dissimilarity in every metropolitan area, then taking a weighted average, giving more weight to areas with more group members.

Table 2.1 showed that African Americans make up just under 12 percent of the population in the United States, while Afro-Caribbeans and Africans account for 0.5 percent and 0.2 percent, respectively. Thus, if these non-Hispanic black groups were distributed randomly (without regard to in-group preferences or discrimination), their isolation index values would be about 12, 0.5, and 0.2, respectively. Likewise, the exposure scores would match the population percentages of non-Hispanic blacks and whites in table 2.1. Dissimilarity is a measure of evenness and thus captures how equally members of a given group are distributed across tracts compared to another group. A dissimilarity score of less than 30 is generally thought to indicate low segregation, scores between 30 and 55 indicate moderate segregation, and scores above 55 indicate high segregation.

Table 2.5 shows that exposure to whites is low and declining for each black group. Africans have the highest exposure to whites (in 2000, just under half of the people in the neighborhood where an average African person lived was white); Afro-Caribbeans now have the lowest exposure to whites (29.9 percent) among black groups. Conversely, dissimilarity scores indicate high, though slightly declining, segregation of all non-Hispanic black groups from whites. All dissimilarity scores from non-Hispanic whites are in excess of 60 percent.

Table 2.5.   Segregation of Black Populations, National Metro Averages

		African Americans	Afro-Caribbeans	African Born
Exposure to whites	1990	33.4%	33.5%	56.7%
	2000	33.3	29.9	46.3
Segregation from whites	1990	68.6	74.1	69.6
	2000	65.0	71.8	67.8
Isolation (exposure to own group)	1990	54.3	12.5	1.8
	2000	49.4	15.3	3.3
Exposure to blacks	1990	56.1	47.3	23.3
	2000	51.8	47.3	28.3
Segregation from African Americans	1990	—	46.6	68.9
	2000	—	42.5	59.2
Segregation from Afro-Caribbeans	1990	62.3	—	66.7
	2000	56.3	—	60.3
Segregation from Africans	1990	75.8	66.1	—
	2000	66.7	60.0	—

The percentage of African Americans in the neighborhood where an average African American person lives declined from 54.3 percent in 1990 to 49.4 percent in 2000. Because of their smaller size, other black groups have much lower isolation scores, though these were on an upward trajectory in the 1990s. While they live in neighborhoods where their own group tends to be a small minority, Afro-Caribbeans' neighborhoods are, on average, close to 50 percent black. Africans, on the other hand, live in neighborhoods where blacks are outnumbered by whites (though they did increase their exposure to blacks from 23.3 percent to 28.3 percent).

Segregation of black groups from one another, as measured by the Index of Dissimilarity, is declining, but it is strikingly high. (Note that these average values are not symmetrical because the average segregation of group x from group y is weighted by the number of group x residents; segregation of group y from group x is weighted by the number of group y residents.) Caution should be exercised in interpreting these figures, however. Because Africans and Afro-Caribbeans are found in very small numbers in many metropolitan areas, the national averages include many values for metro areas where the score is unreliable. It will be more revealing to assess dissimilarity scores among black groups in places like New York, Washington, D.C., and Atlanta, where all three are found in larger numbers. These data are shown in tables 2.6 and 2.7.

Table 2.6 describes residential patterns for Afro-Caribbeans in the ten largest metropolitan areas for this population. Segregation from whites is very high in all of them, increasing in some areas, while declining in others. Exposure to whites, however, varies greatly—from living in neighborhoods that are less than a quarter white and majority black (New York, Miami, and Newark) to living in neighborhoods where whites make up as much as 40 percent of the population (Boston, West Palm Beach, and Orlando). Segregation from African Americans is only in the moderate range (35–45), indicating that Afro-Caribbeans' neighborhoods overlap substantially with those of African Americans. Segregation from Africans is substantially higher, though it remains within the moderate range. New York is the one case where both Afro-Caribbeans and Africans are present in large numbers, and segregation between these two groups is in the high range.

Table 2.7 shows segregation measures in the ten largest metropolitan areas for the African born. Exposure of Africans to whites declined significantly in all ten regions; it was extremely low in New York (17.0 percent) and near or above 50 percent only in Minneapolis–St. Paul, Boston, Dallas, and Philadelphia. Segregation from whites is in the high range in all cases, though falling in some of them. At the same time, Africans' exposure to blacks is growing, though it is much lower for Africans than for Afro-Caribbeans.

The table generally confirms the national pattern in which Africans are surprisingly segregated from African Americans and Afro-Caribbeans, though these values generally declined during the last decade. Washington, D.C., and Atlanta offer the possibility that where their populations are larger, Africans' neighborhoods may overlap more with those of other blacks. However, the case of New York shows that such a tendency is not inevitable.

BLACKS' NEIGHBORHOOD CHARACTERISTICS

Non-Hispanic black groups are residentially segregated from whites and from each other. Do they also live in neighborhoods of different

Table 2.6. Segregation of the Ten Metro Regions with Largest Afro-Caribbean Population in Census 2000

Metro Area	Exposure to whites		Segregation from whites		Exposure to blacks		Segregation from African Americans		Segregation from Africans	
	1990	2000	1990	2000	1990	2000	1990	2000	1990	2000
New York, NY	15.4%	11.8%	81.8%	82.7%	62.2%	64.0%	40.2%	39.2%	62.6%	57.7%
Miami, FL	23.9	15.0	66.6	68.1	49.6	54.1	50.6	47.3	66.1	59.0
Fort Lauderdale, FL	52.8	36.6	56.1	57.2	36.3	43.6	44.4	34.6	69.8	67.5
Boston, MA–NH	42.7	40.7	76.4	73.2	42.8	39.3	41.3	34.9	63.4	54.5
Nassau–Suffolk, NY	45.5	36.7	76.8	75.2	38.0	38.7	40.8	36.4	68.7	48.8
Newark, NJ	26.2	22.9	79.8	78.0	60.8	60.0	40.5	37.8	59.7	47.7
West Palm Beach–Boca Raton, FL	46.1	47.3	69.7	60.2	41.5	34.6	42.7	44.0	83.0	74.4
Washington, D.C.–MD–VA–WV	40.8	34.6	67.0	64.6	43.0	43.3	55.2	48.4	44.9	42.5
Orlando, FL	62.8	42.4	52.9	58.1	26.0	32.6	49.1	40.2	67.3	65.4
Atlanta, GA	48.8	36.2	69.0	61.8	46.6	52.3	53.6	39.8	56.8	48.2

Table 2.7. Segregation of the Ten Metro Regions with Largest African-born Population in Census 2000

Metro Area	Exposure to whites		Segregation from whites		Exposure to blacks		Segregation from African Americans		Segregation from Afro-Caribbeans	
	1990	2000	1990	2000	1990	2000	1990	2000	1990	2000
Washington, D.C.–MD–VA–WV	47.7%	37.5%	62.7%	63.1%	34.6%	36.7%	62.9%	58.2%	44.9%	42.5%
New York, NY	29.9	17.0	71.6	78.0	38.4	47.0	62.1	48.5	62.6	57.7
Atlanta, GA	53.1	39.4	67.2	63.6	39.7	43.2	57.4	54.0	56.8	48.2
Minneapolis–St. Paul, MN–WI	78.0	59.2	73.0	68.4	11.2	21.9	66.1	50.0	79.3	73.5
Los Angeles–Long Beach, CA	44.7	34.4	59.4	59.9	17.1	19.9	68.3	60.6	65.8	61.1
Boston, MA–NH	55.5	47.5	68.2	63.7	22.4	26.6	64.7	48.9	63.4	54.5
Houston, TX	46.8	33.0	68.2	67.9	23.7	27.3	71.3	64.7	61.6	54.8
Chicago, IL	51.7	45.1	78.0	72.7	29.1	31.0	80.5	71.2	73.2	66.3
Dallas, TX	66.4	49.0	64.8	60.0	15.5	19.6	74.3	64.2	72.9	66.4
Philadelphia, PA–NJ	56.8	49.2	78.1	70.2	34.5	38.7	72.2	61.9	68.0	58.8

quality? (For research on this same question in the 1970–1980 period, see Adelman et al. 2001.) This final section of this chapter analyzes selected neighborhood characteristics for the average group member: the neighborhood's median household income (in constant dollars for 1990 and 2000), the percentage of group members who own their homes, and the percentage of residents (over age twenty-five) with a college education. These are characteristics of the neighborhoods in which an average group member lives, rather than of the groups themselves (these were shown previously in table 2.4).

Table 2.8 shows that non-Hispanic blacks, regardless of ethnicity, live in worse neighborhoods, on average, than do non-Hispanic whites, with one exception—Africans exceed whites in the educational attainment of their neighbors.

More relevant here are the differences among black populations:

- *Income:* The average African American lives in a census tract with a median income of $35,679, while the average Afro-Caribbean lives in a census tract with a median income of $41,328. Africans live in more advantaged neighborhoods with a median income of $45,567 (though this is still more than $7,000 below the neighborhood median income of an average non-Hispanic white).
- *Homeownership:* The average African American lives in a tract where 53.1 percent of the residents own their homes. This is higher than the other black groups, and to some extent it reflects the advantage of having lived for more generations in the United States. The average Afro-Caribbean lives in a tract where 49.8 percent of the residents own homes. Although lower than the national aver-

Table 2.8.   Neighborhood Characteristics of the Average Group Member, National Metro Averages

Group	Median Household Income ($)		Percentage Homeowners		Percentage College Educated	
	1990	2000	1990	2000	1990	2000
African American	31,548	35,679	49.8	53.1	14.0	17.5
Afro-Caribbean	39,970	41,328	44.1	49.8	17.5	20.3
African born	44,715	45,567	44.7	47.2	28.8	29.3
Non-Hispanic white	47,683	52,637	67.6	70.7	23.8	29.0

age for African Americans, this deficit is largely due to their concentration in the New York metro area, where this group is mainly
found in inner-city neighborhoods. Regional comparisons of this
neighborhood characteristic show that Afro-Caribbeans fare much
better than African Americans in New York and somewhat better
in Washington, D.C., and Atlanta. The average African lives in a
tract where 47.2 percent of neighbors are homeowners.

* *Education:* The average African lives in a neighborhood where
  29.3 percent of residents have a college education, compared to 29
  percent for an average non-Hispanic white. This reflects the very
  high educational attainment of the Africans who have been able to
  immigrate to the United States. By contrast, the average African
  American lives in a neighborhood where 17.5 percent of residents
  have a college education, while 20 percent of an average Afro-
  Caribbean person's neighbors have a college education.

Table 2.9 provides a closer look at the metro areas where Afro-
Caribbeans are most numerous. Homeownership in their neighbor-
hoods, as noted above, is especially low in New York (and Newark and
Boston as well, where they also are concentrated in the inner city).
Their neighborhoods are relatively less affluent and less educated in
New York. In other metro areas in the table, homeownership in their

**Table 2.9. Neighborhood Characteristics of
the Average Afro-Caribbean Resident**

Metro Area	Median Household Income ($)		Percentage Homeowners		Percentage College Educated	
	1990	2000	1990	2000	1990	2000
New York, NY	39,410	38,758	31.0	35.1	15.5	18.2
Miami, FL	33,665	33,873	53.8	58.1	13.9	15.0
Fort Lauderdale, FL	35,403	39,621	59.2	64.3	13.3	17.0
Boston, MA–NH	40,825	42,463	36.9	42.3	22.5	26.1
Nassau–Suffolk, NY	63,190	64,241	73.7	75.9	21.4	23.5
Newark, NJ	44,036	45,216	39.6	41.9	17.9	20.5
West Palm Beach–Boca Raton, FL	33,061	38,114	54.9	62.2	12.5	17.5
Washington, D.C.–MD–VA–WV	53,864	57,218	51.9	57.6	31.5	35.7
Orlando, FL	38,210	39,252	59.6	60.0	17.2	18.1
Atlanta, GA	46,267	50,911	57.9	61.9	27.1	29.9

neighborhoods is actually well above the national average for African Americans. Afro-Caribbeans live in relatively affluent neighborhoods in Nassau-Suffolk (which is all suburban), Washington, D.C., and Atlanta and in neighborhoods with a relatively high education level in Washington, D.C., Atlanta, and Boston.

Similar information is given in table 2.10 for the top ten metro areas of Africans. Their neighborhoods have especially high levels of education in Washington, D.C., but in several other metro areas, the percentage of neighbors with a college degree is higher than the national average for whites' neighborhoods: Atlanta, Los Angeles-Long Beach, Houston, Chicago, and Dallas. Exceptionally low are the education levels in New York and Philadelphia. Africans also live in especially affluent neighborhoods in Washington, D.C., with a median income of over $57,000—again, well above the national average for whites' neighborhoods. These income levels are lowest in New York and Minneapolis. Finally, Philadelphia stands out for high homeownership in Africans' neighborhoods (over 60 percent), while in New York, homeownership is exceptional low (less than 25 percent).

Table 2.10. Neighborhood Characteristics of the Average African-born Resident

Metro Area	Median Household Income ($)		Percentage Homeowners		Percentage College Educated	
	1990	2000	1990	2000	1990	2000
Washington, D.C.– MD–VA–WV	55,784	57,143	47.0	50.4	37.5	39.5
New York, NY	40,145	35,243	24.3	24.2	22.7	20.3
Atlanta, GA	43,049	48,614	45.1	49.8	30.0	30.5
Minneapolis–St. Paul, MN–WI	36,321	37,679	46.4	44.0	31.2	27.9
Los Angeles–Long Beach, CA	49,075	47,009	41.9	42.9	26.9	29.8
Boston, MA–NH	43,138	42,925	37.9	40.2	27.3	28.2
Houston, TX	41,298	46,531	39.2	48.8	30.9	30.9
Chicago, IL	40,700	45,509	41.0	47.4	30.7	34.3
Dallas, TX	45,671	49,347	38.2	43.6	35.0	33.1
Philadelphia, PA–NJ	43,811	41,647	60.2	60.7	25.4	23.1

CONCLUSION: THE INCREASING DIVERSITY
OF AMERICA'S BLACK POPULATIONS

All of these analyses point in a similar direction. Black Americans of all ethnic backgrounds are highly segregated from whites and disadvantaged in comparison to them. Yet, beneath this communality born of the color line are substantial differences between the majority of blacks with historical origins in the United States and new, growing minorities from the Caribbean and Africa. Nearly 17 percent of recent growth in the black population is due to increases in these new groups. Particularly in metro areas where they constitute 20 percent or more of the black population, an increasingly urgent social and political question is whether common problems associated with race will outweigh differences linked to national origins (Logan and Mollenkopf 2003). Scholars generally agree that the differences are substantial and that black immigrants have limited prospects of assimilation either into mainstream American society or into the African-American minority (Kasinitz 1992; Ho 1991). In some places with a long history of black ethnic diversity, such as New York City, the differences have appeared to be divisive in political races (Rogers 2004). But some studies have shown that majority-black institutions are capable of successfully incorporating newcomers (Foerster 2004).

The newcomers have numerous advantages compared to African Americans. Their own education levels and incomes tend to be higher. Not only do they typically live in somewhat different neighborhoods, but in most metro areas, these neighborhoods have a higher socioeconomic standing.

Comparable diversity has been documented among Hispanics (particularly contrasting South Americans and Cubans with Mexicans, Central Americans, and Dominicans) and Asians (among whom Indians and Filipinos present a very different profile than Chinese or Koreans). The American public is used to thinking in terms of the broader racial and ethnic categories—Hispanic, Asian, black. Certainly in the history of black-white relations in this country, the distinctions between blacks of different social class or national origin have paled in comparison to their common treatment. We may nevertheless be moving into an era when those distinctions become more salient and when we must think not only in terms of majority and minority groups but in terms of a nation of many minorities.

TECHNICAL NOTES: HOW ANCESTRY AND PLACE OF BIRTH ARE USED TO COUNT BLACK POPULATIONS

This chapter extracts information about the non-Hispanic black population from four census data files. Information about group sizes and their social and economic characteristics is from the 1990 PUMS and 2000 PUMS. These are individual-level files with rich detail about people and households, but they lack the geographic detail to place individuals in their neighborhoods.

The 1990 and 2000 PUMS have detailed information on place of birth and ancestry. Ancestry gives the most complete enumeration of black ethnic groups, while place of birth is a secondary selection characteristic. Accordingly, individuals are selected and grouped by the places of birth and ancestries listed in table 2.11.

Summary files from the 1990 and 2000 Census of Population have been used here to describe the residential segregation and characteristics of neighborhoods in which an average member of a non-Hispanic black group lives by metropolitan region. Among non-Hispanic blacks, the best method of identifying Afro-Caribbeans is by ancestry. Using ancestry, however, would inflate the count of Africans because many

Table 2.11.   Major Groups in the 1990 and 2000 PUMS

African American	Country of Birth All others	Ancestry All others, including African
Afro-Caribbean	Caribbean (330–74), except Cuba (271), Dominican (275), Dominican Republic (339), and unspecified Latin American countries (356)	West Indies (300–59)
African	Africa (400–99), except Algeria (400), Egypt (415), Libya (430), Morocco (436), Tunisia (456), and unspecified North African countries (468)	Sub-Saharan Africa (500–99)

Note: Country of birth and ancestry codes shown here are from 1990 PUMS. Census 2000 PUMS identifies equivalent groups, but the codes are different.

blacks who are descended from several generations of forebears in the United States list their ancestry as African. Therefore, only country of birth is used to identify this group, with the accompanying disadvantage of counting only the first generation.

ACKNOWLEDGMENTS

I thank Glenn Deane for his collaboration in preparing the original report and Hyoung-jin Shin for his assistance in the data analysis.

REFERENCES

Adelman, Robert M., Hui-shien Tsao, Stewart E. Tolnay, Kyle D. Crowder. 2001. "Neighborhood Disadvantage among Racial and Ethnic Groups: Residential Location in 1970 and 1980." *Sociological Quarterly* 42: 603–32.

Arthur, John A. 2000. *Invisible Sojourners: African Immigrant Diaspora in the United States.* New York: Praeger.

Dodoo, F. Nii-Amoo. 1999. "Black and Immigrant Labor Force Participation in America." *Race and Society* 2: 69–82.

Foerster, Amy. 2004. "Race, Identity, and Belonging: 'Blackness' and the Struggle for Solidarity in a Multiethnic Labor Union." *Social Problems* 51: 386–409.

Ho, Christine. 1991 *Salt-Water Trinnies: Afro-Trinidadian Immigrant Networks and Non-assimilation in Los Angeles.* New York: AMS Press.

James, Winston. 2002. "Explaining Afro-Caribbean Social Mobility in the United States: Beyond the Sowell Thesis." *Comparative Studies in Society and History* 44: 218–62.

Kasinitz, Philip. 1992. *Caribbean New York.* Ithaca, NY: Cornell University Press.

Kollehlon, Konia T., and Edward E. Eule. 2003. "The Socioeconomic Attainment Patterns of Africans in the United States." *International Migration Review* 37: 1163–90.

Logan, John R., and John Mollenkopf. 2003. *People and Politics in America's Big Cities.* New York: Drum Major Institute for Public Policy.

Rogers, Reuel R. 2004. "Race-Based Coalitions among Minority Groups: Afro-Caribbean Immigrants and African-Americans in New York City." *Urban Affairs Review* 39: 283–317.

Sowell, Thomas. 1978. "Three Black Histories." In *Essays and Data on American Ethnic Groups*, ed. Thomas Sowell. Washington, DC: Urban Institute.

Takyi, Baffour K. 2002a. "Africans in the Diaspora: Black-White Earnings Differences among America's Africans." *Ethnic and Racial Studies* 25: 913–41.

———. 2002b. "The Making of the Second Diaspora: On the Recent African Immigrant Community in the United States of America." *Western Journal of Black Studies* 26: 32–43.

Waters, Mary. 1999. *Black Identities: West Indian Immigrant Dreams and American Realities.* Cambridge, MA: Harvard University Press.

CHAPTER 3

Thinking through Identities: Black Peoples, Race Labels, and Ethnic Consciousness

Lewis R. Gordon

The academic study of black peoples predates the founding of black studies programs in the American academy in 1967 at San Francisco State University (cf. Davies et al. 2003; Gordon and Gordon 2005, 2006). Credit for that early effort is held by W. E. B. DuBois, whose monumental *Philadelphia Negro* (1898) was commissioned by the University of Pennsylvania. Prior to DuBois's effort, the work of black academics took place mostly on the periphery of academic institutions, such as that of Alexander Crummell presented before the American Negro Academy. There was one exception in Western Europe; Anton Wilhem Amo, an eighteenth-century Ghanaian-born philosopher and professor of philosophy at the Universities of Halle and of Jena in Germany, wrote a work in law in 1729 entitled *Disputation de jure maurorum in Europa* (Amo 1968). Returning to the U.S. context, there were, as well, the many studies by Carter G. Woodson, E. Franklin Frazier, John Hope Franklin, and many more. The formation of black studies programs led, however, to the centering of a new kind of question in the study of black folk, and that was the nature of the subject of the field itself (see, e.g., Wynter 2005). The question of black studies thus raised many questions that challenged more than the study of black folk, for how black folks were understood depended on the presumptions of human study at work as well as the historical presuppositions that supported such philosophical anthropology.

Black studies, for instance, in its most basic form, focused on the problematics raised by the existence of black peoples (Gordon and Gordon 2006). But black peoples are not necessarily African peoples

(Lewis Gordon 1995). Black peoples include Australian Aboriginal peoples, many other Pacific Island peoples, various indigenous Asian peoples, and, in some readings, certain peoples of Europe. Yet, as things tend to be in this area of research, this argument itself depends on presuppositions that themselves could be transformed in another reading of black studies. For instance, there is a sense in which black studies raises the question of the human species itself. The human species, *Homo sapien sapiens*, evolved, as genetics, paleoanthropology, and paleoarchaeology reveal, in southern Africa approximately 220,000 years ago. As archaeological evidence continues to unfold in the *Journal of Human Evolution*, humans took to the seas at least fifty or sixty thousand years ago and spread throughout the Southern Hemisphere before making their way into Europe and western Asia about thirty thousand years ago (see Neves and Pucciarelli 1998; Neves, Powell, and Ozolins 1999; Neves et al. 2003). It is pretty certain that those early migrants from the African continent were dark peoples, what we could today call "early Africans," where the term *African* simply refers to people indigenous to the continent of Africa. The morphological transformations that transpired northward, westward, southward have led to a world of "races," but we should bear in mind that by about twenty thousand years ago, the other hominids, such as Neanderthals and *Homo erecta*, died out, leaving *Homo sapien sapiens* as the only hominid species, and although differences in appearance emerged, they are primarily superficial as each group, or race, of these hominids belongs to the same species—namely, *Homo sapien sapiens* or, simply put, the human race. In this sense, then, the story of the human species is one of dark peoples who spread around the planet and whose present descendants are simply genetic variations of those peoples. Black studies, from this point of view, is simply the study of human beings, but with the additional set of questions that emerge from taking into account the impact of race discourse on modern systematic studies of human subjects.

There is, however, another story that would create an isomorphic relationship between black peoples across the globe and black studies. In that account, successions of peoples from Africa migrated from the continent, and only some of them remain morphologically close to their origins, while others were so radically transformed in appearance that they were, in effect, new peoples. Thus, the dark peoples of Asia and the Pacific are simply early people/blacks/Africans, and those that were spread across the globe during modern colonialism and slavery are simply newer blacks/Africans, since lighter Asians and whites have emerged in the interim and have developed different cultural patterns than the peoples more closely connected to the African continent and its antiquity (cf. Jane Gordon 2005).

And then there is a model that separates black African studies from black Asian and Pacific studies. The black African, in this view, represents a unique cultural formation of at least the past ten thousand years, and the creolization or culturally mixed process that emerged with Europe in modernity has led to two kinds of black African cultures—those on the African continent and those spread across the globe, particularly the New World. The latter represent a mixture with indigenous American, European, and Asian cultures.

More recently, members of the black American intelligentsia ushered in a transition from *black* to *African American* as the term by which they would like to be called. It came about as a function of American racial and ethnic discourses (Dawson 2001; Dzidzienyo and Jones 1977). In spite of its political significance, it is difficult to avoid the racial connotations of the word "black." The use of the term *African American* announced an effort to shift from a race-centered discourse of group identity to an ethnic-centered model, one in which a leveled conceptual field would dominate in the stream of hyphenated expressions of national membership (cf. Lewis Gordon 1995; Wynter 2005). Along with Euro-Americans, Asian Americans, and Native Americans, there is the African American, whose continental origins offer a genealogical heritage, a cultural offering for the conglomeration of peoples that embody a republic that supposedly builds citizenship on laws instead of race.

There is, however, the problem of a set of contradictions that emerge from this narrative. The first pertains to Native Americans. The neat continental prefixes fall apart with the term *native*. In effect, it presents a redundant term, best exemplified by the referent of *native* in this case—namely, "American," which leads to the awkward expression "American American." Further problems emerge in that neither *native* nor *American* is the proper term for the peoples of North America since they are introduced colonial terms, pretty much as *Asia* and *Africa* are to their respective continents (cf. Mudimbe 1988; Dussel 1995; Mignolo 2006; Liu 2006). The indigeneity of the native here, then, is paradoxical. For it is indigenous to a world that is more rooted in a temporal-political reality: the founding of the Americas and the history generated by it. In effect, then, all of the listed categories—Native American, Euro-American, Asian American, African American—are indigenous to America (cf. Gordon and Gordon 2006).

The indigenous status of these terms does not, however, mean that they stand on equal footing, for only one among them stands in the role of determining the conditions for the rest. *Euro-America* is, after all, the centered term from which the others emerged. Its significance is both semiotic, or symbolic, and genealogical. From a semiotic perspective, it is a relational term; it is the point from which, in either direction, extremes come into being, as evidenced by the oppositions posed by movements from least light to lightest, from black to white. There is, however, another model, which, instead of settling for whiteness as a center, aims for whiteness as the telos.

An important feature of the terms used in race discourses is that they carry their meaning not only in their content but also in their form, which, in kind, has its own grammar. This is the insight behind analyses that point out that even if the historic people who designate each term were to disappear, the social systems they once inhabited could very well continue to produce new inhabitants for those abandoned spaces. This is certainly the case internal to racial groups in much of the modern world. For instance, in "all-black" settings, there is the unmistakable reproduction of racist differentiation on the basis of skin color, where the options available to lighter-skinned blacks are greater than those for darker-skinned blacks. This is not to say that there are no poor or underprivileged light-skinned blacks, but it defies reality to deny that the association of dark skin with poverty has strong empirical foundations, as Crummell (1992) recognized more than a century ago. Among Native Americans, the situation of light-skinned Indigenous peoples and dark-skinned ones is similar. And the same is so for Asians. These examples illustrate that the formal structure of light-dark/high-low racism persists in those cases (cf. Ifekwunigwe 2004). Such stories fuse with history to offer more genealogical accounts of racial, ethnic, and other identity constructions.

IDENTITIES IN OLD WORLDS AND NEW WORLDS

The year 1492 marked two significant events in the formation of modern racial consciousness. The first was the expulsion of the Moors from Spain in January of that year, under the leadership of Queen Isabella and King Ferdinand. The Moors were Afro-Muslim peoples (often characterized as Berber-Arab) from North Africa who colonized much of the Iberian Peninsula and the southern Mediterranean in the eighth century. The impact of the Moors on this region continues to the present. Much of the southern Mediterranean had become a creolized world of Afro-Arabic and European peoples. This period was marked by constant wars as Christians from the north attempted to push the Moors out, and the Moors strove to advance northward. The achievement of forcing the Moors southward led to the continuance of the conflict on the African continent and the Atlantic Ocean, inaugurating the expansion of Christian Europe and the retraction of the Muslim world as Europeans strove to regain and hold on to northern African territories. For our purposes, it is important to recognize that European expansion entailed a conscious expulsion of brown and black colonizers from European lands, and by the time this effort was successful, a good portion of the Mediterranean was, in fact, both morphologically beige and brown and culturally Afro-Arabic.

The war against the Moors took to the seas and inaugurated the process of expansion that created the modern world. This expansion of Mediterranean cultures led, as Enrique Dussel (1996, 2003) has shown, to the realignment and reorientation of geographical centers in the Old World, a world that was, at least in perception, significantly smaller. That world saw itself as west of center, which, at the time of the Renaissance, was India. The founding of the New World in 1492 announced the existence of a planet much larger than expected by the world governed by commerce along the Mediterranean Sea (cf. Fernández-Armesto 1987). The economy that grew across the Atlantic Ocean, which strove to look so far westward that this vision eventually returned from the east, nearly dried up the Mediterranean-oriented economies from Asia Minor, and as India declined in focus, a new center came about as Europe was born in proverbial mind and spirit. This Europe began to expand itself, and in such efforts, its various national identities were solidified and spread abroad: New England; Hispaniola; Francophone territories; Lusophone ones; some Germanic and Dutch regions here and there; Swedes and Norwegians in North America; and more.

The people who lived in those places "discovered" during this expansion found themselves facing a fate similar to much of the fauna being cleared by the conquerors to create what eventually became European countries abroad. As those people became extinct in the Caribbean, the solution was to import labor, and the story of the Atlantic slave trade began. We should bear in mind that the emergence of that trade and the period of Moorish occupation were not the beginnings of the relationship between Europeans and the peoples of the African continent. There were always (black) Africans in Europe from the moment early humanity decided to cross the terrain that connected present-day northeastern Africa with the Middle East, and given how early human beings took to the seas, no doubt this was also the case across the Mediterranean. The multiraciality of Europe and of the crews that set sail from there, then, already suggests that the neat constellations of "Euro" and "Afro" should be rethought in heterogeneous terms. Similar reflections apply to Asia, where today the lighter northeastern populations dominate images of a continent that is, in fact, marked by a history of dark indigeneity from the shores of Japan to the islands of the Philippines and westward to the shores of the Indian subcontinent (cf. Lewis Gordon 1995; Barnes et al. 1995).

Africa, as well, was and continues to be a continent so richly mixed that it is difficult to imagine a time when it was the sole continent with human beings and that those bipeds of 220,000 years ago were mostly, if not exclusively, dark hued. The continent's story, as we've already seen, involves inhabitants leaving in many directions and their descendants returning with a markedly different appearance as the demands of adaptation made their impact. By the time of the medieval and modern slave trades—which took human beings from the continent through the Arab trade routes and the East Indian Ocean, in addition to the Atlantic—the rich diversity of humankind may have reached its zenith.

Accompanying the expansion of countries whose consolidation became known as Europe were emerging differences in the order of knowledge through which human beings were classified. As scholars such as V. Y. Mudimbe (1988), Oyèrónké Oyewùmí (1997), and Cornel West (2002) have shown, drawing upon the resources of archaeological and genealogical poststructuralism, the emergence of systematic forms of inquiry premised upon white supremacy as the basis of human normality resulted in notions of deviation that structured black people in a derivative relationship with whites. In other words, a link between the formation of knowledge and processes of inquiry, on the one hand, and mechanisms of power and the effecting of new and differentiating forms of life/identities, on the other, emerged with their correlative subjectivities. From aesthetic criteria for human beauty to measurements of intelligence, blacks became the comparison model of deviation instead of ever serving as the standard. Even worse, the very production of their classification—as blacks at the least, "niggers" at worst—was a function of a logic that was not their own; blacks are, in other words, as Frantz Fanon (1967) declared, white constructions.

The account suffers, however, in that it simply declares the conditions for the emergence of certain forms of phenomena; it does not articulate the lived reality of such phenomena, especially in terms of the consciousness that experiences them. For even such a consciousness would be subjected to discursive determinations of its emergence; it would, in other words, be accepted if, and only if, theorized *from its outside*, that is, in terms of what constitutes it as such. So, meaning, form, definition, and determination cannot make sense *inside of* things. Given the conceptual work brought to bear in making things meaningful, there is always an outside, public, hence social, dimension to the constitution of meaning. We should thus study not the essence of the thing but how such an essence is formed. A problem is raised, however, by a thing that is capable of raising such questions, a thing that can raise the question of its own meaning and subjectivity. In effect, it subjects itself, or is able to raise the problem of its existence to itself. This means that it faces a paradox: in the face of the rejection of an inner logic of the self, it poses the question of itself as an external matter *from inside of itself*. This rather complex development amounts to saying that the thing in question is not fully a thing. It is a human being.

The human being poses a challenge to mechanisms of discursive closure. This means that there is always a world of relations of subjectivities and intersubjectivities, of a shared experience of meanings that are both given and being made. This dialectical relationship of subjection and intersubjectivity is a manifestation of what is often called *agency*. That human beings are aware of, or have to interpret and even apprehend, their situations means that the archaeological and genealogical accounts of the constitution of racialized forms of life tell only a part of the story. Missing, as well, are the varieties of ways subjects of racism live in their historical and everyday social situations. That they live a constant struggle for the assertion of their humanity means that social lines are constantly challenged, expanded, and retracted, and in their course, a more dialectical story unfolds.

The DuBoisian concept of double consciousness is a case in point. In one instance, it is simply an effect of the system—blacks seeing themselves as seen by the dominating perspectives and resources of meaning in an antiblack racist society. On the other hand, as Paget Henry (2005) points out, there is potentiated double consciousness, where there is realization of the false, universalistic claims of the system of oppression, where blacks realize that the reality of injustice posed as justice in a racist system hides the racism *as racism* by (as DuBois [1898, 1903] also observed) making black people into problems instead of engaging black people as people facing problems. The latter expectation requires an admission of a social relationship between blacks and nonblacks, in short, the reality of intersubjective or shared participation in the constitution of meaning in the world.

That black people have posed much difficulty for the modern world is a sign of a healthy consciousness. It means a refusal to submit to attempts of human erasure. It is not that all black individuals subscribe to such resistance. It is simply sufficient that enough resistance has existed from the start of racialized slavery in the sixteenth century to make the anthropological question of what it is to be a human being a constantly unfolding discourse and material praxis of the modern age. For black people, the concrete formulation is the reduction of blacks to forms of inert labor, as labor without a point of view, as property. Even for many freed blacks, the institutional imposition of labor with blackness meant a constant struggle for the assertion of claimed freedom in a world that had no room for blacks to have leisure time; to be black and not laboring amounted to an illicit laziness. But even more, the plethora of lines drawn against human assertion meant a constant struggle against illegitimate being. Any category of social life becomes stained with indiscretion in black form; how does one "live" when one lacks a right to exist?

Fanon observed in *Black Skin, White Masks* (1967) that when black people live only among black people, the canceling out of racial subordination enables a coherent negotiation of health and pathology. Blacks who have contact with the world of antiblack racism face, however, the absence of any coherent notion of normality. To be black, in effect, is to be pathological. Since Fanon was writing about blacks in the Caribbean and Africa, as well as about cases of blacks in Europe, there is something already strange about models of antiblack racism that treat only U.S.-born blacks as its recipients. Yet, even so, in some places in the world, certain dimensions of antiblack racism do not, indeed cannot, function as they do in the United States because of the unique reality of black forces of domination and power. In much of Africa in the last half of the twentieth century, for instance, generations of Africans have been raised in a world of no direct contact with white supremacist rule. The embodiment of exploitation and brutality for them has been primarily black, and even Eurocentrism, which teaches that it is culturally best to be a European, is often brought through black-run European institutions ranging from church to school to police to government. The same applies to much of the Afro-Caribbean since the late 1970s. In the consciousness of such blacks, then, the dimension of antiblack racism that associates being black with lacking power does not hold at the national level. Power in such social worlds is mediated by and through black bodies. And it is, in fact, in cases where the grammar of Eurocentric antiblack racism takes the form of economic opportunities correlated with skin color, where the majority of the middle and upper classes amounts to a concentration of the lighter-skinned blacks, that a form of black consciousness emerges in the simple thesis that although all may be black, some are blacker than others, and it is worst to be the blackest.

Returning to the U.S. experiment, issues of ethnicity and race begin to emerge as the ethnic effort of "African" faces the specificity of Euro-American ethnic individuation. Euro-Americans do not, after all, live as such but as Italian Americans, Anglo-Americans, French Americans, Swedish Americans, and so on. Among Asians, there are Chinese

Americans, Japanese Americans, and Korean Americans. To meet a Yoruba American, Asanti American, or Zulu American, however, involves meeting someone more recently arrived than the others. Although some African Americans have traced their roots to these groups, these links are clearly only biological-genealogical, and with few exceptions—those being people from places where it was possible to live as in the past—most African Americans live through the cultures created in, that is, indigenous to, the New World. The term *African*, then, here signifies a creolized or mixed convergence of cultures from the continent of Africa, one that, mixed with Native America and Europe, with occasional Asian influences, constitutes a new culture. Yet, although new, this culture is not radically so, for in the modern world, as we have been relating, there is the weight of race, where, as Alain Locke (1989) and Fanon (1967) observed, "Negroes" became the shadow that was more real than the people from whom they were cast.

For Africans and Afro-Caribbean immigrants to the United States, this means entering a world half-blind with a naive consciousness. Many know of the antiblack racism that saturates the American state and civil society, but the history of black emergence in the United States suggests a challenge hardly fathomable to immigrant populations. After all, most immigrants, especially those from poverty-stricken countries with brutal state leadership, are empirical exemplars of the thesis that one leaves a situation that is truly bad. How, then, could they ever imagine how bad the United States could be if they are migrating to it?

The question itself is, however, fallacious because it presupposes that oppression could function as a constant term, as a substance or a thing. Oppression is hardly a constant or self-sustained phenomenon. It is a function of human relations. As a consequence, it is always relative to sets of conditions that are constantly changing. Consider it this way: oppression is a relationship between choices and options. Choices are the activities through which a human being emerges as a meaningful being. Options are the objective conditions that impose limits on choices. Options can be physical, such as mountain, a valley, or the air we breathe. They can also be social, such as the institutions by which we live. Institutions can, however, have the effect of material reality. An institution can pose limits that can be as unsurpassable as a steel fence. When institutions are equalized, no one suffers the difference in the choices they have to make. This is the insight behind republicanism, where laws are not arbitrary and are equally applicable to everyone. But where there is a discrepancy, where only some people are subject to limiting institutions and others in fact have supporting institutions, the meaning of choices takes a different turn. Those with more options may live a reality that is outwardly oriented, or what Fanon (1967) calls "actional." Those who run out of options, however, in fact, those against whom institutions are built, find themselves locked in or limited in terms of their actional reach. The social world does not, in other words, respond to their overtures or efforts at participation. They find themselves using up their resources or options before others do, and in such instances, they often find themselves living as though locked into their own bodies. In fact, physicality is associated with nearly all oppressed subjects because the social world does not extend their human reach; they literally have to move physically through the world and move things. In a world in which such touch is, however, illicit, the probability of violation is increased, and oppressed subjects eventually become isomorphic with violence.

A response to the dangers of violating others when physically reaching out is to shut oneself down, to focus instead on adjusting, fixing, molding oneself. In effect, the oppressed subject moves from reaching out to others (the social world) to inwardly directed agency. As even those resources become limited, where acting on oneself is regulated, action disappears into adverbial fantasy (how one lives one's inaction) to the point of implosivity, of living as though incapable of making any choices at all.

The black immigrant to the United States knows that there are limited options in the country he or she may be leaving, but the error is to assume that the absence of those limitations in the United States means that there are no other limitations in everyday aspects of American social life. One can be "foreign" for only so long as new generations are born into a new country whose social institutions change more slowly than such generations emerge. Eventually, the governing logic no longer becomes the normative space of the country left behind but that of the one that, for newer generations, constitutes "home." This home-grown logic of options brings along its own contradictions as the transition is made from seeing-oneself-through-the-eyes-of-others toward potentiated consciousness.

THE CREOLIZED COMMUNITY

The brilliant work of Claudia Milian Arias (2001, 2002, 2006), Johnnella Butler (2006), and Nelson Maldonado-Torres (2002, 2005) has challenged many of the constructions that have undergirded the traditional model of black and Latino studies. Although this volume focuses predominantly on blacks in Anglophone settings, Milian Arias's work provides a good case to rethink the black American in terms of the mixed and creolized categories of Latino and Latin American understandings of New World studies and, in so doing, to raise intriguing questions about their Caribbean correlates. The black American and even the African American, she argues, exemplifies not one theoretical model but the convergence of at least two: double consciousness and borderland theory.

According to Milian Arias, DuBois's insight into double consciousness articulated the lived reality of color, but it conveys the theme of crossing borders. DuBois argued that the call for the black American *only to be an American* required an erasure of the self in a world that had already collapsed Americanness into whiteness and white views of the self, including of the black self. For the social and political reality of American society was such that it placed borders not only on the movement of black Americans but also on American thought and political identity. The issue is that borderland theory is associated with Latino studies, as people whose relationship to the country in which they live is one of constant "foreignness" (Anzaldúa 1999). This "elsewhereness" is marked through language, skin color, and other cultural emblems. Milian Arias reminds us, however, that these two worlds of double consciousness and borders have been historically misrepresented as separate and have created a narrative in which there was no Latin dimension of North American black culture and no black dimension of Latin American ones (cf. Nascimento 1980).

In the standard model of African America, Southern slaves were forced to create a Baptist Christian culture infused with soul food, spirituals, and the blues (cf. Stuckey 1987; Palmer 2000). Mixture, in this model, is discussed almost entirely in terms of the model of the mulatto, the individual who is a mixture of white and black. So, the model of Negroes and mulattos, which eventually became Negroes and "coloreds," then, for a time, simply coloreds (as in white and colored sections under Jim Crow), before becoming "blacks" and then "Blacks," dominated much of the narrative about African Americans. The problem with this model, however, is that although it is true about many African Americans, not all African Americans are a product of it. Its falseness can easily be shown at the level of demographics. Although the vast majority of slaves at the time of the Civil War were fifth-generation Americans, scholars have often overlooked the constant flow of blacks across borders that functioned differently in the past than the present. Selling slaves between Louisiana and the states prior to the Louisiana Purchase is a case in point. The flow of slaves up the Mississippi River from the Gulf of Mexico suggests that black creolization could have been more than the Baptist framework, and Catholic influences should be brought into the mix. In addition, that 30 percent of the imported slaves were Muslim and that some among them were Hebrews or Jews raises questions of retention of African versions of these religions as well as other African religions that acquired new form in the Americas (cf. Austin 1997). Moreover, the flow of Caribbean slaves and freedmen and women from places where freedmen and women outnumbered whites enabled the preservation of cultural and religious practices—known today as "roots" religions—that were more African than European (Chevannes 1998). A similar observation applies to the Cape Verdean population, whose major migration, mainly for work in the shipping and whaling industry, began in the first quarter of the nineteenth century in Massachusetts and parts of Rhode Island (Wonkeryor 2006). The black populations who moved westward found themselves in places where Spanish was the dominant language, and more significantly, a number of blacks mixed in with the Native American populations in all regions of North America and lived by their cultural practices.

Here is a case in point. It is always a delight to take a white non-American on a tour of the Southern United States. I had the occasion to do so with someone who was well versed in black American literature, especially that describing the South. What surprised this scholar on her first visit through North Carolina, South Carolina, Georgia, and then northern Florida was how *mixed* the black populations appeared. She did not realize how much of African America resembles certain parts of Latin America. This scholar had visited Africa many times and had worked primarily in northern urban cities of the United States; she thus had visions of a purer African-American blackness in the South. Instead, she discovered that many were mixed with Native Americans and whites. This is not to say *no* black Americans were closer in appearance to the people of the shores of African from which their ancestors were stolen. The coastal Carolinas offer such examples, and there are tiny communities in the Florida Keys and some parts of Georgia that would make a Fante or an Asante wonder if he or she had really left home.

I mention this story because of how much it makes sense but is often overlooked in the ideological notions of a pure New World blackness. In my experience of teaching black studies classes over the past decade, for instance, I have yet to teach a class in which, with the exception of students immediately from Africa, there are New World black students whose ancestry does not include white, Native American, or Asian elements, or some mixture thereof. In one recent class, every black American student was also a Native American.

In many ways, this realization of black America as a creolized community has always been hidden in plain sight, as it were. It is there in novels and autobiographies, in confessions of being able, even in the age of Jim Crow, to ride occasionally in the white section by claiming to be Latin American. James Weldon Johnson's protagonist claimed to be Latin American at one point in *The Autobiography of an Ex–Colored Man* so that he could ride in the white section of a train, and there are examples of Caribbean figures even in Ralph Ellison's *Invisible Man*. The late Ossie Davis often recounted pretending to be Caribbean when he moved from the South to the Northeast. And even among Caribbeans, such as Harry Belafonte, there were those who pretended to be from other islands than their places of birth; there were Jamaicans who pretended to be Trinidadians, Haitians who pretended to be Martinicans, and many other variations thereof. This chamaeleonism was a function of how each group was located or perceived in the social hierarchies of each city or region.

Even historic moments speak of a more fluid black reality than present models claim. This was certainly so in the formation of influential black institutions. The American Negro Academy, for instance, had, in addition to DuBois, Johnson, and Crummell, the Jamaican Claude McKay and the Puerto Rican Arthur Schomburg. The organizing genius of Jamaican-born Marcus Garvey at the dawn of the twentieth century is well known. And more, there was the constant flow of such figures as the Trinidadians Claudia Jones and C. L. R. James, among others. In short, to be black in America did not necessarily mean having a family with a single narrative of blackness, and continued migration and intermarriage will increasingly challenge old meanings of the label "African American". In many U.S. cities today, to say that an African American will be joining the conversation does not mean that one can predict the immediate ancestry of that individual. Returning to the semiotic markers discussed earlier, this means that in spite of the ethnicizing efforts behind the term *African American*, it has clearly been reinscribed as a racial formation, as Michael Omi and Howard Winant (1994) would say, one that functions both internally and externally since it is the racial imposition on the term *black* that leads African diasporic immigrants eventually to be absorbed into the term African Americans, albeit very new and culturally more diverse ones.

This is not to say that there is not an ugly side to this process of mixing and working through the politics of racial formation. In hardly the first instance of such enmity, Henry Louis Gates Jr. and Lani Guinier recently made headlines voicing their concerns about the presence of Afro-Caribbean and African students and scholars in U.S. elite universities as beneficiaries of programs supposedly designed exclusively for U.S.-born blacks with all grandparents being descendants of slaves in this country (see Rimer and Arenson 2004). The discussions that followed revealed several striking features of their depiction of the indicted populations. First, they presented U.S.-born blacks as suffering a legacy of slavery as though slavery did not exist in the Caribbean or on the African continent. Some discussions focused on the question of U.S. responsibility to descendants of U.S. slaves, as though the sphere of U.S. influence on slavery was limited to its shores. The history of Haiti, for instance, is one of the United States' doing everything in its power to cripple the black republic and lock it into de facto, if not de jure, slavery (cf. Fischer 2004). And U.S. foreign policy to this day has been one of forcing dependency in the Caribbean (see, e.g., Thompson 1997). Second, they seem to have implied that the only slots available in U.S. institutions for blacks should be reserved only for U.S.-born blacks. It is, in other words, a standard, xenophobic in orientation, not applied to whites or Asians. Moreover, what is odd about this characterization is the presumption that multiple-generation U.S.-born blacks have a singular racial and ethnic ancestry. Harold Cruse (1967), in his critical discussion of African American and Caribbean black nationalism in *The Crisis of the Negro Intellectual*, reminds us, "In America, the Negro group is more an ethnic, than a racial group—meaning a group of mixed African, Indian, and white strains" (557). He could add to that list Afro-Caribbean mixtures of the same and note that an increased percentage of individuals with that white mixture derives from more recent generations of immigrants from Europe than from slave ancestors.

Returning specifically to Gates and Guinier, their criticism of the presence of black immigrants in U.S. elite universities did not in any way address another dimension of the opportunities available to blacks in such institutions—namely, that light-skin blacks continue to be the majority population of blacks at such institutions. Gates and Guinier are exemplars of this phenomenon, as are most of their black colleagues and students in the Ivy League and peer institutions. Gates's and Guinier's backgrounds are also ironic to the point of hypocrisy since, as Gates discovered in his recent documentary *American Lives* (2006), his lineage contains European ancestors, and Guinier's mother is white American and her father was a black Jamaican. But these details reveal some of the silliness of the opportunism and chauvinism of this path of reasoning, for pointing these contradictions out does not demonstrate that many of these individuals do not deserve to be where they are. We should not, however, forget that racism in many ways subverts categories of assessment, which means that it prefers to make exceptions the rule for one group over others. That the overwhelming proportion of blacks is brown or darker skinned makes unavoidable the conclusion that skin color influences the opportunities available in most of the world.

I have encountered the dynamics of this dimension of intrablack conflict since my childhood years. I was born on the island of Jamaica to a family of Afro-Jewish and Chinese descent and left there to join my mother in New York City at the age of nine. My mother was dark skinned, and I remember her recounting, with great disdain, how lighter-skinned Jamaicans with fewer credentials than hers had job opportunities unavailable to her. She lived in a world in which she had to be four times as good as the whites and twice as good as the lighter-skinned blacks to move ahead. I have many memories of how many people in Jamaica and in the United States responded to me as the darkest of my mother's children and of their responses to other children who were darker than me. My early years in the United States were spent in the South Bronx, on the southern side of a neighborhood bordering an Italian neighborhood to the north and a black and Puerto Rican neighborhood to the south. There were not many Anglophone Caribbean people living there. The black population, as I remember us, was pretty much as I have been describing in this chapter. We ranged from the very light to the very dark. Everyone was related to someone who came from somewhere else, be it the southern United States or other countries. Those whose relatives were from the South, even the darkest among them, were invariably mixed with Native Americans (cf. Forbes 1993). I remember visiting my father in Jacksonville, Florida, during the early years of the 1970s, and there was not much of a difference culturally. We all listened to the same music: a conglomeration of rhythm and blues, soul, reggae, and salsa. It never occurred to me that the worlds of my Jamaican family and black American friends were being portrayed in academic writings as so radically different. Even at the level of food, where at first there was more difference in recipes than in what was eaten, a mixture of U.S. soul and Caribbean creole foods was already evolving. Many restaurants in black neighborhoods today offer such a mixture. As I got older, I began to see a growing rift in the various communities. By the time I was a teenager, we had moved to the Northeast Bronx, and there I found myself suddenly in a community where, unquestionably, most blacks were Caribbean. In some sociological texts, this Caribbean community has been portrayed as a "model minority," a narrative that pits them against the non-Caribbean blacks who preceded them, as well as against Hispanophone and Francophone Caribbeans and Africans.

The Caribbean blacks see themselves as harder working than the black populations that preceded them, thus able to take advantage of what the United States has to offer. They do not take into account the double-edged standards of American citizenship and, as Percy Hintzen has pointed out in *West Indian in the West* (2001; cf. also Rogers 2006), the rather low standards of "middle-class" access they in fact embody. Even more, by way of example, consider that although the term *black* may shift from region to region in the New World, one constant is its association with crime. For instance, the demographics of people incarcerated in New York City, Atlanta, and Newark are well known in terms of *race*. But what might we find if we were to examine them in terms of *ethnicity*? The large Caribbean populations in those cities may discover that while they may "succeed" as Caribbeans they "fail" as blacks. Against the Hispanophone and Francophone populations, the Anglophone Caribbean immigrant critics do not take into account the oscillating dynamics of racial and ethnic identification and that the Anglophonic centrism of the United States suggests different opportunities for black English-speaking immigrants than black Hispanophone and Francophone ones. We see here a return of the semiotic markers and the grammar of racist discourse.

Since my years in New York City, I have lived in the Midwestern United States and then in New England. I have done much traveling and, in the course of my professional life, have chaired a department of Africana studies, which enabled me to learn from my colleagues' research on the African diaspora. Let me simply bring up some observations.

We have already seen that the multiethnic dimensions of black communities should be taken into account. Amid these categories, an often overlooked group is black Latino-Caribbeans and black Latino–Central and–South Americans (Hernández 2003; Palmer 1996; Grosfoguel 2003; Lewis Gordon 2005). The complex "black Latinos," depending on which island or country they come from, often mix with the black Caribbeans in one context and the black Americans in another. An exception seems to be Dominicans, who in some cities, such as Providence, Rhode Island, and New York City, have developed an independent and often self-isolating social structure that mirrors, to some extent, Haitians in Boston and Miami. Black Puerto Ricans seem to have a stronger ongoing relationship with black Americans, as we saw as far back as the days of Schomburg at the turn of the century, than with Anglo-Caribbeans, although, as in all human relationships, there are exceptions. I recall being attacked in a park by a group of older black and white boys in the South Bronx of my childhood because they thought I was Puerto Rican. Costa Ricans, Venezuelans (many of whom are also Trinidadians), black Cubans (many of whom are of Jamaican descent), Panamanians (many also of Jamaican extraction, descended of migrant workers who came to build the Panama Canal), and Belizians (many also of Jamaican descent) tend to mix in with Jamaican and other predominantly black Caribbean communities. Many black Latinos do not subscribe to the racial category black, or they will conflate ethnic categories with racial ones to be identified singularly in terms of their nationality. Because of the creolized national identity, they often attempt to assert that category as a racial-ethnic one over and against the racialized one of "black" or the ethnicized one of "African American." This is an ironic commonality (among many) between the Hispanophone Caribbean and the Anglophone Caribbean, for it reveals their similarity in the face of their continued affirmed difference. Nearly all of the arguments issued by Milian Arias above, for instance, could be applied to the island of Jamaica, whose landscape reveals its Spanish and creolized origins in spite of its Anglocentrism and claims of Africanness in the face of East Indian and Chinese influences.

Yet, we cannot overlook certain features of black Anglophonic Caribbean influences in U.S. cities like New York, Mount Vernon, and Atlanta, and in much of southern Florida. The second and subsequent generations of these Caribbean immigrants are increasingly growing up in a new kind of American and Caribbean environment, one that echoes where they have come from and is changing where they are; they discover that their Caribbean identity is more indigenous to the United States than the region's archipelago.

In academic environments, these changes are reflected in the absence of homogeneous blackness in black studies programs, although not all scholars in the field are happy about this. My own experience has ranged from black studies at Lehman College of the City University of New York, which was multiethnically black, to African American studies at Yale, which was multiethnically black and multiracial but dominantly light skinned and theoretically informed by ideas from Britain and Europe, to Purdue University, which was entirely black and in which I was the only member of the department that was born abroad. Then, I taught at Brown University, where, for the first time, I had a Caribbean colleague, in Africana studies, before joining Temple University, where I am not in African American studies but relate much to the U.S.- and African-born faculty here.

WITHIN THE FAMILY

Over the years, I have met many French people who deny antiblack racism in France, the very country that stimulated the writings of Anténor Firmin (1999), Aimé Césaire (2000), and Frantz Fanon (1967). I meet many black Americans and Caribbeans who claim to love England, while the blacks who live there tell a story of violent thugs brutalizing blacks with near impunity. Swedes and Norwegians are appalled by the United States and South Africa, while they defend the benefits of their past efforts at eugenics and continued efforts at tightly controlled and limited immigration from black countries. In fact, most of Europe has signed on to the Schengen Treaty, which places additional restrictions on people from countries with predominately black populations. I hear Latin American scholars speak of how race configures differently in Latin America, but we should recall that it was through traveling through such countries that Marcus Garvey's black political consciousness was radicalized, and one need simply look at any popular self-representation from television to newspapers in those countries, ironically with proportionately larger black populations than in the United States, to observe the politics of race by virtue of its absence: regarding the visual presence of blacks in popular culture, the United States is way ahead of all Latin American countries (cf. Rout 1976).

But this back-and-forth biting is, in the end, a function of the logic of borders and racist distributions of social goods. It is a fight over scraps, and, unfortunately, there are many who are willing to wage such battle. The force of how racial-ethnic mythologies function in contemporary race discourses comes to the fore. Where there is a phobia of some kind, be it race phobia or xenophobia, the result is always related to the superfluity of numbers (cf. Lewis Gordon 1995, 1997, 2000). It reminds me of the racist situations in which I was seen *only* as black.

In those cases, I alone represented *blacks*, which, of course, meant *too many blacks*. The logic of superfluity, or exponentiality, means that one should never, in truth, have more than one since one is already a plenitude. Such overdetermination is, as well, a function of a distorted social world, where the meaning of black appearance lacks a condition of intersubjective possibility. It is, literally, as if to posit the emergence of an alien life form. Blacks are overdetermined from without, as Fanon (1967) would say, which means that there is a denied inner life or point of view. As a result, the notion of a black point of view loses its meaning since the means of differentiation are also eliminated. Without the articulation of such difference, there is no basis to claim that one point of view is different from another. They collapse into the same, consequent hyperequality to the point of becoming all-as-the-same. So many, in other words, are always echoed out of so few. To be black in such a world is to face being always "too many" even in a world of alarming mortality rates for blacks.

It is perhaps the nature of the situation that purgative moments emerge. The racial logic of insider and outsider depends, after all, on the false notion that conflicts do not occur from within. In many ways, since African America never really embodied the homogenous image that dominates many textbooks, this battle between insider and outsider Africans in America has been, and continues to be, an ongoing family affair.

REFERENCES

Amo, Wilhelm. 1968. *Anton Wilhelm Amo Antonius Gvilielmus Amo Afer of Axim in Ghana: Translation of His Works*. Halle-Wittenberg, Germany: Martin Luther University.

Anzaldúa, Gloria. 1999. *Borderlands/La Frontera: The New Mestiza*. 2nd ed. San Francisco: Aunt Lute.

Austin, Allan D. 1997. *African Muslims in Antebellum America: Transatlantic Stories and Spiritual Struggles*. New York: Routledge.

Barnes, Robert Harris, Andrew Gray, and Benedict Kingsbury, eds. 1993. *Indigenous Peoples of Asia*. Ann Arbor, MI: Association for Asian Studies.

Butler, Johnnella. 2006. "Black Studies and Ethnic Studies: The Crucible of Knowledge and Social Action." In *A Companion to African-American Studies*, ed. Lewis R. Gordon and Jane Anna Gordon, 76–95. Malden, MA: Blackwell Publishers.

Césaire, Aimé. [1972] 2000. *Discourse on Colonialism*, trans. Joan Pinkham. New York: Monthly Review Press.

Chevannes, Barry, ed. 1998. *Rastafari and Other African-Caribbean Worldviews*. New Brunswick, NJ: Rutgers University Press.

Crummell, Alexander. 1992. *Destiny and Race: Selected Writings, 1840–1898*, ed. Wilson Jeremiah Moses. Amherst: University of Massachusetts Press.

Cruse, Harold. 1967. *The Crisis of the Negro Intellectual: A Historical Analysis of the Failure of Black Leadership*. New York: Quill.

Dawson, Michael C. 2001. *Black Visions: The Roots of Contemporary African-American Political Ideologies*. Chicago: University of Chicago Press.

Davies, Carole Boyce, Meredith Gadsby, Charles Peterson, and Henrietta Williams. 2003. *Decolonizing the Academy: African Diasporic Studies*. Trenton, NJ: Africa World Press.

DuBois, W. E. B. 1903. *The Souls of Black Folk: Essays and Sketches*. Chicago: A. C. McClurg and Company.

Dussel, Enrique. 1995. *The Invention of the Americas: Eclipse of "the Other" and the Myth of Modernity*, trans. Michael D. Barber. New York: Continuum.

———. 1996. *The Underside of Modernity: Apel, Ricoeur, Rorty, Taylor, and the Philosophy of Liberation*, ed. and trans. Eduardo Mendieta. Atlantic Highlands, NJ: Humanities Press.

———. 2003. *Beyond Philosophy: Ethics, History, Marxism, and Liberation Theology*, ed. and trans. Eduardo Mendieta. Lanham, MD: Rowman & Littlefield.

Dzidzienyo, Anani, and Rhett Jones. 1977. "Africanity, Structural Isolation and Black Politics in the Americas," *Studia Africana*, no. 1 (spring): 32–44.

Fanon, Frantz. 1967. *Black Skin, White Masks*, trans. Charles Lamm Markman. New York: Grove Press.

Fernández-Armesto, Felipe. 1987. *Before Columbus: Exploration and Colonization from the Mediterranean to the Atlantic, 1229–1492*. Philadelphia: University of Pennsylvania Press.

Firmin, Anténnor. 1999. *Equality of Human Races: A Nineteenth Century Haitian Scholar's Response to European Racialism*, trans. Asselin Charles. New York: Garland Publishing Company/Taylor and Francis.

Fischer, Sibylle. 2004. *Modernity Disavowed: Haiti and Cultures of Slavery in the Age of Revolution*. Durham, NC: Duke University Press.

Forbes, Jack D. 1993. *Africans and Native Americans: Color, Race and Caste in the Evolution of Red-Black Peoples*. Urbana: University of Illinois Press.

Gordon, Jane Anna. 2005. "Challenges Posed to Social-Scientific Method by the Study of Race." In *A Companion to African-American Studies*, ed. Lewis R. Gordon and Jane Anna Gordon. Malden, MA: Blackwell Publishers.

Gordon, Lewis R. 1995. *Bad Faith and Antiblack Racism*. Amherst, NY: Humanity Books.

———, ed. 1997. *Existence in Black: An Anthology of Black Existential Philosophy*. New York: Routledge.

———. 2000. *Existentia Africana: Understanding Africana Existential Thought*. New York: Routledge.

———. 2005. "Black in Latinas and Blacks in Latin America: Some Philosophical Considerations." In *Latinas in the World-System: Towards the Decolonization of the U.S. Empire in the 21st Century*, ed. Ramón Grosfoguel, Nelson Maldonado Torres, and José David Saldívar. Boulder, CO: Paradigm Publishers.

Gordon, Lewis, and Jane Anna Gordon, eds. 2005. *Not Only the Master's Tools: African-American Studies in Theory and Practice*. Boulder, CO: Paradigm Publishers.

———. 2006. "On Working through a Most Difficult Terrain: Introducing *A Companion to African-American Studies*." In *A Companion to African-American Studies*, ed. Lewis R. Gordon and Jane Anna Gordon. Malden, MA: Blackwell Publishers.

Grosfoguel, Ramón. 2003. *Colonial Subjects: Puerto Ricans in a Global Perspective.* Berkeley: University of California Press.

Henry, Paget. 2005. "Africana Phenomenology: Its Philosophical Implications." *CLR James Journal* 11, no. 1 (summer): 79–112.

Hernández, Tanya Katerí. 2003. "'Too Black to Be Latino/a': Blackness and Blacks as Foreigners in Latino Studies." *Latino Studies* 1, no. 1 (March): 152–59.

Hintzen, Percy C. 2001. *West Indian in the West: Self-Representations in an Immigrant Community.* New York: New York University Press.

Ifekwunigwe, Jayne O., ed. 2004. *"Mixed Race" Studies: A Reader.* London: Routledge.

Liu, Lydia H. 2006. *The Clash of Empires: The Invention of China in Modern World Making.* Cambridge, MA: Harvard University Press.

Locke, Alain. 1989. *The Philosophy of Alain Locke: The Harlem Renaissance and Beyond.* Philadelphia: Temple University Press.

Maldonado-Torres, Nelson. 2002. "Post-imperial Reflections on Crisis, Knowledge, and Utopia: Transgresstopic Critical Hermeneutics and the 'Death of European Man,'" *Review: A Journal of the Fernand Braudel Center for the Study of Economies, Historical Systems, and Civilizations* 25, no. 3: 277–315.

———. 2005. "Toward a Critique of Continental Reason: Africana Studies and the Decolonization of Imperial Cartographies in the Americas." In *Not Only the Master's Tools: African-American Studies in Theory and Practice,* ed. Lewis R. Gordon and Jane Anna Gordon, 51–84. Boulder, CO: Paradigm Publishers.

Mignolo, Walter. 2006. *The Idea of Latin America.* Malden, MA: Blackwell Publishers.

Milian Arias, Claudia. 2001. "Breaking into the Borderlands: Double Consciousness, Latina and Latino Misplacements." PhD diss., Brown University.

———. 2002. "New Languages, New Humanities: The 'Mixed Race' Narrative and the Borderlands." In *A Companion to Racial and Ethnic Studies,* ed. David Theo Goldberg and John Solomos, 355–64. Malden, MA: Blackwell Publishers.

———. 2006. "Differences are Relational: Dialoguing with African American and Latino Studies." In *A Companion to African American Studies,* ed. Lewis R. Gordon and Jane Anna Gordon. Malden, MA: Blackwell Publishers.

Mudimbe, V. Y. 1988. *The Invention of Africa: Gnosis, Philosophy and the Order of Knowledge.* Bloomington: Indiana University Press.

Nascimento, Elisa Larkin. 1980. *Pan Africanism and South America: Emergence of a Black Rebellion.* Buffalo, NY: Afrodiaspora.

Neves, Walter A., Joseph F. Powell, and Erik G. Ozolins. 1999. "Modern Human Origins as Seen from the Peripheries." *Journal of Human Evolution* 37, no. 1 (July): 129–33.

Neves, Walter A., André Prous, Rolando González-José, Renato Kipnis, and Joseph Powell. 2003. "Early Holocene Human Skeletal Remains from Santana do Riacho, Brazil: Implications for the Settlement of the New World." *Journal of Human Evolution* 45, no. 1 (July): 759–82.

Neves, Walter A., and Hector Pucciarelli. 1998. "The Zhoukoudian Upper Cave Skull 101 as Seen from the Americas." *Journal of Human Evolution* 34, no. 2 (February): 219–22.

Omi, Michael, and Howard Winant. 1994. *Racial Formation in the United States: From the 1960s to the 1990s.* 2nd ed. New York: Routledge.

Oyewùmí, Oyèrónké. 1997. *The Invention of Women: Making an African Sense of Western Gender Discourses.* Minneapolis: University of Minnesota Press.

Palmer, Colin. 1996. "Africans in Hispanic America." In *Encyclopedia of Latin American History and Culture.* Vol. 1, ed. Barbara Tenenbaum, 21–23. New York: Scribner's.

———. 2000. "The African Diaspora." *Black Scholar* 30, nos. 3–4 (fall/winter): 56–59.

Rimer, Sara, and Karen W. Arenson. 2004. "Top Colleges Take More Blacks, but Which Ones?" *New York Times Education Supplement*, available at www.nytimes.com/2004/06/24/education/ 24AFFI.final.html?ei=5007&en=92df04e0957d73d3&ex=1403409600&partner=USERLAND &pagewanted=all (last accessed February 27, 2007).

Rogers, Reuel. 2006. *Afro-Caribbean Immigrants and the Politics of Incorporation: Ethnicity, Exception, or Exit*. New York: Cambridge University Press.

Rout, Leslie B., Jr. 1976. *The African Experience in Spanish America: From 1502 to the Present*. Cambridge: Cambridge University Press.

Stuckey, Sterling. 1987. *Slave Culture: Nationalist Theory and the Foundations of Black America*. New York: Oxford University Press.

Thompson, Alvin. 1997. *The Haunting Past: Politics, Economics and Race in Caribbean Life*. Kingston, Jamaica: Ian Randle Publishers.

West, Cornel. 2002. *Prophesy Deliverance: An Afro-American Revolutionary Christianity*. Anniversary edition. Philadelphia: Westminster Press.

Wonkeryor, Edward Lama. 2006. "Diversity in the United States: The Experience of African Immigrants." *Oxford Roundtable Forum*. Harris Manchester College, Oxford University, Oxford, England, March 12–17, 2006.

Wynter, Sylvia. 2005. "On How We Mistook the Map for the Territory, and Re-Imprisoned Ourselves in Our Unbearable Wrongness of Being, of *Désêtre*: Black Studies toward the Human Project." In *Not Only the Master's Tools: African-American Studies in Theory and Practice*, ed. Lewis R. and Jane Anna Gordon. Boulder, CO: Paradigm Publishers.

CHAPTER 4

Marriage and Family Socialization among Black Americans and Caribbean and African Immigrants

Harriette Pipes McAdoo, Sinead Younge, and Solomon Getahun

People of African descent in America belong to three major groupings: descendants of enslaved Africans, immigrants from Caribbean countries and their descendants, and immigrants from countries on the African continent and their descendants. The growing proportion of these native and foreign-born black populations in the United States has posed a challenge for the study of marriage, parenting, and family-socialization patterns especially of contemporary immigrants from the Caribbean and Africa. We note that the proportions of Afro-Caribbean and African immigrants are small (see chapter 2) compared to other immigrants from Europe, for instance, but these proportions are no different from other immigrants, such as those from Asia, who are more visible and have captured more investigative attention. As America becomes more diverse, and as more people of color are born in or voluntarily migrate to the United States, the cultural landscape is being transformed, and the worldviews of these contemporary groups contribute to the discourse on, or narratives of, people of color living in America. We focus on Anglophone, or English-speaking, Afro-Caribbean immigrants and English-speaking immigrants from Africa (e.g., Nigeria and Ethiopia) in our comparative discussions in this chapter.

People of African descent in America are a heterogeneous group to be sure; yet, they share a number of noteworthy characteristics. Billingsley (1968), for instance, has maintained that five general statements characterize families of all people of African descent: they are extended in form, they have fictive kin who become as close to the family as blood kin, they have supportive family patterns, they have flexible family boundaries, and they have flexible gender roles in child rearing. There are notable similarities in socialization in particular, and in patterns of family formation in general, but, clearly, there are also differences based on contextual influences or the evolution of approaches to living based on different historical experiences. While there may be similarities in approaches to marriage and parenting across these groups, however, there are also notable differences within each group in terms of family trajectories based on education and financial resources.

One central institution to the "black experience," indeed, to all collective experiences, is the family. The role of any family is to provide support and codes of conduct for individuals within a milieu. At the same time, ideas or concepts of family functioning are culturally bounded and dictated by historical vicissitudes. When these culturally relative ideas are generally applied to diverse forms of family functioning, they tend to yield misinformed or erroneous generalizations. This has been the case, for the most part, with descriptions of native Americans of African descent, as their history in America shows. Due to this history, we find that, among native Americans of African descent, there are families who have become educationally and financially solvent and moved on up the rungs of the socioeconomic ladder, as well as those who have remained poor over generations in this land of wealth. While their beginnings as groups of enslaved Africans may be similar, their family histories over generations are different. The story for immigrant Caribbean and African families in America may be different, though not dissimilar, in their experience of racial typing in their land of settlement. Historically, immigrant Caribbean and African families have been characterized by higher-than-average educational and financial standing, and contemporary Caribbean and African families may be no different in that they may have family patterns that are strongly dependent upon their originating educational and financial status before coming to this country. For all three groups, however, their family and life trajectories are influenced by their goal of attaining middle- and upper-class status in this American society.

Our purpose in this chapter, then, is to focus on the family characteristics of these groups. We provide a general description of family functioning for each of these three groups by profiling families within the framework of their cultural traditions. Our profile of each group evokes similarities and differences that exist across families in these groups, but we also note that there are significant gaps in the data on marriage, parenting, and socialization patterns, especially for the immigrant black groups. For this reason, we also provide suggestions to stimulate discussion for future research. We begin our discussions by profiling the black American family; we next present Caribbean and African immigrant families.

BLACK AMERICANS

America shares a common British heritage with the Anglophone Caribbean and Anglophone African countries. However, America differs from Africa and the Caribbean in the specific form of chattel slavery it adopted and the subsequent race- and class-based social systems that developed as a result. Throughout their history in America, black Americans have experienced many changes in their status, and from slavery until contemporary times, blacks in America have faced a number of challenges that have had particularly salient effects on the family. The current family formation of many black Americans is the culmination of vestiges of a preslavery West African heritage, the system of chattel slavery, social class, and acculturation into Euro-American culture. Throughout this time, the black family has been continuously labeled as deviant and pathological, while little regard has been given to the historical sociocultural influences on the family functioning of blacks or the resilience and strengths displayed by black families.

In an effort to control the enslaved and dominate African slaves more completely (Frazier 1951; Blassingame 1972; Boyd-Franklin 1989), some slave masters made systematic efforts to destroy family structures by promoting a casual attitude toward families (Frazier 1951). As an adaptive coping response, the black family has existed, and continues to exist, in many variations, often comprising several different households embedded in a larger network of extended family networks (Billingsley 1968; Nobles 1997). Loyalty to family and the ability to adapt to adverse circumstances allowed blacks to overcome many negative forces by reasserting their ties of affection and using extended kinship ties, a strong spiritual/religious orientation, and a focus on the importance of multigenerational networks (Sue 2005). These coping mechanisms continue to exist today. Below, we present two core topics of socialization, namely, parenting styles and religion, to describe patterns of family structures among black Americans.

Parenting Style

In the postemancipation period, family socialization played an important role in the lives and development of freed blacks. Under the system of slavery, enslaved males were disempowered and unable to protect their families. The general marginalization of the black male has had long-lasting effects upon black family relationships. Currently, 41 percent of African-American adults are married in contrast with 62 percent of whites and 60 percent of Latinos (U.S. Census Bureau 2004). Overall black males (47 percent) are more likely than their white counterparts (28 percent) to be single, divorced, or widowed. The slight gender imbalance of black males (48 percent) to black females (52 percent) that places a strain on black male-female relations is set in the context of high homicide, incarceration, and poverty rates among black males. Estimates from the Current Population Survey (Census Bureau 2005) show that over half of black children are currently living in single-parent homes although black nonresident fathers have a higher rate than white and Hispanic nonresident fathers of visiting their children and partaking in primary-care duties (Coles 2001). Data from the National Survey of Families and Households indicate that black males are more likely to be single full-time fathers than their white and Hispanic counterparts (Eggebeen, Snyder, and Manning 1996).

Whether part of a single- or a two-parent household, black parents rely on relatives and friends to play supportive roles in child-rearing practices. For many African Americans, extended kinship support is an adaptive strategy that allows for the sharing of resources and the opportunity for extended kin to help influence children's positive development. African American parenting styles vary and are influenced by sociodemographic factors, including education and socioeconomic status (McAdoo et al. 2005). Early investigations of African American families suggested that these families were characterized by high levels of power assertion, unrealistic expectations of obedience, and low tolerance for child input (Baumrind 1971). Such findings often resulted from comparative studies of black and white families that yielded an incomplete portrayal of African American child rearing. In a more recent study of working- and middle-class African American mothers, a child-oriented approach to discipline was demonstrated among the women participants (Bluestone and Thomas-LaMonde 1999).

In comparison to whites, African American parenting styles have generally been characterized as authoritative and as using physical punishment more frequently. According to Diana Baumrind's (1971) model of parenting styles, an *authoritative* parenting style is characterized as being highly demanding and highly responsive; otherwise stated, it is high in both warmth and control. Moreover, authoritative parents remain receptive to the child's view but take responsibility for firmly guiding the child (Baumrind 1996). Authoritative parenting styles have been linked to positive adolescent development. Comparative studies of black and white parenting styles demonstrate that Baumrind's model may be applicable to racial ethnic minorities and must be considered with caveats since parenting styles are qualitatively different across racial groups. When whites are used as the standard, black parenting styles may be interpreted inaccurately.

In contrast to authoritative parents, Baumrind characterizes *authoritarian* parents as firm disciplinarians who lack the warmth of the authoritative parent, whereas *permissive*, or indulgent, parents are characterized as being high in warmth but lacking focus on discipline and control. Several researchers have begun to argue that authoritarianism is not as detrimental to African American children's academic achievement as it is to that of European American children. Scholars reason that because African American children, especially boys, are often exposed to the harsh realities of the inner city, firm parental control is adaptive in these environments, and emotional warmth may be expressed slightly differently than in comparison groups (Mason et al. 1996; Ogbu and Gibson 1991).

In order to be successful in American society, African Americans must teach their children how to deal with racial discrimination and prejudice (Hill 1997). Black parents often stress education as a means of upward mobility and a way to combat racism (Higginbotham and Webber 1992). In addition to the important role parents play in child socialization, another traditionally salient institution in the African American family is religion and spirituality.

Religion and Spirituality

A strong religious and spiritual orientation has remained a significant aspect in the lives of African Americans. Religious practices are often strongly reinforced within the African American community and many of these religious practices were initially influenced by traditional African practices (DuBois 1903). Melville Herskovits (1930) argues that religious practices are often the only surviving social institution of Africa, with the African influence strongest in the South (e.g., style of worship, music) (cf. Pipes 1992). Although enslaved Africans brought their spiritual belief systems with them to America, once in America, they were forced to become Christians, and during this period, they integrated their various traditional belief systems into Christianity. (Notably, African Americans resisted Christianity at first because it condoned slavery and the oppression of nonwhites).

Today, African Americans are represented in a diverse array of religious orientations. Religion remains an important factor in the lives of black Americans and the socialization of black children. Studies show that black American students are more likely than other students to believe in God, to pray, and to attend religious services frequently (Astin et al. 2005). A number of empirical studies have found that religiosity among blacks acts as a buffer against stress, deters risky behaviors among both adolescents and adults (e.g., substance use, sexual intercourse), and contributes to overall psychological well-being (Bachman et al. 2003; Hardy and Raffaelli 2003). The black church not only plays a therapeutic and religious role in the lives of African Americans, it fulfills social needs. Regardless of religiosity, African Americans have traditionally gone to church to seek friends and to pray. Historically, courtships often took place in the church, for that was often the only time that people in the community were able to get together (Woodson 1921). Services were often long, and the women brought dinner and supper. Meals would often be followed by one or two more sermons and many spirituals.

The black church is one of the oldest institutions in the U.S. black community and continues to be one of the institutions in which African Americans are able to have complete control over their lives and activities. As an important resource for the African American community, religious participation provides spiritual assistance, norms for moral and interpersonal behaviors, and a source of social support for parents as well as children (Chatters et al. 2002).

CARIBBEAN IMMIGRANT FAMILIES IN AMERICA

The Caribbean is the source of the earliest and largest voluntary black migration into the United States, so it comes as little surprise that, like the African American family, the Caribbean family has often been erroneously viewed as pathological because it differs from European or Western concepts of healthy family functioning. Today, Afro-Caribbeans, along with African-born blacks, make up a growing proportion of the U.S. black population, resulting in the fusion of a variety of cultures and ethnic groups with American society. There are approximately 1.5 million Afro-Caribbeans living in the United States; however, this number only reflects first-generation documented immigrants who report their status to the U.S. Census Bureau and does not account for the children of Caribbean immigrants, the second-generation, who may identify as Afro-Caribbean but are considered to be American according to their U.S. nativity. Therefore, the actual number of individuals who identify as Afro-Caribbeans likely exceeds 1.5 million. Long after migrating to the United States, many Afro-Caribbean immigrants maintain a strong ethnic and national identity, which is often passed down with great effort to successive generations.

This section focuses on the Anglophone, or English-speaking, Caribbean people, including people from Guyana, Trinidad and Tobago, Barbados, and Jamaica. It must be noted that the institutional life of the Anglophone Caribbean is a diverse culmination of African, Asian, East Indian, European, and, to a lesser extent, indigenous (e.g., Arawak and Carib) cultures. Each Caribbean country's unique culture distinguishes it from its neighbors; however, many commonalities link them, and when Anglophone immigrants arrive in the United States, many may adopt a pan-Caribbean or West Indian identity (Butterfield 2004).

Studies on the social and economic profiles of African Americans and their black immigrant counterparts report that Afro-Caribbeans and Africans have slightly higher levels of socioeconomic status than their African American counterparts (see chapter 5). Afro-Caribbean immigrants in the United States have been referred to as the "black success story" due to the large number of individuals who come to the United States and realize the American dream of upward mobility. The differences in social mobility between African Americans and Afro-Caribbeans have been used to draw comparisons and reinforce stereotypes about foreign-born versus American-born blacks. These stereotypes influence intraracial relations. Subsequently, the economic successes of immigrant blacks have been used as an argument against the oppressive claims of racism and discrimination that are said to impede the opportunities for upward mobility for native-born African Americans. However, the advantage of *selective migration* is often excluded from these discussions, as is the fact that black immigrants continue to have lower median incomes in comparison to white Americans and white immigrants.

It has been suggested that in large metropolitan cities with substantial numbers of black immigrant communities, there is less interaction between black immigrant groups and black Americans (and Americans in general), which reduces immigrants' need to fully integrate into American society. Contrary to this belief, there is evidence that Afro-Caribbeans' neighborhoods in large metropolitan cities tend to overlap substantially with African Americans' neighborhoods (Logan and Deane 2003). The integration of Afro-Caribbean individuals and their successive generations into mainstream American society is largely influenced by familial functioning, socioeconomic status, and the region of the country in which they reside. Some black immigrants who arrive in the United States with the hope of attaining the American dream fall prey to the belief that embracing a "black identity" or "assimilating" into black America will inherently lead to downward social and cultural mobility (Waters 1994; Zhou 1997). Therefore, some immigrants choose to assimilate into white "mainstream" culture or not to assimilate at all. This controversial and often misunderstood topic has received wide attention and provides further fuel for the myth of the "model minority." Interestingly, with the proximity and shared experiences of all blacks in America, regardless of ancestry, acculturation for all groups is inevitable. Against this background, we describe Caribbean families in America by focusing on three topics; namely, marriage and socialization patterns, gender roles, and the influence of religion on family life.

Marriage and Socialization

Just as there is a sex-ratio imbalance in the African American community (i.e., women outnumber men), Caribbean women make up approximately 57 percent of the total British West Indian population in the United States (Census Bureau 2006). In 2000, 20 percent of British West Indian males and 18 percent of British West Indian females over the age of fifteen reported being married (these numbers exclude separated couples). Although marriage is a valued union, it is not the only type of family pattern among Caribbean people (Brice 1982). Among some social classes, marriage is clearly not the norm in the Caribbean, and female-headed households are both more common and less taboo than in the United States (Safa 1998). Unions where men and women choose to live together and have children without being married are acceptable among many segments of the population in the Caribbean.

In the postemancipation period, neocolonial institutions, such as the church and the educational system, sought to destroy the social and economic independence experienced by Caribbean women by promoting marriage as prestigious and morally superior (Momsen 2002). Yet, many Caribbean women resisted formal marriage because of "the familial patriarchal ideology which allowed domestic violence, loss of parental rights and a double standard of sexual freedom" (Momsen 2002, 46). In today's Caribbean, many women choose economic autonomy and personal freedom outside of marriage; this tradition of independence continues to exist among Caribbean immigrants residing in the United States, and there seems to be little change regarding common law unions among many Caribbean immigrants in America.

The children of Caribbean immigrants who grow up in the United States may seek mates who can relate to their own experiences but often have a difficult time dating if they do not reside in one of the large metropolitan cities where a large proportion of Caribbean immigrants resides. The second generation must choose whether to marry someone directly from their parent's home country, someone more assimilated into American society with a similar background as their own, or someone from outside of their national and racial group altogether (see chapter 8). This can be especially complex for the individuals of mixed heritage who, in the Caribbean, may be classified in their own category but, in the United States, have to submit to broad and explicit racial classifications. According to a study of interracial couples by Suzanne Model and Gene Fisher (2001), Afro-Caribbean men and women who arrived in the United States as adults or teenagers were more likely to have native white partners than African American men and women. Overall, the likelihood of Afro-Caribbean men and women marrying outside of their race was higher for those who arrived as children or were born in the United States than for those who arrived as teens or adults. Whether one marries within their racial or ethnic group or not, the children of these relationships must negotiate their parent's traditional culture versus the host culture in which they are raised, and this can often be a point of contention in the parent-child relationship.

The transmittal of customs, values, norms, and beliefs takes place at various ecological levels, such as family, school, church, and community (Bronfenbrenner 1979). Although rapid urban migration has dispersed family and community networks, both African Americans and Afro-Caribbean families continue to draw support from a notably wide range of kin, including not just parents and children, but also siblings, aunts, uncles, and even fictive kin (Chamberlain 2003). These cultural practices do not continue unchanged once migration has occurred; they are restructured, redefined, and renegotiated in new environments, and immigrants continue to draw on premigration family experiences, norms, and cultural frameworks as they carve out new lives for themselves in the United States (Hondagneu-Sotelo 1994). Although immigrants are unable to reproduce their old cultural patterns exactly when they move to a new land, these patterns continue to have a powerful influence in shaping family values and norms, as well as actual patterns of behavior that develop in the new setting.

In the Caribbean, child care is typically provided by a grandmother or aunt living nearby, enabling the mother to work outside of the home. Once families migrate to the United States, it is not unusual for the caregiver to be sent for from the country of origin (Thompson and Bauer 1995). These caregivers, who are typically elders in the family, may also act as socialization agents for second-generation children. Though empirical research on Afro-Caribbean families residing in the United States remains limited, it appears that these premigration customs continue to exist in the United States (Chamberlain 2003).

Of note, too, is how newly arrived family members and second-generation children undergo the process of racial socialization in America. The nuclear and extended families promote or inhibit the integration of newly arrived family members or second-generation children into American, or more specifically black, society. There has been some debate regarding the process of racial socialization of second-generation Caribbean immigrants into black American culture, and some scholars suggest that first-generation black immigrants in particular see themselves as immigrants first and feel that their immigrant status may protect them from the negative stereotypes associated with being black American, although this attitude varies across social classes (Portes and Zhou 1993; Waters and Eschbach 1995). A study by Waters (1999) found that a strong West Indian identity was most lacking among the children of the most economically disadvantaged immigrants. Her sample consisted of children of economically disadvantaged Caribbean immigrants living in New York City who were raised in harsh and economically depressed conditions, indicating that socioeconomic status has an impact on one's level of social and ethnic identity among the children of Caribbean immigrants. Waters claims that in these circumstances, the Caribbean identity of second-generation children may be repressed by the forces of daily life in the American ghetto. For these second-generation immigrants, the effort to move ahead in American society means that, because of the salience of race in the United States, they will be subject to the same levels of racism and discrimination as native-born African Americans. Waters's assertions are limited in that she did not study a comparison group of Caribbean immigrants of higher socioeconomic status who tend to distance themselves from families of lower socioeconomic statuses, including those within their own ethnic groups (Butterfield 2004).

It has been demonstrated that some Caribbean immigrants and their children attempt to avoid racism directed toward the African American community by emphasizing ethnic over racial identity. Distinctive cultural traits and continued ties to their homeland, for instance, have been used to emphasize differences from black Americans. First-generation Afro-Caribbean immigrants are at times stereotyped by whites as "hardworking," and some immigrants use these stereotypes to their advantage in order to negotiate racially hostile environments.

Gender Roles

Throughout the Caribbean, there are significant differences among various groups in terms of gender roles, and these differences are often a reflection of color, class, political views, religious affiliation, age, physical ability or disability, and the culture of the island of residence. In terms of gender roles, the Caribbean family has traditionally been viewed as patriarchal, with a structure that is vertical and hierarchical (Baptiste, Hardy, and Lewis 1997). Gender roles are traditionally sharply defined, and in the Caribbean, men have traditionally tended to have greater societal entitlement and privileges than women. Caribbean families have traditionally been explicitly male dominant. Upon arrival in the United States, however, many Anglophone Caribbean couples tend to adopt the prevailing gender roles for men and women. Generally, these roles are more egalitarian and less explicitly male dominant and allow women greater equality than in the Caribbean (Baptiste, Hardy, and Lewis 1997; Momsen 2002). Yet, research on immigrant families also indicates a greater restriction and monitoring of daughters versus sons due to the expectation that daughters must embody traditional ideals of behavior compared to sons (Dion and Dion 2001). As such, among Caribbean immigrants, while daughters are expected to seek educational and career opportunities, they are also expected to adhere to traditional family values. The values regarded as most important are often those that are directly related to specific cultural behaviors, practices, and family relationships.

Within the Caribbean's traditional division of household labor, the majority of women perform most of the household and child-rearing tasks, regardless of their employment status. Men are perceived to be responsible primarily for the economic support of the family, even when women work outside the home. At the same time, it is not uncommon for women in professions like nursing to be the primary or sole provider. While traditional notions of the Caribbean family are patriarchal in nature, there is also what some refer to as a "more common" typology of Caribbean families in which women are economically and otherwise responsible for the day-to-day living arrangements of their families and households (referred to as matrifocal households). In these types of households, males typically do not enjoy the dominant presence they have in the nuclear family structure.

The contemporary Caribbean family has been characterized as "patriarchy in absentia" (Momsen 2002, 48) due to matrifocal familial patterns and gender-specific migration patterns. In these circumstances, males who migrate out of the Caribbean for economic reasons tend to leave women in charge of their families. It is not uncommon for young women to have their first child while still living at home with their mothers, while male relatives act as paternal role models for sisters, cousins, nieces, and nephews. Women in most Caribbean countries have long held the right to own land and valued education as a method for upward mobility.

Religion and Spirituality

Religion is a dominant element in the lives of Afro-Caribbean individuals, and its value is typically reinforced within the family structure. In a national survey conducted by the Institute for Social Research at the University of Michigan, 91 percent of Afro-Caribbeans residing in the United States said that religion was important in their lives. A mosaic of religious and spiritual systems, including Christianity, Buddhism, Hinduism, Judaism, Islam, Obeah, and Rastafarianism, can be found in modern Anglophone Caribbean. Unlike Christianity and traditional African belief systems, Hinduism and Islam were largely brought to the Anglophone Caribbean by East Indian indentured servants.

Religions like Vodun, Santeria, and Espiritismo are more commonly associated with the Hispanophone and Francophone countries of the Caribbean, although elements of all of these religions can be seen throughout the entire Caribbean.

Enslaved Africans arrived in the Caribbean with their own religious beliefs and spiritual practices. During slavery, the Black Codes specified that Christianity would be imposed on the enslaved in order to control and assimilate the Africans into European culture. Protestant missionaries began arriving in the region in the late eighteenth century, providing slaves, and later the newly emancipated, with religious education. And yet, a small percentage of escaped slaves, or *maroons,* were able to retain a significant level of traditional African practice and religion.

Despite the constraints of linguistic heterogeneity and practices among some of the early Africans, the regional commonalities of oral tradition, proverbs, songs, and practices from their original homelands prevailed to infuse Christianity with traditional West African cultural practices. The combination of African and European practices is palpable in modern Caribbean society as evidenced by dance, music, Carnival, and rites of passage. Contemporary research on the religious practices of Caribbean immigrants have examined religion and spiritual belief systems in terms of how religious practices provide a way to cope with the stresses of the immigrant experience (Gregory 1999). In a study on religious faith and support at the end of life, Jonathan Koffman and Irene Higginson (2002) compared first-generation Afro-Caribbeans and whites in the United Kingdom and found that Afro-Caribbeans relied on religion and culture as a coping mechanism. Another study conducted by Ami Rokach (1999) examined cultural background and coping in a group of North American, South Asian, and West Indian individuals residing in Canada. The findings from this study indicated that women from South Asia and the West Indies (Guyana, Jamaica, Barbados, and Trinidad and Tobago) reported being more religious, and their religious beliefs and practices influenced their lifestyles, customs, and overall ability to cope with loneliness. Continued research into the role of religion in the lives of Afro-Caribbeans residing in the United States will expand this discourse (see chapter 6).

In sum, Afro-Caribbean parents in the United States must raise their children to be successful members of American society and at the same time inculcate in them Caribbean traditional values. The children of Caribbean immigrants in the United States face a choice regarding whether they will identify as black Americans by yielding to acculturation or assimilation pressures, whether they will maintain an ethnic identity reflecting their parents' national origins while pursuing social mobility in the United States, or whether they will adopt both a racial and ethnic identity, which may not necessarily be antithetical (Bonnet 1990; Foner 1987; Fouron 1987; Kasinitz 1992; Ostine 1998; Waters 1994; Butterfield 2004). While some first-generation black immigrants in the United States have distanced themselves from black Americans, stressing their national origins and ethnic identities, the children of these immigrants are faced with overwhelming pressures to identify only as "blacks" (Stafford 1987; Foner 1987; Kasinitz 1992). The children of black immigrants, who lack their parents' distinctive accents and experiences, can choose to be even more invisible as ethnics than their parents or must actively work to assert their ethnic identities.

AFRICAN IMMIGRANT FAMILIES IN AMERICA

In this last section of the chapter, we present what we know about African immigrants and describe the African immigrant family by presenting premigration characteristics (the heterogeneity of these immigrants, the "push" factors for migration, who migrates; and gender inequality) and postmigration themes (familial structures, sources of familial tensions, health status). We note that the study of contemporary African immigrant families in America requires further rigorous research to distill the myriad of phenomena that immigrants encounter, including the adjustment problems they face, how they cope with changing gender roles in the family, issues related to child rearing, the effect of the generation gap on familial relations, white racial discrimination and African-American ethnic bias and the context of arrival and reception, language barriers, and the predictors of downward mobility. We also note that in order to understand contemporary African immigrant families in America, we have to find out whether variations in the ethnicity and religion of African immigrants lead to differences in their family structures in the United States (cf. Takyi 2002).

Premigration Characteristics

Although Africans residing in the United States share a common experience as immigrants, there is a large degree of heterogeneity within African communities and the immigration experience. In terms of regional representation, West Africans are the largest group of African immigrants in the United States. They represent more than 30 percent of all Africans in America, followed by East Africans, who make up more than 25 percent, and North Africans, who constitute more than 20 percent. Approximately 7 percent of the remainder are from southern Africa, while middle Africa represents less than 3 percent. Of these groups, Nigerians (West Africa) and Ethiopians (East Africa) represent the largest number of immigrants from sub-Saharan Africa. These data show that African immigrants in America are ethnically diverse, and at times they are acutely divided in terms of regional or ethnic origin. For example, Nigerians are divided into Igbo (Ibo), Hausa, and Yoruba, among other ethnic groups, while Ethiopians identify themselves as Amhara, Oromo, and Tigre. Despite the palpable ethnic heterogeneity, in general, there is a dearth of empirical studies that examine African immigrant issues from an ethnic, national, or regional origins perspective, and for the most part, African immigrants have remained "invisible" sojourners in America (Apraku 1991; Arthur 2001; Takyi 2002). Instead, most studies have treated these immigrants as a homogeneous group. Existing studies on African immigrants have been conducted in relation to black diaspora formation (cf. Okpewho, Davies, and Mazrui 1999) and have emphasized communality and "Africanness" more than the complex identities of Africans from various parts of Africa and the differences in their manners of entry and reception.

The increasing African presence in the United States that began in the early 1960s was the outcome of a diverse, yet interrelated, set of factors. Socioeconomic and political problems on the African continent and the revocation of restrictive immigration laws in the United States led to the current increased presence of African immigrants in the United States (Rumbaut 1996; Warner 1998). At one time or another, many post-1960s African immigrants were victims of military dictatorship, interethnic conflict, economic hardships, or a combination of the three. It is such misfortunes that have driven highly educated professionals out of their home countries. Currently, African immigrants in the United States account for a small proportion of the U.S. population compared with immigrants from other continents, but the number of Africans coming to the United States is continually increasing.

The majority of African immigrants reside in metropolitan areas, and one-third of them are concentrated in three states, New York, California, and Texas, although significant enclaves of immigrants and refugees can be found in places like Maryland and Minnesota (see chapter 1). It is noted that the longer African immigrants reside in the United States, the more likely they are to become dispersed across the country (U.S. Department of Homeland Security 2003).

Being part of the post-1960s immigration, a considerable proportion of black Africans immigrating to the United States were professionals who came to further their education but failed to return home. As a whole, this particular group of immigrants is highly representative of the educated elite of their countries of origin. Consequently, this particular type of immigrant projected the image of the "highly educated African" in the United States (Apraku 1991; Getachew and Maigenet 1991). At the same time, the majority of the post-1960s African immigrants who came to the United States as students and professionals were disproportionately men.

During the colonial period, education in Africa was less available to the masses, while the sons and daughters of African chiefs and kings had relatively easy access. This difference between the rulers and the ruled was further heightened in the postcolonial period when education became the sole requirement for employment and social mobility. Hence, though exceptions could be made for talented individuals, those Africans who came to the United States in the 1960s and 1970s were often members of the middle and upper classes. This disparity was further characterized by gender inequality in terms of access to opportunities (Robertson 1995). A corollary of this phenomenon is that African males have been the beneficiaries of a mostly patriarchal system that has provided them with greater access to education and prosperity while relegating women to domestic roles (Arrighi and Maume 2000). Historically, African women have not had the same access to education as men (although this is clearly changing as evidenced by the increasing number of women who are being educated in Africa), and flows of immigration to the United States reflect this. On the other hand, women's reproductive labor, or motherhood, has been the basis of women's empowerment in many African societies, even when they did not have access to education. In fact, the attainment of motherhood for married African women often moves them out of the subordinate position of "wife" to the exalted category of "mother" (Sudarkasa 2004). Whether this change in women's status ameliorates their subordinated domestic role in their country of origin and enhances their domestic status once they migrate to the United States is a question that remains to be answered.

Postmigration Themes

The migration patterns that favor African males are reflected in the male-female sex-ratio imbalance of immigrants of marriageable age who remain in the United States. Overall, 52 percent of African immigrants in the United States are male, although within specific populations, the imbalance is greater; for instance, among Nigerians, male immigrants outnumber their female counterparts by approximately 24 percent. The trend is similar for Ethiopian immigrants in America, according to the U.S. Census Bureau (2006).

Among African immigrants in the United States who are married, family conflicts are noted as one of the impediments to their adjustment. Family problems among African immigrants can arise due to attempts to retain premigration ideas of gender roles and family functioning. A married African couple residing in the United States may find it difficult to function in an environment different from the one they were accustomed to in their home country, where African conjugal families, unlike Western nuclear families, are not structural and spatial isolates (Sudarkasa 2004). Also, immigrant couples must submit to the transformation of gendered domestic roles, enhancing the role of women and their capacity to participate as equals in household decision making after immigration (Pedraza 1991; Gabaccia 1994; Gold 1989). Ultimately, immigrant couples recreate or modify their traditional roles to participate fully in the American social milieu.

As with black Americans and Caribbean-born blacks (and indeed all groups), family is a central institution in the life of the African immigrant, and the extended family structure is the norm rather than the exception. Additionally, many black Africans share with their African American and Afro-Caribbean counterparts a collective or communalistic cultural orientation (Triandis 1995). In some traditional African extended families, the care and upbringing of children is never left exclusively to the parents. The extended family is always involved; members of the extended family, particularly women, are seen, and see themselves, as resources for each other in the rearing of their children (Sudarkasa 1973). In the United States, however, African immigrants tend to be more geographically dispersed, and it is difficult to rely on extended family.

In terms of parenting, African immigrants in the United States have to contend with issues similar to those highlighted in the previous section on Caribbean immigrants. The tensions that second-generation African immigrant children experience are no different from those reported for Caribbean families: these include the pressure to assimilate and become Americanized while at school and outside the home. As African immigrants establish roots in the United States, they do not completely relinquish their cultural or religious traditions from their country of origin and strive to pass these on to their children (Livingston and Sembhi 2003). What the research does not tell us is how second-generation African children cope with the tensions that may arise if they do not adopt the way of life preferred by their parents or how these second-generation children deal with acculturation pressures and peer pressure at school while submitting to the traditional values and other cultural expectations of their parents. Neither do we know how African immigrant parents are dealing with such circumstances.

While immigrants in general face a number of problems, including stress related to acculturation, change, and loss (Koehn 1991; Kamya 1997; see also chapter 9) the health of African immigrants when they arrive in the United States is generally not as adversely affected as might be expected since these immigrants reportedly have fewer health problems, including hypertension and reproductive health issues, as compared with African Americans (Read, Emerson, and Tarlov 2005; Singh and Siahpush 2002). However, with increased time spent in the United States, the health advantage erodes as a result of increased risk-taking behavior, poor diet, lack of exercise, and loss of protective factors, such as extended family support (cf. Marmot and Syme 1976; Singh and Siahpush 2002).

Finally, we note that a concomitant condition of the immigrant experience, regardless of marital status, is loneliness, cultural isolation, and unfamiliarity with American mainstream customs. As seen in other immigrant groups, these can lead to a diminished sense of subjective well-being (Stoller and McConatha 2001). Hugo Kamya's (1997) study of African immigrants who had resided in the United States for at least three months demonstrated the importance of spiritual well-being in buffering the negative effects of stress associated with trying to integrate into a new host country. While we do not have data on the spirituality and religiousness of African immigrants, we can conjecture that the role of religion or spirituality in the lives of these immigrants is similar to that identified for Caribbean immigrants.

FUTURE DIRECTIONS

The contemporary migration of Africans and Afro-Caribbeans presents a necessary challenge to the existing thinking and discourse on the black experience in ethnic-minority research. Our review highlights parenting styles, marriage patterns, the prevalence of extended family structure, gender roles among the three black groups, and the emergent tensions that immigrant families face as they mold new identities. While our data, and therefore our discussions, may be incomplete, our conclusions are no less salient: the marriage and socialization patterns of these groups may have several similarities, but they are also characterized by heterogeneity in ethnic identity. To make precise statements about the level of difference and similarity, we have to obtain more comprehensive empirical data (quantitative or qualitative) for all groups on the variety of topics we have raised.

We argue that while the shared experience of racial identity may shape the everyday experiences of these blacks in America, this characteristic alone is not sufficient to capture the family dynamic of blacks of all ethnicities in America. At the same time, as a result of couplings and convergences of experiences over the years in America, individuals from all of these groups will create families embracing different values, structures, and parenting approaches that will be American in nature. The challenge for researchers is to investigate these emergent patterns of family functioning.

REFERENCES

Apraku, Kofi K. 1991. *African Emigres in the United States.* Westport, CT: Praeger.

Arrighi, Barbara A., and David J. Maume. 2000. "Workplace Subordination and Men's Avoidance of Housework." *Journal of Family Issues* 21: 464–87.

Arthur, John. 2001. *Invisible Sojourners: African Immigrant Diaspora in the United States.* Westport, CT: Praeger.

Astin, Alexander W., H. S. Astin, J. A. Lindholm, A. N. Bryant, K. Szelenyi, and S. Calderone. 2005. *The Spiritual Life of College Students: A National Study of College Students' Search for Meaning and Purpose.* Los Angeles: Higher Education Research Institute.

Bachman, Jerald G., Tony N. Brown, Thomas A. Laveist, and John M. Wallace Jr. 2003. "The Influence of Race and Religion on Abstinence from Alcohol, Cigarettes and Marijuana among Adolescents." *Journal of Studies on Alcohol* 64: 843–48.

Baptiste, David A., Kenneth V. Hardy, and Laurie Lewis. 1997. "Family Therapy with English Caribbean Immigrant Families in the United States: Issues of Emigration, Immigration, Culture and Race." *Contemporary Family Therapy* 19: 337–59.

Baumrind, Diana. 1971. "Current Patterns of Parental Authority." *Developmental Psychology Monograph* 4: 1–103.

———. 1996. "Parenting, the Discipline Controversy Revisited." *Family Relations* 45: 405–14.

Billingsley, Andrew. 1968. *Black Families in White America.* Englewood Cliffs, NJ: Prentice Hall.

Blassingame, John W. 1972. *The Slave Community: Plantation Life in the Antebellum South.* New York: Oxford University Press.

Bluestone, Cheryl, and Catherine S. Tamis-LeMonda. 1999. "Correlates of Parenting Styles in Predominantly Working- and Middle-Class African American Mothers." *Journal of Marriage and the Family* 61: 881–93.

Bonnet, Aubrey. 1990. "West Indians in the United States of America: Some Theoretical and Practical Considerations." In *Emerging Perspectives on the Black Diaspora*, ed. A. Bonnet and G. L. Watson, 149–63. Lanham, MD: University Press of America.

Boyd-Franklin, Nancy. 1989. *Black Families in Therapy: A Multisystems Approach.* New York: Guilford Publications.

Brice, Janet. 1982. "West Indian Families." In *Ethnicity and Family Therapy,* ed. M. McGoldrick, J. K. Pearce, and J. K. Giordano, 123–63. New York: Guilford Publications.

Bronfenbrenner, Urie. 1979. *The Ecology of Human Development: Experiments by Nature and Design.* Cambridge, MA: Harvard University Press.

Butterfield, Sheri Ann. 2004. "Challenging American Conceptions of Race and Ethnicity: Second Generation West Indian Immigrants." *International Journal of Sociology and Social Policy* 24: 75–102.

Chamberlain, Mary. 2003. "Rethinking Caribbean Families: Extending the Links." *Community, Work and Family* 6: 63–76.

Chatters, Linda M., Robert J. Taylor, Karen D. Lincoln, and Tracy Schroepfer. 2002. "Patterns of Informal Support from Family and Church Members among African Americans." *Journal of Black Studies* 33: 66–85.

Coles, Roberta L. 2001. "The Parenting Roles and Goals of Single Black Full-Time Fathers." *Western Journal of Black Studies* 25, no. 2: 101–16.

Dion, Karen, and Kenneth Dion. 2001. "Immigrant Perspectives and Adaptations Gender and Cultural Adaptation in Immigrant Families." *Journal of Social Issues* 57, no. 3: 523–49.

DuBois, W. E. B. 1903. *The Souls of Black Folk.* New York: Modern Library.

Eggebeen, David, Tasha Snyder, and Wendy D. Manning. 1996. "Children in Single-Father Families in Demographic Perspective." *Journal of Family Issues* 17: 441–65.

Foner, Nancy. 1987. *New Immigrants in New York*. New York: Columbia University Press.

Fouron, Georges. 1987. "The Black Immigrant Dilemma in the United States: The Haitian Experience." *Journal of Caribbean Studies* 3: 242–65.

Frazier, E. Franklin. 1951. *The Negro Family in the United States*. New York: Dryden Press.

Gabaccia, Donna. 1994. *From the Other Side: Women, Gender, and Immigrant Life in the U.S., 1820–1990*. Bloomington: Indiana University Press.

Getachew, Metaferia, and Shifferraw Maigenet. 1991. *The Ethiopian Revolution of 1974 and the Exodus of Ethiopia's Trained Human Resources*. Lewiston, NY: E. Mellen Press.

Gold, Steven J. 1998. "Differential Adjustment among New Immigrant Family Members." *Journal of Contemporary Ethnography* 17: 408–34.

Gregory, Sheila. 1999. *Black Women in the Academy: The Secrets to Success and Achievement*. Lanham, MD: University Press of America.

Hardy, Sam A., and Marcela Raffaelli. 2003. "Adolescent Religiosity and Sexuality: An Investigation of Reciprocal Influences." *Journal of Adolescence* 26: 731–39.

Herskovits, Melville. 1930. *The Anthropometry of the American Negro*. New York: Columbia University Press.

Higginbotham, Elizabeth, and Lynn Weber. 1992. "Moving Up with Kin and Community: Upward and Social Mobility for Black and White Women." *Gender and Society* 6: 263–77.

Hill, Nancy. 1997. "Does Parenting Style Differ Based on Social Class? African American Women's Perceived Socialization for Achievement." *American Journal of Community Psychology* 35: 675–97.

Hondagneu-Sotelo, Pierrette. 1994. *Gendered Transitions: Mexican Experiences in Immigration*. Los Angeles: University of California Press.

Kamya, Hugo. 1997. "African Immigrants in the United States: The Challenge for Research and Practice." *Social Work* 42: 154–65.

Kasinitz, Philip. 1992. *Caribbean New York: Black Immigrants and the Politics of Race*. Ithaca, NY: Cornell University Press.

Koehn, Peter H. 1991. *Refugee from Revolution: U.S. Policy and Third-World Migration*. Boulder, CO: Westview Press.

Koffman, Jonathan, and Irene J. Higginson. 2002. "Religious Faith and Support at the End of Life: A Comparison of First Generation Black Caribbean and White Populations." *Palliative Medicine* 16: 540–41.

Livingston, Gill, and Sati Sembhi. 2003. "Mental Health of the Ageing Immigrant Population." *Advances in Psychiatric Treatment* 9: 31–37.

Logan, John R., and Glenn Deane. 2003. "Black Diversity in Metropolitan America." Albany: University of Albany.

Marmot, Michael G., and S. Leonard Syme. 1976. "Acculturation and Coronary Heart Disease in Japanese-Americans." *American Journal of Epidemiology* 104, no. 3: 225–47.

Mason, Craig A., Ana M. Cauce, Nancy Gonzales, and Yumi Hiraga. 1996. "Neither too Sweet nor too Sour: Problem Peers, Maternal Control, and Problem Behavior in African American Adolescents." *Child Development* 67, no. 5: 2115–30.

McAdoo, Harriette P., Sinead N. Younge, Hester H. Hughes, C. Henshaw, and Marissa Murray. 2005. "Use of Coping Resources among African American and Latino Parents of Children with Special Needs: Implication for Interventions." *Race and Society* 6: 125–40.

Model, Suzanne, and Gene Fisher. 2001. "Black-White Unions: West Indians and African Americans Compared." *Demography* 38: 177–85.

Momsen, Janet. 1994. *Women and Change in the Caribbean*. London: James Curry Publishing.

———. 2002. "Gender, Migration, and Domestic Service." *Annals of Association of American Geographers* 92: 609–10.

Nobles, Wade. 1997. "African American Family Life: An Instrument of Culture." In *Black Families*, ed. H. P. McAdoo, 83–93. Thousand Oaks, CA: Sage.

Ogbu, John U., and M. A. Gibson, eds. 1991. *Minority Status and Schooling*. New York: Garland Publishing Company.

Okpewho, Isidore, Carole Boyce Davies, and Ali A. Mazrui. 1999. *The African Diaspora: African Origins and New World Identities*. Bloomington: Indiana University Press.

Ostine, Regine. 1998. "Caribbean Immigrants and the Sociology of Race and Ethnicity: Limits of the Assimilation Perspective." *Research Perspectives* 4, no. 1: 1–10.

Pedraza, Silvia. 1991. "Women and Immigration: The Social Consequences of Gender." *Annual Review of Sociology* 17: 303–25.

Pipes, William H. 1992. *Say Amen Brother! Old-time Negro Preaching: A Study in American Frustration*. Westport, CT: Greenwood Publishing Group.

Portes, Alejandro, and Min Zhou. 1993. "The New Second Generation: Segmented Assimilation and Its Variants." *Annals of the American Academy of Political and Social Science* 530: 74–96.

Read, Jennan Ghazal, Michael O. Emerson, and Alvin Tarlov. 2005. "Implications of Black Immigrant Health for U.S. Racial Disparities in Health." *Journal of Immigrant Health* 7: 205–12.

Robertson, Claire. 1995. "Women in the Urban Economy." In *African Women South of the Sahara*, ed. M. J. Hay and S. Stichter, 44–65. London: Longman Group Limited.

Rokach, Ami. 1999. "Cultural Background and Coping with Loneliness." *Journal of Psychology* 133: 55–62.

Rumbaut, Reuben. 1996. "Unraveling a Public Health Enigma: Why Do Immigrants Experience Superior Perinatal Health Outcomes." *Research in the Sociology of Health Care* 13: 335–88.

Safa, Helen. 1998. "Race and National Identity in the Americas." *Latin American Perspectives* (Special Issue) 25, no. 3: 3–20.

Singh Gopal K., and Mohammed Siahpush. 2002. "Ethnic-Immigrant Differentials in Health Behaviors, Morbidity, and Cause-Specific Mortality in the United States: An Analysis of Two National Data bases." *Human Biology* 74: 83–109.

Stafford, Susan B. 1987. "The Haitians: The Cultural Meaning of Race and Ethnicity." In *New Immigrants in New York*, ed. N. Foner, 131–58. New York: Columbia University Press.

Stoller, Paul, and J. McConatha. 2001. "City Life: West African Communities in New York." *Journal of Contemporary Ethnography* 6: 651–77.

Sudarkasa, Niara. 1973. *Where Women Work: A Study of Yoruba Women in the Marketplace and in the Home*. Anthropological Papers 53. Ann Arbor: University of Michigan Museum of Anthropology.

———. 2004. "Conceptions of Motherhood in Nuclear and Extended Families, with Special Reference to Comparative Studies Involving African Societies." *Jenda: A Journal of Culture and African Women Studies* 5, available at www.jendajournal.com/issue5/sudarkasa.htm (last accessed February 27, 2007).

Sue, Derald. 2005. *Multicultural Social Work Practice*. Hoboken, NJ: John Wiley and Sons.

Takyi, Baffour K. 2002. "The Making of the Second Diaspora: On the Recent African Immigrant Community in the United States of America." *Western Journal of Black Studies* 26: 32–43.

Thompson, Paul, and Elaine Bauer. 1995. "Jamaican Transnational Families: Points of Pain and Resilience." *Wadabagei: A Journal of the Caribbean and Its Diaspora* 3: 1–36.

Triandis, Harry C. 1995. *Individualism and Collectivism*. Boulder, CO: Westview.

U.S. Census Bureau. 2004. "National Population Estimates—Characteristics." Washington DC: Government Printing Office.

——. 2005. "Living Arrangements of Black Children under 18 Years Old." Current Population Survey. March and Annual Social and Economic Supplements. Washington DC: Government Printing Office.

U.S. Census Bureau, Population Division. 2006. "Foreign-Born Population of the United States from the American Community Survey: 2003." Washington DC: Government Printing Office.

U.S. Department of Homeland Security, Office of Immigration Statistics. 2003. "2002 Yearbook of Immigration Statistics." Washington DC: Government Printing Office.

Warner, Stephen R. 1998. "Immigration and Religious Communities in the United States." In *Gatherings in Diaspora: Religious Communities and the New Immigration*, ed. S. R. Warner and J. G. Wittner, 3–34. Philadelphia: Temple University Press.

Waters, Mary. 1994. "Ethnic and Racial Identities of Second-Generation Black Immigrants in New York City." *International Migration Review* 28: 795–820.

——. 1999. *Black Identities: West Indian Immigrant Dreams and American Realities*. New York and Cambridge: Russell Sage Foundation and Harvard University Press.

Waters, Mary, and Karl Eschbach. 1995. "Immigration and Ethnic and Racial Inequality in the United States." *Annual Review of Sociology* 21, no. 1: 419–46.

Woodson, Carter G. 1921. *The History of the Negro Church*. Washington DC: Associated Publishers.

Zhou, Min. 1997. "Growing Up American: The Challenge Confronting Immigrant Children and Children of Immigrants." *Annual Review of Sociology* 23: 63–95.

CHAPTER 5

Earnings, Wealth, and Social Capital: A Review of Debates and Issues

Yoku Shaw-Taylor and Steven A. Tuch

The current earnings debate focusing on differences between native black Americans and Caribbean immigrants or Caribbean black Americans was perhaps instigated by Thomas Sowell's (1978) claim that the cultural traditions of native black Americans contributed to their lower earnings (money or income received for work or services) as compared to Caribbean black immigrants. Sowell (1978) identified earnings differences between native black Americans and Caribbean black Americans in favor of the latter and provided evidentiary data to support long-held views about a certain Caribbean cultural distinctiveness in terms of work ethic and prosperity (cf. Johnson 1958, 153; Reid 1939, 121; Glazer and Moynihan 1964, 35; Osofsky 1971, 133; Light 1972, 33). In the main, these views were based on Caribbean black Americans in New York City, where a significant proportion of them reside. The debate has now expanded to include African immigrants, and in this chapter, we review the emerging literature and studies on earnings that have compared, in the main, native black Americans to Caribbean black immigrants, as well as the few studies that have included African black immigrants or African black Americans (Butcher 1994; Dodoo 1997).

In addition to the review of the earnings debate, we discuss black wealth (assets that are directly convertible to money). The work of E. Franklin Frazier in 1957 perhaps spurred a closer reflexive look at the wealth of black Americans; he contended that black Americans "had little experience with the real meaning of wealth and they lack[ed] a tradition of saving and accumulation" (230). The argument was that native black Americans were predominantly wage earners and salaried professionals with little wealth in America compared to other groups. Into this social circumstance of unequal wealth (cf. Oliver and Shapiro 1997), Caribbean black Americans and, more recently, African black Americans have entered, beckoned by economic opportunity in the United States. As of this writing, intraracial data on wealth are non-existent, so we present data on black wealth as measured by the Census Bureau's Survey of Income and Program Participation (SIPP) in four years; this serves as the context for discussing the distribution of wealth among black Americans. Together, earnings (income) and assets and liabilities (wealth) capture material property; these are the "two most important components of economic stratification of the U.S. population" (cf. Davern and Fisher 2001). Income demonstrates current flow of capital or monetary resources, and wealth is the cumulative level of economic resources available.

We also discuss social capital (social connections, valued credentials, property and property rights) as a comprehensive look at the aggregate of resources. The concept of social capital is sociologically not new (cf. Portes 1998, 2) because it captures how the social organization of relationships and social networks affect our collective and individual lives. The work of Pierre Bourdieu is important in this regard; by emphasizing the accumulation and conversion of social relationships/networks into economic capital, Bourdieu (1986) inspired a rethinking of the aggregate of resources available to individuals within communities. Our discussion makes a distinction between macro ideas of social capital—the kind that Robert Putnam (1995, 2000), for instance, ascribes to whole communities and societies—and the micro concepts of social capital—the kind that accrues to individuals through membership in social networks. For migrants, social capital is operationalized more precisely in terms of how community members are able to support and sponsor immigration by facilitating contacts, providing work for newer immigrants, and thereby increasing the accumulated knowledge and resources for immigration (cf. Massey, Goldring, and Durand 1994; Zhou and Bankston 1994). Among natives, the accumulation and availability of social capital is facilitated by the exchange of information about business and education opportunities (for instance) and entrepreneurship (cf. Oliver and Shapiro 1997, 190; 2001).

EARNINGS

Studies informing the earnings debate following Sowell (1978) have been based on a typical model (Chiswick 1979; Borjas 1985; Farley and Allen 1987; Dodoo 1991; Model 1991, 1995; Butcher 1994; Daneshvary and Schwer 1994; Kalmijn 1996; cf. Dodoo and Takyi 2002), which uses probability samples of males (and in very few cases, females [Model 1991, 1995]), ages twenty-five to sixty-four, drawn from census data in various years to examine the correlates of earnings. The census definition of earnings is "money, wage or salary income [that] is the total income people receive from work performed as an employee during the income year. This includes wages, salary, armed forces pay, commissions, tips, piece-rate payments, and cash bonuses" before taxes, bonds, and pension and union deductions (Census Bureau 2005, 6). The core correlates of these earnings estimations are measures of human capital (cf. Schultz 1961; Becker 1975), operationalized as level of English proficiency (or literacy), education or years of schooling, and labor force participation or experience. Prior to the publication of Sowell's (1978) work, Herbert Gutman's (1976) publication of occupational data for Caribbean black Americans and native black Americans provided initial quantitative data for comparing human capital endowments between the two groups (pp. 512 and 518, tables A-42 and A-49). Based on the 1925 New York State census, Gutman's data showed that, proportionately, more native black Americans were laborers compared with a slightly higher rate of skilled workers among Caribbean black Americans in New York City.

In a 1994 publication, Kristin Butcher provided an updated look at earnings by introducing immigrant black Africans into the ongoing debate about whether Caribbean black Americans were more successful as compared to native black Americans. In comparison to Butcher's study, contemporary discussions about earnings differences have aggregated all black immigrants, combining Caribbean immigrants with comparatively recent African immigrants (Chiswick 1979; Dodoo 1991), or they have excluded African black immigrants in their comparison of differences between Caribbean immigrants and native black Americans (Model 1991, 1995; Daneshvary and Schwer 1994; Kalmijn 1996). In a different approach to these study designs, Augustine

Kposowa (2002) excluded Caribbean immigrants from his study of earnings differences. It is notable that Butcher's study also directly addressed the issue of selectivity: she compared native black American "movers," or those who migrate to and reside in a state other than their state of birth, to "nonmovers," or those who do not migrate.

Other studies have reported immigrants from Africa as a homogenous group; for instance, Barry Chiswick (1978, 1979, 1986) analyzed whether immigrants from Africa earned less in the American labor force when compared to immigrants from Europe, Latin America, and Asia. George Borjas (1987) listed Egypt as the only African country in his estimations. Estimations that use such broad aggregations conceal the effects of race; for instance, Egyptians are culturally not perceived as black. Broad aggregations yield imprecise estimations about the reality being measured because they obscure important distinctions in the data (cf. Smelser, Wilson, and Mitchel 2001, 5). F. Nii-Amoo Dodoo and Baffour Takyi (2002), for example, analyzed probability samples from the 1990 census and reported that despite comparable levels of human capital, annual earnings of white African immigrants (predominantly from Egypt and South Africa) were higher than for black African immigrants (predominantly from Nigeria and Ethiopia). Konia Kollehlon and Edward Eule (2003) came to a similar conclusion in their analysis of the earnings of white versus black Africans in the United States. While Nasser Daneshvary and R. Keith Schwer (1994) used regions of origin that listed entire continents as correlates in their estimations, they distinguished between black immigrants and non-black immigrants.

Below, we begin our discussion of the array of studies on earnings among black Americans by presenting Butcher's (1994) analysis for all three groups, then reviewing other studies that used 1980 census data and one that used 1970 data. The rest of the section then discusses studies that used 1990 census data.

Butcher's study used 1980 census data, and her analyses of wage differences showed that among the employed, African black Americans, on average, earned 13 percent less than Caribbean black Americans and native black Americans. African black Americans, on average, worked fewer weeks but were more educated (with proportionately more college years) than the other two groups. Between native black and

Caribbean black Americans, the earnings differences were negligible, but favored Jamaican Americans, who, as a Caribbean subgroup, also had comparatively higher employment rates. Multivariate analyses of 1980 earnings for these three groups from Butcher's paper show that whereas Caribbean black Americans had a higher likelihood of employment based on the same levels of education, they did not earn more than native black Americans, and after twenty years, the weekly earnings of immigrant black men were no different from those of native black Americans. Among those with higher levels of education (ten to sixteen-plus years), native black Americans had higher employment rates and earned more than the other groups; among the less educated (nine to eleven years), immigrant blacks tended to have higher rates of employment and earned more than native black Americans. Notably, Butcher uncovered a similarity in earnings and employment between native black American internal migrants and Caribbean black immigrants; this finding undermines the singular explanation that a distinct Caribbean cultural drive makes them more successful than native black Americans in the labor force.

In their monograph cataloging quality of life in America by race, Reynolds Farley and Walter Allen (1987) also used 1980 census data to report, among other things, on wage, education, and employment differences between native and foreign-born blacks, between blacks and whites, and by gender. Unlike Butcher, Farley and Allen present foreign-born blacks as an undifferentiated group. Farley and Allen found that foreign-born black men, who were predominantly of Caribbean origin (90 percent of the sample), on average had more education and higher labor force participation rates. Earnings estimates for men were reported by controlling for number of years of schooling (five and two years of college, versus two years of high school) and controlling for place of birth (New York, the South, "elsewhere"). These estimates showed that native black men consistently outearned foreign-born blacks among professional workers with five years of college and among technical workers with two years of college. Among administrative support workers, foreign-born black men earned more than native blacks. Overall, native black men earned 82 percent of earnings accruing to whites, and foreign-born black men earned 4 percent less than native black Americans. Hourly earnings, however, were almost the same for both groups when other variables, such as human capital and experience, were entered into a multivariate model.

These results are not dissimilar from the results of analysis of same census data performed by Suzanne Model (1991), who set out to examine whether Caribbean immigrants were a "black success story." Although Model did not include African immigrants in her estimations, she expanded her analysis by reporting wage differentials by gender; she found that for males, West Indian or Caribbean immigrants earned, on average, 88 percent of the income of native black Americans with comparable human capital endowments, whereas Caribbean immigrant females earned 95 percent of the income of their native black American counterparts. The groups had comparable employment rates. Wages did not vary significantly even when West Indian or Caribbean country of origin (Jamaica, Trinidad and Tobago, U.S. Virgin Islands, Puerto Rico, Dominican Republic, Haiti, Other) was introduced into the models; comparatively for both men and women, the black Hispanic groups from Cuba and Dominican Republic showed a handicap in literacy, and immigrants from Haiti showed a handicap in literacy despite an educational advantage. Model (1991) concludes that the cultural superiority of any group is simply nonexistent based on her analysis of 1980 census data and that "by 1980 any advantage that some Caribbean subgroups enjoyed over native born blacks in the past [had] disappeared" (273). Model was reacting to earlier studies using 1970 census data (Sowell 1978; Chiswick 1979) that found earnings advantages for immigrant blacks from the Caribbean.

Dodoo (1991) also used a probability sample of males from the 1980 census to design a study similar to Model's. Like Model, Dodoo's examination of wage differentials excluded African immigrants and aggregated all black immigrants into a "black foreign-born" category. The results of Dodoo's study are similar to those reported by Butcher (1994) and Model (1991) in terms of differentials between Caribbean black American and native black American males. He concludes that native black American males earned slightly more than Caribbean males based on slightly higher labor force participation. Foreign-born blacks showed, on average, more years of education, but native black Americans had more work experience. The idea that human capital endowments favored Caribbean black Americans and yielded higher annual earnings for them did not appear to be true based on this analysis of data from the 1980 census.

In another approach, Kposowa (2002) excluded Caribbean immigrants, the largest segment of black immigrants, from his study; he used 1980 and 1990 census data to examine differences among native black Americans, African black immigrants, native white Americans, and white immigrants. His analysis demonstrated that black African immigrants on average had more education and lower labor market experience in 1980 and earned less than the other groups, although their earnings returns were closer to parity with native black Americans in 1990, and their hours of work were similar to native white Americans in 1990. Daneshvary and Schwer's analysis of 1980 census data, published in 1994, compared wages of black immigrants, nonblack immigrants, and native black Americans and yielded similar patterns of differences favoring native black Americans as reported by Farley and Allen (1987) and Dodoo (1991).

Notably, Chiswick's pioneering analysis based on 1970 census data and published in 1979 provided an initial examination of earnings differences using human capital endowments (training, education) and demographic variables (including age, marital status, area of residence). Chiswick used tests of mean differences to examine the effect of human capital on earnings, which were methodological improvements on Sowell's 1978 analysis. His results showed that black immigrants (less than one-tenth of whom were from Africa and approximately equal proportions of whom came from English-speaking and non-English-speaking Caribbean Islands) on average had more schooling and outearned native black Americans. Chiswick also demonstrated the effect of length of time in the United States on earnings. When he compared native black Americans to immigrant blacks, his analysis revealed that immigrant blacks earned 2 percent less if their stay in the United States was ten years, but earned more after a period of twenty years in the country. This finding supported his original thesis (Chiswick 1978) that earnings of immigrants increased as their job skills became more relevant. He argued that these patterns are similar to observed trends for other groups. However, since he did not include labor market participation rates in the United States as a correlate, it is impossible to identify this effect on the earnings advantage of black immigrants from the Caribbean.

Since Sowell (1978) and Chiswick (1979) found that Caribbean immigrants earned more than native black Americans, subsequent studies based on 1980 data have found patterns that discount an earnings advantage for Caribbean immigrants and suggest that the Caribbean earnings advantage, if it exists, does not turn up consistently. But the studies by Butcher (1994), Farley and Allen (1987), Model (1991), Dodoo (1991), and Daneshvary and Schwer (1994) also did not capture the dynamism of social reality in terms of the variations in human capital of successive cohorts of disaggregated black immigrants and the effect of years spent in the United States. These studies used cross-sectional data, which offer indirect evidence of the effect of time in United States since migration (or what Borjas termed "period effects" [1994, 1675]), because they produce point estimates of earnings. Such study designs also assume that human capital endowments and other predictive variables of earnings for immigrants do not vary from cohort to cohort (Borjas 1985, 1987, 1994). At the same time, analyses using pooled data from cohorts of immigrants are unable to examine the effect of work-related immigrant experiences of the same group as they increase their knowledge and skills within the American labor market. We turn our attention now to studies using 1990 census data.

In a 1997 publication, Dodoo updated the intraracial estimations of earnings differences among all three groups: native black Americans, Caribbean black Americans, and African black Americans. Dodoo was updating Butcher's (1994) inclusive study, and his study design included terms for cohorts of immigrants in four waves (pre-1965, 1965–1974, 1975–1984, 1985–1990). The 1997 update to Butcher's work benefited from increasing focus on and scrutiny of the design of studies investigating wage differences between Caribbean black Americans and native black Americans (cf. Model 1995; Kalmijn 1996) and the performance of immigrants in the American labor market (cf. Borjas 1994. For instance, in analyzing pooled probability samples from census data, Model (1995) revised her study design to include three cohorts of Caribbean black immigrants (1970, 1980, and 1990), and Matthijs Kalmijn (1996) attempted to estimate "duration effects" (period effects) or the impact of length of time in the United States on wages.

Dodoo's (1997) analysis of 1990 census data showed that average earnings of both Caribbean black Americans and African black Americans were depressed by recent arrivals (1985–1990), which highlights the cohort effect argued by Borjas (1985). When human capital measures were added to the model, earnings for Caribbean black immigrants showed an 8 percent advantage over those of native black Americans, whose earnings were now not markedly different from those of African black Americans—this, even though African black Americans, on average, had more years of schooling and more college degrees and worked slightly more hours in 1989. This finding shows that among these three groups higher education alone (whether a degree was obtained in America or not) does not yield higher earnings. Dodoo speculates that, perhaps, African black Americans are rewarded poorly for their education because they are in "mismatched" jobs for which they are overqualified and underpaid.

In his analysis of 1990 census data, Kalmijn (1996) compared Caribbean black immigrants to native black Americans by examining the effect of Caribbean origins; his models included terms for Hispanic Caribbean, French Caribbean, and British Caribbean, who were operationalized as first-generation immigrants reporting Caribbean ancestry. Kalmijn emphasized the heterogeneity of Caribbean Americans in order to test the relative effect of literacy or "linguistic group" as a factor in the level of human capital. Kalmijn also estimated wage differences between generations by explicitly including second- and later-generation Caribbean black Americans. In becoming more like native black Americans than their parents were, Kalmijn (1996) hypothesized that second- and later-generation Caribbean black Americans will receive a negative period effect in terms of earnings because they are less likely to speak with the accent of their parents, which may signal their "Caribbeanness" to members of the dominant group, and they are therefore less likely to experience favoritism when compared with native black Americans. This assumption was a derivative of the discourse on second-generation experience (cf. Portes 1996; Portes and Zhou 1993).

In his tables, Kalmijn (1996) reported that Caribbean black Americans whose parents were from the British Caribbean showed higher hourly earnings and more years of schooling, on average, than native black Americans; Caribbean black Americans from the French Caribbean and Hispanic Caribbean showed a consistent disadvantage when compared to immigrants from the British Caribbean and native black Americans. These results held up only slightly in the multivariate analyses when the full complement of human capital variables were included in the model as controls: male Caribbean black Americans from British Caribbean showed, on average, 1 percent higher earnings and 5 percent higher occupational status. The progeny of Hispanic Caribbean and French Caribbean immigrants were also consistently and similarly disadvantaged when compared to the progeny of British Caribbean immigrants and native black Americans. Kalmijn's (1996) estimations of generational wage differences showed that "Caribbean blacks who were born in the U.S. [had] higher earnings and occupational status than Caribbean immigrants upon arrival" (928). In general, however, Kalmijn's estimations of generational differences are limited because the specification of the model was not based on a pooled sample of longitudinal data.

Model (1995) also used 1990 census data to reexamine earnings differences; her design, like Kalmijn's (1996), excluded African black Americans. However, her reexamination is more rigorous as she used probability samples from 1970, 1980, and 1990 and estimated wage differences by gender (ages twenty-five to sixty-four). She used data from the New York Metropolitan Statistical Area (MSA) and restricted her analyses to British West Indians. Model's analyses showed that for census years 1970 and 1980, labor force participation rates favored foreign-born Caribbean males (first-generation Caribbean Americans) as compared to native black Americans and Caribbean Americans born in the United States; by 1990, however, native black Americans outearned the other groups, even though first-generation immigrants in 1990 worked more hours and their level of schooling was comparable to that of native black Americans. From 1970 to 1990, native black Americans males showed increases in education. Wage differences and years of schooling in 1970, 1980, and 1990 favored Caribbean females born in America when compared to immigrants and native black Americans, although immigrants worked more hours in 1980 and 1990. Model reported that foreign-born Caribbean men and women had higher labor force participation rates than native blacks. She found that for men, the human capital endowments of immigrants varied little, while they declined for women for the years analyzed. Model's design, however, does not directly address how earlier cohorts affect her earnings results. For instance, the stock of foreign-born in the 1980 cohort includes the foreign-born who arrived in 1970, and the stock of foreign-born in 1990 includes the foreign-born who arrived in 1970 and 1980, if we take for granted that return migration is random and is not marked (cf. Borjas 1985). Model (1995) concluded that "there is nothing here to suggest cultural advantages or employer favoritism" (548–49). Although she speculated that employers might prefer Caribbean workers, she argued that employers "do not pay West Indians higher salaries."

By including African black Americans, the studies conducted by Butcher (1994) and Dodoo (1997) expand the earnings debate beyond mere reaction to Sowell's (1978, 42) findings that West Indians in America outperform native blacks in personal and family income, education, and "learned" professions because West Indians have, for example, a "distinct aversion to manual labor." The other studies, in direct reference to Sowell's study in 1978, have deepened our understanding of the complex nature of earnings attainment in the United States for native black Americans and Caribbean black Americans. From the results of these studies, our review yields two consistent findings when comparing earnings differences among Caribbean black Americans, native black Americans, and African black Americans: (1) first-generation immigrant blacks show a somewhat higher rate of participation in the labor force (Farley and Allen 1987; Model 1995; Dodoo 1997). Butcher (1994) found this to be so for immigrants with nine to eleven years of education, but Dodoo (1991) reported higher labor participation rates for native black Americans; and (2) Duration in the United States, or the period effect, is a significant variable that may efface the returns from education for first-generation immigrants (Kalmijn 1996; Dodoo 1997; Kposowa 2002; cf. Chiswick 1978; Borjas 1985).

Labor Force Participation as Migration Investment

Immigration flow is not a random selection process because potential immigrants and successful immigrants undergo a migration decision that, among other things, takes into consideration the earnings opportunities in the host country as compared with the home country and net migration costs (cf. Borjas 1994). For African black immigrants, the core question about whether to migrate, especially when migration entails transcontinental travel, involves not merely pull factors based on the perception that the host country has more dispersion of earnings distribution or economic opportunities; the decision also involves the realization that the costs of return migration are high. As such, those who decide to migrate, whether with superior human capital endowments or not, develop investment incentives to migrate that support the assumption that "selection biases *do* exist" (Borjas 1987, 535, emphasis in original) to migrate within populations. Self-selection to migrate does not mean that immigrants have superior human capital endowments, although this has been the case in past immigration flows (cf. Chiswick 1978). Borjas (1987) and Chiswick (1986) have noted that in recent years skill levels have declined due to visa preferences given to kin of immigrants, and in many cases, kin may possess lower levels of human capital when compared with original immigrants.

On arrival in the host country, the determination to succeed leads these immigrants to be highly productive. The studies reviewed above show consistently that immigrant blacks have higher employment rates, and although they may not earn as much as native blacks, their labor force participation demonstrates that they oftentimes work more hours than the natives. Butcher's (1994) analysis of native black movers, or migrants within America, and nonmovers confirms the proposition of selectivity: movers on average earned 35 percent more than nonmovers with the same human capital endowments.

It is not cultural distinctiveness that drives these immigrants (who, after all, have a lot of catching up to do when they arrive in the United States) to participate in the labor market at higher rates. Rather, it is high motivation since they have invested in the migration process, and their successes in their new country are returns on this investment, even in the face of racial stereotyping and discrimination. So-called culturally distinct attributes, such as reliability and willingness to work, may be features of immigrant status and not national origin, and "distinct" cultural values have nothing to do with such fundamental decisions about costs and opportunities. If we were to use cultural distinctiveness to describe the human capital characteristics of contemporary African black immigrants, we would have to estimate the main or interaction effects of place of origin, as Model (1991, 1995) and Kalmijn (1996) have done for Caribbean immigrants. In the case of African immigrants, we would have to disaggregate immigrants from Nigeria into their respective ethnic groups, such as the Yoruba, Ibo, Hausa, Fulani, Nupe, Igede, and Jukun among others; we would also have to disaggregate immigrants from Ethiopia into their respective ethnic groups, such as Galla and Amhara, among others. And from Ghana, we would have to do the same to account for the Fante, Asante, Ga, and Ewe, among others. Immigrants from Nigeria, Ethiopia, and Ghana constitute the majority of black Africans in America, and whereas these ethnic groups may share some common characteristics, such as speaking different dialects of the same language (e.g., Fante and Asante), many of them have culturally distinct features, such as language, ideas about religion, and written or oral traditions.

And for African black Americans, the color line bears a significant wage disadvantage as they leave their place of birth where racial discrimination is virtually absent (or has been toppled, as in South Africa) and go through the calculus to settle in America, where they are penalized for being black: African black Americans, on average, earn 19 percent less than African white Americans with similar human capital and labor market experience (Dodoo and Takyi 2002; cf. Kollehlon and Eule 2003). Dodoo and Takyi (2002) observe that "although any conclusion of discrimination must be made with caution, the variations in occupational distribution, given the similarity in education, make us more inclined to accept discrimination as the primary explanation for the wage gap" (931). For black Africans, the decision to migrate to America also involves an encounter with the continuing significance of race in terms of wages (cf. Wilson 1980; Farley and Allen 1987; Cancio, Evans, and Maume 1996).

Period or Assimilation Effects

The comparative earnings disadvantage of African black Americans in light of their superior education levels (and sometimes comparable human capital endowments) appears to underscore the impact of period effects. Chiswick (1978) explained the period effect in his study of white immigrant men: "Recent immigrants to the United States are likely to have less of the characteristics associated with higher earnings than the native born. Being recent arrivals, they have less knowledge of the customs and language relevant to U.S. jobs, have less information about U.S. job opportunities, and have less firm-specific training" (899). This is the adjustment period (cf. Farley and Allen 1987, 366) during which migrants acquire knowledge, skills, and the requisite experience for the labor market. Chiswick (1978) hypothesized that the "knowledge gap" between natives and migrants is most marked during these years. Eventually, earnings rise in correlation with experience in the host country. For migrants with low human capital endowments, the adjustment may take longer in terms of comparative earnings as they navigate the labor market (Borjas 1985, 1994; Chiswick 1986).

The period effect has also been described as the "assimilation" effect (Borjas 1987, 531; Dodoo 1997, 541; Butcher 1994, 266; Kalmijn 1996, 923), a depiction that dovetails with Milton Gordon's (1964, 71) synthesis of assimilation ideas when he described entry into organizations of the host country as structural assimilation, which is the second stage of the process of incorporation. Chiswick (1978) originally estimated this period to last from ten to fifteen years in his comparison of earnings between white foreign-born and native white Americans, and Borjas (1985, 479) confirmed the period effect to be so when immigrant whites are compared to native white Americans, although the rate of convergence was slower for other nonwhite groups (e.g., black immigrants).

This process of catching up may be hindered or facilitated by the context of reception. Alejandro Portes and Rubén Rumbaut (1996) observe that immigrant integration into the economy is based on the characteristics of the (ethnic) community that receives them and in which they reside; these communities provide "sources of information about outside employment [and] sources of jobs inside the community" (86–89). The community networks also provide cultural information and knowledge about the host country in terms of prejudice and discrimination. At the same time, these contexts of reception can slow the process of assimilation if the community is characterized by low-status jobs with restricted opportunities for social mobility. Reception into the labor market is also defined by racial attitudes or the level of accept-ance of the host country. In this regard, Dodoo (1997) argues that the lower earnings of African black Americans may be related to "extreme negative stereotyping" of African descendents and "condescending as-sumptions" held by people of European descent (530). This argument disregards period or assimilation effects and suggests that the so-called favorable status accorded black immigrants in comparison to native blacks (Waters 1999, 102) may be a Caribbean phenomenon or ethnic-ity specific. For African black Americans, the period effect, or number of years in the United States, might explain their relative earnings dis-advantage considering that they have, on average, more years of schooling.

WEALTH

Studies and writings about the wealth of native black Americans, un-like those about earnings or income, are mainly presented in compari-son to whites and not to Caribbean black Americans or African black Americans. This is because extant data on wealth are available for the racial category "black" or "African American," which represents all black Americans. These studies have variously focused on the magni-tude of disparities between white and black Americans (Terrell 1971; Franklin and Smith 1977; Henretta 1979; O'Hare 1983; Tidwell 1987; Oliver and Shapiro 1989; Gittleman and Wolff 2000), predictors and correlates of wealth inequality or the effects of asset allocations (Smith 1975; Margo 1984; Long and Caudill 1992; Chiteji and Stafford 1999; Altonji, Doraszelski, and Segal 2000; Straight 2002), processes of wealth accumulation (Soltow 1972; Parcel 1982; Brimmer 1988; Blau and Graham 1990), policies to ameliorate wealth inequality (Duncan 1969; Browne 1974; Conley 2000), and wealth and the economic sta-tus of blacks generally (cf. Vatter and Palm 1972; Oliver and Shapiro 1997, 2001). The focus on black wealth generally (and comparisons to white wealth) is understandable because the aforementioned studies used data that relied on stratified samples whose categories or strata of Caribbean born and African born may be too small for estimating wealth. Mostly, these two groups are subsumed under the larger "black" racial category.

Financial data in these studies have come mainly from surveys including the Survey of Economic Opportunity (SEO), Survey of Consumer Finances (SCF), Survey of Financial Characteristics of Consumers, Panel Study of Income Dynamics (PSID), Current Population Surveys (CPS), National Longitudinal Surveys, and the Survey of Income and Program Participation (SIPP). Studies on savings have used the Study of Consumer Purchases and the Survey of Consumer Expenditures; James Smith (1975) and Stephen Franklin and Smith (1977) used estate tax returns and death certificates for decedents in Washington, D.C., to examine asset allocations and margins of wealth inequality, respectively. The SEO was the first survey to capture data on assets and net worth by race when it began in 1967 (Terrell 1971; Galenson 1972), but the SIPP, which began in 1984, uses a large sample size—thirty-seven thousand households were interviewed for the panels reported in 2000 data—and contains an extensive array of assets and liabilities questions compared to the other surveys.

However, the SIPP is deficient in that the survey questionnaire item that asks about country of origin does not include a category for people from Africa. This makes it impossible to estimate wealth differences among African black Americans, Caribbean black Americans, and native black Americans using the SIPP. One advantage of the SIPP is that it has provided a standard definition of wealth by consistently measuring the same attributes of wealth or net worth (assets minus debts) over the past twenty years (Smith 1975, 332; Wolff and Marley 1987, 3; Wolff 1991, 94).

Assets are operationalized as follows: (1) interest-earning assets held at financial institutions, including passbook savings accounts, money market deposit accounts, certificates of deposit, and interest-earning checking accounts; (2) other interest-earning assets, including money market funds, U.S. government securities, and municipal or corporate bonds; (3) stocks and mutual fund shares; (4) mortgages held for sale of real estate and amounts due from sale of business or property; (5) regular checking accounts; (6) U.S. savings bonds; (7) real estate; (8) individual retirement accounts (IRAs) and Keough accounts; and (9) motor vehicles.

Debts are operationalized as follows: (1) secured liabilities, including mortgages on real estate, debt on a business or profession, vehicle loans, and margin and broker accounts; and (2) unsecured liabilities, such as credit card and store bills, medical bills, educational loans, and loans from individuals and financial institutions (cf. Davern and Fisher 2001).

However, Melvin Oliver and Thomas Shapiro (1989, 1997) developed an alternate measurement of wealth called net financial assets, which is a more precise measure of "financial assets normally available for present or future conversion into ready cash [or] liquid sources of income and wealth that can be used for a family's immediate well-being" (1997, 60). Net financial assets exclude equity in vehicles and homes and dramatically reduce estimates of net worth. For instance, while the mean net worth of blacks based on 1988 SIPP data is $23,818, the mean net financial assets is $5,209. In this chapter, we restrict our discussions to the conventional net worth measure.

The focus on black-white differences in wealth is important and has rightly dominated the discussion about the distribution of wealth in United States: inequality in wealth is palpable. Oliver and Shapiro (1997) report this succinctly when they estimated that "white [households] possess nearly 12 times as much median net worth as blacks, or $43,000 versus $3,700" (86). These stark estimates show the vast inequality that is consistently documented and catalogued. Notably, the discourse on intergenerational transfers (Brittain 1973, 1978; Menchik 1979; Kotlikoff and Summers 1981, 1988; Modigliani 1988; Blinder 1988; Kessler and Masson 1989; Clignet 1992; Menchik and Jianakoplos 1997; Oliver and Shapiro 2001) has informed us about the significance of parental transfers to children and how such transfers constitute approximately 18 to 34 percent of all wealth accumulation and contribute to generational wealth inequality among classes and between white and black families in the United States.

Longitudinal data from the SIPP documenting the assets and wealth (net worth) of black households from 1984 to 2000 (see table 5.1) provide context for our discussion of intraracial differences. The discussion is bounded by the unavailability of wealth data on Caribbean black and African black Americans.

Table 5.1 shows that home ownership among blacks has increased only slightly since data collection began for the SIPP. Homes account for approximately 44 percent of all wealth in the United States (Luckett

Table 5.1.   Asset Ownership Rates for Black Households

Asset Type	1984	1988	1995	2000	Percent Change 1984–2000	Percentage Distribution of Wealth by Asset Type, 2000
Home	43.8%	43.5%	45.2%	46.8%	6.8%	62.0%
Rental property and other real estate	9.9	9.0	7.0	4.5	−54.5	8.5
Stocks and mutual fund shares	5.4	6.9	5.2	10.2	88.9	4.0
Interest-earning accounts	45.9	46.4	47.5	42.4	−7.6	7.4
U.S. savings bonds	7.4	11.0	8.9	6.9	−6.8	0.3
IRA or Keogh accounts	5.1	6.9	7.9	6.5	27.5	2.3
401K and thrift savings plan*	—	—	—	19.6	—	6.7
Regular checking accounts	32.0	30.1	31.9	30.0	−6.3	0.5
Own business or profession	4.0	3.7	2.9	4.7	17.5	5.2
Motor vehicles	65.0	64.7	73.2	70.2	8.0	9.7
Other assets	0.7	0.8	0.7	0.9	28.6	0.9

Source: Survey of Income and Program Participation.
*This variable was not reported in 1984, 1988, or 1995.

2001). The proportion of black households owning their own businesses has increased, but the ownership rate of rental property and other real estate has declined. Table 5.1 also shows the net worth of black Americans by percentage distribution of asset types; this column shows that the home is the biggest component of wealth for most black American households.

Table 5.2 summarizes net worth data by presenting the distribution of actual wealth for black households for the same periods of the SIPP reported in table 5.1. This table shows that in 2000, almost one-third of black households did not possess any net wealth to speak of. For comparative purposes, overall, 15 percent of Americans, and 12.7 percent of white Americans, are documented as having no wealth. For black Americans, the proportion of households with negative or zero wealth has practically stayed the same since the SIPP began, but the proportions of households with positive wealth have increased over the survey years.

What can we make of these data in terms of the wealth of native black Americans, Caribbean black Americans, and African black Americans? We highlight four research issues that frame the literature on the wealth of black Americans: (1) the propertyless class of blacks, (2) historical patterns of wealth accumulation within the native black American population based on skin tone, (3) transnational wealth accumulation, and (4) conspicuous consumption among the black middle class.

Table 5.2.   Net Worth Rates for Black Households

Wealth	1984	1988	1995	2000	Percent Change 1984–2000
Zero or negative	30.5%	29.1%	21.7%	29.1%	–4.6%
$1–$24,999	44.7	42.5	45.4	34.9	–21.9
$25,000–$49,999	11.7	12.9	12.6	12.7	8.5
$50,000–$99,999	9.3	10.3	14.0	12.6	35.5
$100,000–$499,999	3.8	5.1	6.1	10.1	165.8
$500,000 and over	0.1	0.1	0.2	0.6	500.0

Source: Survey of Income and Program Participation.

We note the unrelenting category of blacks with no wealth over the survey years; the proportion of this group is higher among black Americans than it is in the general American population. This is William Wilson's (1987) "underclass," made up of those who remain predominantly low-income wage earners and accumulate net of socioeconomic disadvantage (Wilson 1987, 120). Wilson noted that while the black middle class has experienced increases in its professional, managerial, technical, and administrative ranks, with concomitant increases in income, home ownership (outside of inner-city neighborhoods), and college enrollment (see Wilson 1987, 109–10), there is a growing underclass of blacks who are poorly educated, experience long-term joblessness and poverty, and become welfare dependent. The underclass is caught in the inner city where single heads of households dominate, family and community lives are unstable, and incomes are low (Wilson 1987, 7–9). This so-called schism frames the overall picture of wealth distribution in the black American population and confirms the significance of attributes such as education and income to wealth; Michael Davern and Patricia Fisher (2001) for instance observe a "strong positive association between net worth and income" (ix) based on an analysis of 1995 and 1993 SIPP data. This relationship is consistent and was reported also by Shawna Orzechowski and Peter Sepielli in their 2003 report on net worth and asset ownership (cf. Oliver and Shapiro 1997).

Historically, among native black Americans, the distribution of wealth has been related to skin color, which evolved as a mark of social status in their race-conscious society (cf. Frazier 1957; Landry 1987; Russell, Wilson, and Hall 1992). Frazier (1957) wrote that the populations of mixed ancestry who came to dominate leadership roles in the black American community were the ones with initial access to education in the segregated world of America immediately before and after the Civil War. This pattern of privilege and access to the means of achieving wealth (or social capital; see next section) based on shades of color, also called colorism, has been documented in contemporary research.

In their paper examining the significance of color among blacks, Michael Hughes and Bradley Hertel (1990) concluded that respondents judged by interviewers to be of lighter skin had "greater education, occupational prestige, personal income and family income than those with darker skin" (1109). Hughes and Hertel based their analyses on the National Survey of Black Americans and were updating several studies that had posited and documented class distinctions and levels of income and wealth based on shades of lightness or darkness among black Americans. The relationship between skin tone and class hierarchy was also reported by Verna Keith and Cedric Herring (1991), whose analysis showed that "both personal and family income increase significantly with lighter complexion" (768). Moreover, darker-skinned respondents in the survey were more likely to be victims of discrimination. Keith and Herring (1991) concluded that "the effects of skin tone are not only historical curiosities from a legacy of slavery and racism, but present-day mechanisms that influence who gets what in America" (777). Mark Hill (2000) came to a similar conclusion in his longitudinal study of African American men reared in the South: "Men identified as mulatto enjoyed modestly higher adult socioeconomic attainment compared with men identified as black" (1454). Colorism has also been shown to be gendered, as skin color tends to have greater effect on women's access to education, occupation, and income (cf. Keith and Herring 1991).

In his paper titled "Aristocrats of Color," Willard Gatewood (2000) writes about the accounts of white investigators who were interested in social hierarchy among black Americans in the late 1800s and early 1900s: "What they concluded as a result of first-hand observation, rather than by any close objective analysis, was the existence of a black elite, small in number and light in complexion" (112). Other accounts about the black American social hierarchy during this period illustrate how people of darker complexion are able to penetrate the upper echelons of black society: "a man without a distinguished family background and of dark complexion had no chance of being accepted into the highest circles unless he possessed an advanced degree" (Gatewood 2000, 118).

The idea, of course, is not that complexion alone is a determinant or predictor of class, income, and wealth but, rather, that it is a significant correlate. In color-conscious societies, it has been demonstrated consistently that phenotypic designations and classifications that favor the dominant group also overlap consistently and significantly with class status in terms of income and wealth (cf. the status of so-called coloureds in South Africa and Brazil's multilayered classification system; see Marger 1994). The documentation of a certain advantage of lighter skin within the black American population is not an artifact of sociological analysis. We pose the question, how does the category of the underclass, those with negative or no wealth, overlap with the category of blacks, especially women, who are darker skinned?

One pattern of wealth accumulation that characterizes Caribbean and African black Americans is that, whereas native black Americans acquire wealth primarily in the United States, some Caribbean and African black Americans accumulate net worth not only in America but in their countries of origin, especially in the case of first-generation immigrants (cf. Portes 2003). Money transfers and other forms of relocations and investments (as noted and documented by Foner 1987, 2000; Basch, Glick Schiller, and Blanc 1994; Glick Schiller 1999; Levitt and Waters 2002) have created flows of capital that are not concentrated in either the country of settlement or the country of origin. The strength of the American economy allows Caribbean and African blacks (described as transmigrants—see chapter 1) in America to construct homes, buy property, and garner other forms of material wealth in their countries of origin, even as they earn income and accumulate what little wealth they can in the United States. This process of capital accumulation and organization across national and state lines clearly extends the fields of nationality (Glick Schiller 1999; cf. Sassen 2000). Roger Waldinger and Michael Lichter (2003, 11) note that, over time, the links generated by transmigrants across two countries increase the net returns of migration by lowering the costs of movement and consolidating and expanding the network of contacts across two countries.

This is not the same for native black Americans, whose wealth is concentrated in the United States. Indeed, the wealth data reported by SIPP actually captures attributes of native black Americans who still constitute the overwhelming majority of the black American population.

A final note on the accumulation of assets and net worth examines the portfolio choices and consumption patterns of middle-class blacks (cf. Chiteji and Stafford 1999; Brimmer 1988). In an analysis of 1984 PSID data focusing on African American households, Ngina Chiteji and Frank Stafford (1999) found that the likelihood of ownership of a specific portfolio composition was related to parental asset ownership, suggesting a strong impact of social learning in acquiring assets: "a young family's likelihood of owning transaction accounts and stocks is affected by whether parents held these financial assets" (380). In their analyses of 2000 SIPP data, Orzechowski and Sepielli (2003) compared the asset distribution of black Americans to the general American population; they reported that black households hold a higher proportion of their net worth in durable goods, such as housing and vehicles, and significantly less of their wealth in stocks, mutual funds, and interest-earning assets compared with the general population. These data raise the question of whether these asset choices are different among the three black groups. We discuss consumption patterns next.

In his 1957 publication *Black Bourgeoisie*, Frazier first made the argument that middle-class black Americans engage in conspicuous consumption, "constantly buying things—houses, automobiles, furniture and all sorts of gadgets . . . [as] they accumulate things" (230; cf. Hare 1965). In a subsequent study, St. Clair Drake and Horace Cayton (1970) characterized the consumption patterns of the typical black middle-class family in Chicago as follows: "With limited resources, the problem of striking a balance between the conspicuous consumption necessary to maintain status, and long range goals like buying property and educating children, becomes a difficult one" (668).

The idea of conspicuous consumption, first posited by the sociologist Thorstein Veblen, holds that there is an intersection of the social value for status and economic behavior that drives people to purchase material things as a useful way of earning esteem in society and demonstrating substantial financial resources (cf. Henslin 1996, 277;

Curry, Jiobu, and Schwirian 1997, 169). According to Veblen (1934), "conspicuous consumption of valuable goods is a means of reputability to the gentleman of leisure [and] since the consumption of these more excellent goods is evidence of wealth, it becomes honorific; and conversely the failure to consume in due quantity and quality becomes a mark of inferiority and demerit" (74–75).

When Oliver and Shapiro (1997) examined the savings patterns of middle-class blacks using SIPP data, they concluded that their findings did not support the conspicuous consumption argument as allocations of income to savings did not vary from that of comparable middle-class whites. In *The New Black Middle Class*, Bart Landry (1987) examined the issue of conspicuous consumption among middle-class blacks; he concluded that, except for clothes, middle-class blacks generally had lower rates of acquisition of durable and material goods (e.g., automobiles, major appliances, furniture) than middle-class whites. These data demonstrate that middle-class blacks do not exhibit consumption patterns that are starkly at variance with their socioeconomic status. And yet, blacks are less likely to retain their middle-class status as compared with whites: data from 1976 showed that only 58 percent of all black males from middle-class families maintained their middle-class position versus 82 percent of white males. Landry's (1987) work on the evolution of middle-class blacks discusses the context for their consumption patterns; he tracks the travails of the emergent black middle class in the early 1900s, noting their growth from 13 percent of the general black population in the 1960s to approximately 25 percent in the 1970s (compared with approximately 44 percent and 50 percent of whites, respectively, during the same period).

While providing a profile of consumption and economic behavior among black Americans, we are unable to determine from these data whether Caribbean and African middle-class blacks exhibit similar consumption behaviors, and if there are discernable differences, what may account for them. For first-generation immigrants, these data do not allow us to examine how transnational links affect economic behavior; nor do they allow us to tell whether subsequent generations of Caribbean and African black Americans are able to retain the middle-class status of their forebears at higher rates than native black Americans.

SOCIAL CAPITAL

In this last section of the chapter, we focus on social capital as a cumulative resource for individuals in the community. We discuss differential ownership of the components of social capital (cultural, human, and economic) by comparing Caribbean black Americans and African black Americans to native black Americans.

Portes (1998) credits Pierre Bourdieu for providing the "first systematic contemporary analysis of social capital" (3). Bourdieu (1986) defined it as "the aggregate of the actual or potential resources which are linked to possession of a durable network of more or less institutionalized relationships of mutual acquaintance and recognition, or in other words, membership in a group" (248). James Coleman (1988) is often cited as having contributed to the current application of the term; he writes that "social capital inheres in the structure of relations between [social] actors and among actors" (S98). Coleman's discussion recognizes the significance of human capital in the creation of social capital. In *Foundations of Social Theory*, Coleman (1990, 302) notes that social capital involves particular social relationships and actions that facilitate the maintenance of collective assets within the social structure.

Coleman's emphasis on group-level actions is consonant with the perspective of Putnam (1995, 2000), who popularized the concept in his work on civic traditions in modern Italy and his arguments about the decline of community in the United States. Putnam's concept of social capital is based on participation in social and voluntary organizations in democratic societies. The extent of social capital in a society is indicated by the level of participation in social organizations that promote community well-being. Putnam (1995) defines social capital as "features of social organization, such as trust, norms, and networks, that can improve the efficiency of society by facilitating coordinated actions" (167). Communitarian ideas (see, for instance, *The Essential Communitarian Reader*) are also in the vein of restoring the informal social bonds and "moral voices" of the so-called responsive community. Putnam credits L. J. Hanifan (1916), an educational reformer, with using the term to refer to "those intangible substances [that] count for most in the daily lives of people: namely good will, fellowship, sympathy, and social intercourse" (quoted in Putnam 2000, 19). These ideas about social capital take for granted the notion that economic exchange or action and social relations are embedded in each other: economic actions are intrinsically interwoven with social relationships (Granovetter 1985). Also taken for granted is the idea that social capital can be extensive and can take the form of "bridging capital" (Putnam 1995), which exists beyond primary groups (family, extended family, church) to include relationships with people outside of one's primary groups or in groups with which one has "weak ties" (Granovetter 1973).

Notably, contemporary ideas about social capital (cf. inter alia, Loury 1977; Burt 1992; Portes and Sensenbrenner 1993; Portes 1998; Fukuyama 1995; Flap 1991; Lin 1999, 2001) are all in consensus about the importance of social relationships in the production of social capital. As such, the concept captures a dimension of the social organization of human lives and how relationships and social networks, especially informal networks, affect our collective and individual lives. Sociologically, these concepts are fundamental to social morphology because social action, in the form of chosen behaviors, occurs within social structures that facilitate the reproduction of these relationships.

Macrolevel definitions of the concept describe resources for community well-being and development, which accrue to communities or organizations as a "public good" in the form of trust in social institutions and collective norms that are collinear with civic engagement. These resources or social capital at the community level depict familiar classical sociological ideas about the maintenance of social integration, solidarity, and cohesion through generalized reciprocity. The work of Putnam is an exemplar of this framework (cf. the work of Toennies, Durkheim, and the functionalist tradition; cf. the World Bank's Social Capital Research program). Thus, at the aggregate community level, the social capital idea describes "civicness," or "features of social organization, such as trust, norms, and networks, that can improve the efficiency of society by facilitating coordinated actions" (Putnam 1995, 167). "Civil society," or what sociologists have called the social order (and the multiplexity of processes involved in maintaining cohesion), has been used as the context for expounding on social capital (cf.

Edwards, Foley, and Diani 2001). This framework provides explanations of larger social processes in terms of group orientations and organizational cultures and posits social capital as a community, societal resource.

Microlevel definitions emphasize how membership in informal networks yield access to information, access to influential people or social ties that are able to exert influence, and access to human capital endowments that serve as personal capital or one's social credentials. Memberships allow individuals to maintain their status within the opportunity network (cf. Lin 2001). All of these attributes ultimately increase one's stock of social capital.

Three types of capital form the basis of an individual's social capital: human capital, cultural capital, and economic capital. Human capital is measured in terms of training, education, knowledge, and skills (cf. Schultz 1961; Becker 1975). Cultural capital is manifested in the knowledge of the dominant culture and its values and in opportunity networks acquired through the schools one attends, family connections, and informal occasions, where certain class attributes are gained. Bourdieu (1986) maintains that the acquisition of cultural capital is "work on oneself [self-improvement]," which leads to "embodied capital" (244). At the same time, individuals can possess "objectified" cultural capital in the form of material objects, such as paintings, books, and the like (cf. Weber's status groups in Runciman 1978). Bourdieu's (1986) notion of institutionalized cultural capital, however, overlaps with features of human capital in the form of education and academic or vocational qualifications.

All forms of capital are convertible to a most important third kind, economic capital in the form of income, wealth, or both, so that one's store of social capital is an index of access to opportunity structures in the society. Putnam (2000), in his arguments and discussions about the reduction in and determinants of civic engagement in the United States, reiterates the importance of income and wealth; he observes that "well-to-do, highly educated people—those who have more personal and financial resources—are more likely to volunteer, to donate money, and to give blood. In particular, education, is one of the most powerful predictors of virtually all forms of altruistic behavior, even after controlling for other possible predictors" (118; see also 67).

As with all social relationships, opportunity networks more often than not develop among individuals with common socioeconomic characteristics or lifestyles (cf. Lin 2001, 39). Portes (1998) explains this well: "Whereas economic capital is in people's bank accounts and human capital is inside their heads, social capital inheres in the structure of their relationships with others. To possess social capital, a person must be related to others, and it is those others, not himself, who are the actual source of his or her advantage" (7).

For immigrant black Americans, the assimilation effect (Chiswick 1978, 1979; Borjas 1985, 1987) is the primary disadvantage in the acquisition of economic capital. First-generation immigrant blacks have to contend with the assimilation effect of fifteen to twenty years to reach parity with or exceed natives in terms of earnings, even if they have comparable human capital endowments. This lag in economic capital acquisition is clearly linked to their lack of cultural capital or knowledge of opportunity networks. However, as second and subsequent generations become Americanized and racialized, cultural capital increases, and knowledge of the dominant values becomes part of the stock of the embodied social capital. Even as the assimilation effect disappears, the development of transnational identities (being American and maintaining close ties to the country of origin of forebears) becomes another dimension of social capital of the second and subsequent generations if transnational ties expand and yield economic capital (e.g., business opportunities in the "old" country) or human capital (e.g., acquisition of language skills). Milton Vickerman's (2002) research, however, suggests that transnational ties may be merely expressive or symbolic and are hardly instrumental in yielding any form of capital, except in reinforcing lineage and ethnicity in a racialized American society. He observes that, whereas second-generation Caribbean blacks "maintained contact, [they] attached less significance to such contacts than did their parents" (Vickerman 2002, 362). This is especially so because these Caribbean black Americans lived in communities with a critical mass of other Caribbean black Americans.

Cultural capital in the form of knowledge of the American landscape, awareness of personal rights, and certain values of entitlement distinguish native blacks especially from first-generation Caribbean and

African blacks. However, it is important to note that the advantage of cultural capital—including knowledge of dominant values and opportunity networks acquired through the schools one attends, family connections, and informal occasions—is moderated by human capital endowments and the demands of the labor market. In competing with immigrants for entry-level jobs, native blacks with no skills are effectively forced out of opportunity networks because these niches have been taken over by immigrant groups aided by employer preferences. For instance, in her study of entry-level, unskilled workers, Mary Waters (1999) documented the sentiment of managers in relation to recruiting native blacks (native Americans in general): "Native-born applicants are less likely than immigrants to accept the manager's request for commitment to an unspecified set of tasks. Rather than seeing employment as a favor worthy of one's loyalty to the company and to the manager, the American worker sees the job situation as a contract" (111). Waldinger (1996, 7) documented this process of job displacement for unskilled native blacks in New York City; he observed that within the current labor market, the low-skilled or uneducated members of the black American community are unable to access the new niches forged by the growing middle class because the former do not have the human capital endowments needed in these new opportunity networks.

Entry-level, low-skill jobs may be more accessible, but employer preferences for poorly educated immigrants and the development of immigrant network recruitment effectively exclude low-skilled native blacks, whose cultural capital (however modest it may be, based on knowledge of the community, schooling in the community, knowledge of dominant values, and the like) is effectively neutralized by their lack of human capital. Waldinger and Lichter (2003) documented the significance of network hiring as immigrant job holders regularly transmit information about job openings or employment opportunities to kin and others in the immigrant community: "Networks tying veterans to newcomers allow for rapid transmission of information . . . ; the networks send information the other way, as well, telling bosses about applicants, thus reducing the risks associated with hiring. Once in place, the networks reproduce themselves: incumbents recruit friends and relatives, while entrepreneurs gravitate to the cluster of business opportunities already identified by their associates in the community" (12). Employer preferences for uneducated immigrants is also based on the fact that these immigrants will accept low wages and are not encumbered by the low status of entry-level jobs. At the same time, employer recruitment processes involve a rank order of ethnic preferences, which places native black Americans at the bottom of the hierarchy (see Neckerman and Kirschenman 1991; cf. Thurow 1968, 1975; Hodge 1973; Reskin and Roos 1990). For low-skilled and uneducated blacks (cf. Wilson's [1987] underclass), their cumulative stock of social capital is further effaced in a society that is still bounded by racial thinking.

For middle-class black Americans, the accumulation of human capital and their stock of cultural capital enable them to be competitive in the labor force, so they are able to maintain networks of opportunities and preferences within American society (cf. Fraser 1994). Oliver and Shapiro (1997) document the development of opportunity networks within the black American community in the form of promotions of entrepreneurship programs, education, self-employment initiatives, and the production of clearinghouses for business and investment opportunities. Oliver's (1988) assessment of community networks in Los Angeles led him to conclude that within the black community there is an "elaborate organization of personal networks that tie people together within and outside the community in bonds of support and sociality" (639). These bonds engender the production and distribution of emotional and material support and the transfer of wealth to progeny.

And for middle-class black immigrants, opportunity networks may be yielded first by human capital endowments through professional relations. To the extent that first-generation immigrant Caribbean and African black professionals remain legal residents and are able to match their human capital endowments to market demands, they will be able to transfer their class status from their countries of origin and maintain that status in America (cf. Jasso, Rosenzweig, and Smith 2002). However, compared to native black Americans, these middle-class first-generation black immigrants will still experience a lag in overall social capital because of their relative lack of cultural capital, which transfers into a short-term deficit in economic capital.

Ultimately, cultural capital and human capital are convertible to economic capital. The economic basis of society, which was critically posited by Karl Marx, provides a fundamental framework for assessing the significance, or "weight," of social capital in the social milieu. The rich and very rich do not have the same need for social capital or social connectedness to gain access to opportunity networks as the middle class, the working class, the working poor, and the poor. The grand narrative of the economic basis of society (as espoused by neo-Marxists and conflict theorists) is the analytical insight that "human societies [are] networks of privilege and domination, moving through long slow shifts in resource" (Collins 1990, 84). In this vein, Lorraine McCall (2001) noted the inverse relationship between access to social capital and social disadvantage (based on lack of employment, strong family support, and educational opportunities).

Among black Americans, acquisition of social capital is mediated by societal prejudices and ethnic preferences wherever opportunity networks exist. In a racialized society, however, such preferences may also suggest social distancing from the favored immigrants. Waldinger and Lichter (2003) reasoned that ethnic prejudices favoring immigrant blacks reveal a certain perception of their "otherness" (see chapter 1) on the part of employers because "the qualities that make for good underlings may well preclude the potential for relationships of an intimate sort. . . . American employers value immigrants precisely because they are not like us" (17). If, indeed, recruitment preferences among employers favor immigrants because they are hardworking and exhibit none of the entitlement attitudes associated with Americans, then as successive generations of Caribbean and African blacks become Americanized and lose their makers of "otherness," they will also lose their place in the rank order of recruitment preferences. Becoming American, on the other hand, will ultimately increase their stock of social capital, especially in the form of cultural knowledge.

REFERENCES

Altonji, Joseph G., Ulrich Doraszelski, and Lewis Segal. 2000. "Black/White Differences in Wealth." *Federal Reserve Bank of Chicago Economic Perspectives* 24, no. 1 (first quarter): 38–50.

Basch, Linda, Nina Glick Schiller, and Cristina S. Blanc. 1994. *Nations Unbound: Transnational Projects, Postcolonial Predicaments and Deterritorialized Nation-States.* Langhorne, PA: Gordon and Breach Science Publishers.

Becker, Gary S. 1975. *Human Capital: A Theoretical and Empirical Analysis, with Special Reference to Education.* New York: National Bureau of Economic Research.

Blau, Francine D., and John W. Graham. 1990. "Black-White Differences in Wealth and Asset Composition." *Quarterly Journal of Economics* 105, no. 2 (May): 321–39.

Blinder, Alan S. 1988. "Comments on Chapter 1 and Chapter 2." In *Modelling the Accumulation and Distribution of Wealth,* ed. Denis Kessler and André Masson, 68–76. Oxford: Clarendon Press.

Borjas, George J. 1985. "Assimilation, Changes in Cohort Quality, and the Earnings of Immigrants." *Journal of Labor Economics* 3, no. 4 (October): 463–89

———. 1987. "Self-Selection and the Earnings of Immigrants." *American Economic Review* 77, no. 4 (September): 531–53.

———. 1994. "The Economics of Immigration." *Journal of Economic Literature* 32, no. 4 (December): 1667–1717.

Bourdieu, Pierre. 1986. "The Forms of Capital." In *Handbook of Theory and Research for Sociology of Education,* ed. John G. Richardson. New York: Greenwood Press.

Brimmer, Andrew F. 1988. "Income, Wealth and Investment Behavior in the Black Community." *American Economic Review, Papers and Proceedings of the One-hundredth Annual Meeting of the American Economic Association* 78, no. 2: 151–55.

Brittain, John A. 1973. "Research on the Transmission of Material Wealth." *American Economic Review Papers and Proceedings of the Eighty-fifth Annual Meeting of the American Economic Association* 63, no. 2 (May): 335–45.

———. 1978. *Inheritance and the Inequality of Material Wealth.* Washington DC: Brookings Institution.

Browne, Robert S. 1974. "Wealth Distribution and Its Impact on Minorities." *Review of Black Political Economy* 4, no. 4 (summer): 27–37.

Burt, Ronald S. 1992. *Structural Holes: The Social Structure of Competition.* Cambridge: Harvard University Press.

Butcher, Kristin F. 1994. "Black Immigrants in the United States: A Comparison with Native Blacks and Other Immigrants." *Industrial and Labor Relations Review* 47, no. 2 (January): 265–84.

Cancio, Silvia A., T. David Evans, and David J. Maume, Jr. 1996. "Reconsidering the Declining Significance of Race: Racial Differences in Early Career Wages." *American Sociological Review* 61 (August): 541–56.

Chiswick, Barry R. 1978. "The Effect of Americanization on the Earnings of Foreign-born Men." *Journal of Political Economy* 86, no. 5 (October): 897–921.

———. 1979. "The Economic Progress of Immigrants: Some Apparently Universal Patterns." In *Contemporary Economic Problems 1979,* ed. William Fellner, 359–99. Washington DC: American Enterprise Institute.

———. 1986. "Is the New Immigration Less Skilled Than the Old?" *Journal of Labor Economics* 4, no. 2 (April): 168–92.

Chiteji, Ngina S., and Frank P. Stafford. 1999. "Portfolio Choices of Parents and Their Children as Young Adults: Asset Accumulation by African-American Families." *American Economic Review Papers and Proceedings of the One Hundred Eleventh Annual Meeting of the American Economic Association* 89, no. 2 (May): 377–80.

Clignet, Remi. 1992. *Death, Deeds and Descendents: Inheritance in Modern America.* New York: Aldine de Gruyter.

Coleman, James S. 1988. "Social Capital in the Creation of Human Capital." *American Journal of Sociology* 94: S95–S121.

———. 1990. *Foundations of Social Theory*. Cambridge, MA: Belknap Press of Harvard University Press.

Collins, Randall. 1990. "Conflict Theory and the Advance of Macro-Historical Sociology." In *Frontiers of Social Theory*, ed. George Ritzer, 68–87. New York: Columbia University Press.

Conley, Dalton. 2000. "Getting into the Black: Race, Wealth and Public Policy." *Political Science Quarterly* 114, no. 4: 595–612.

Curry, Tim, Robert Jiobu, and Kent Schwirian. 1997. *Sociology for the Twenty-first Century*. Upper Saddle River, NJ: Prentice Hall.

Daneshvary, Nasser, and R. Keith Schwer. 1994. "Black Immigrants in the U.S. Labor Market: An Earnings Analysis." *Review of Black Political Economy* (winter): 77–98.

Davern, Michael E., and Patricia J. Fisher. 2001. *Household Net Worth and Asset Ownership: 1995*. U.S. Census Bureau, Current Population Reports, Household Economic Studies, Series P70–71. Washington DC: Government Printing Office.

Dodoo, F. Nii-Amoo. 1991. "Earnings Differences among Blacks in America." *Social Science Research*, no. 20: 93–108.

———. 1997. "Assimilation Differences among Africans in America." *Social Forces* 76, no. 2 (December): 527–46.

Dodoo, F. Nii-Amoo, and Baffour K. Takyi. 2002. "Africans in the Diaspora: Black-White Earnings Differences among America's Africans." *Ethnic and Racial Studies* 25, no. 6 (November): 913–41.

Drake, St. Clair, and Horace Cayton. 1970. *Black Metropolis: A Study of Negro Life in a Northern City*. 2nd ed. New York: Harper and Row.

Duncan, Otis D. 1969. "Inheritance of Poverty or Inheritance of Race?" In *On Understanding Poverty*, ed. Daniel P. Moynihan, 85–110. New York: Basic Books.

Edwards, Bob, Michael W. Foley, and Mario Diani, eds. 2001. *Beyond Tocqueville: Civil Society and the Social Capital Debate in Comparative Perspective*. Hanover, NH: University Press of New England.

Etzioni, Amitai, ed. 1998. *The Essential Communitarian Reader*. Lanham, MD: Rowman & Littlefield.

Farley, Reynolds, and Walter R. Allen. 1987. *The Color Line and the Quality of Life in America*. New York: Russell Sage Foundation.

Flap, Henk D. 1991. "Social Capital in the Reproduction of Inequality." *Comparative Sociology of Family, Health and Education* 20: 6179–6202.

Foner, Nancy, ed. 1987. *New Immigrants in New York*. New York: Columbia University Press.

———. 2000. *From Ellis Island to JFK: New York's Two Great Waves of Immigration*. New Haven and New York: Yale University Press and Russell Sage Foundation.

Franklin, Stephen D., and James D. Smith. 1977. "Black-White Differences in Income and Wealth." *American Economic Review, Papers and Proceedings of the Eighty-ninth Annual Meeting of the American Economic Association* 67, no. 1 (February): 405–09.

Fraser, George. 1994. *Success Runs in Our Race: The Complete Guide to Effective Networking in the African-American Community*. New York: Avon Books.

Frazier, E. Franklin. 1957. *Black Bourgeoisie*. New York: Free Press.

Fukuyama, Francis. 1995. "Social Capital and the Global Economy." *Foreign Affairs* 74, no. 5: 89–103.

Galenson, Marjorie. 1972. "Do Blacks Save More?" *American Economic Review* 62, nos. 1–2: 211–16.

Gatewood, Willard. 2000. "Aristocrats of Color: The Educated Black Elite of the Post-Reconstruction Era." *Journal of Blacks in Higher Education* 29 (autumn): 112–18.

Gittleman, Maury, and Edward Wolff. 2000. "Racial Wealth Disparities: Is the Gap Closing?" Working Paper 311, Jerome Levy Economics Institute, Bard College.

Glazer, Nathan, and Daniel P. Moynihan. 1964. *Beyond the Melting Pot: The Negroes, Puerto Ricans, Jews, Italians and Irish of New York City.* Cambridge, MA: MIT Press.

Glick Schiller, Nina. 1999. "Transmigrants and Nation-States: Something Old and Something New in the U.S. Immigrant Experience." In *The Handbook of International Immigration,* ed. Charles Hirschman, Philip Kasinitz, and Josh DeWind, 94–119. New York: Russell Sage Foundation.

Gordon, Milton M. 1964. *Assimilation in American Life: The Role of Race, Religion and National Origins.* New York: Oxford University Press.

Granovetter, Mark S. 1973. "The Strength of Weak Ties." *American Journal of Sociology* 78: 1360–80.

———. 1985. "Economic Action and Social Structure: The Problem of Embeddedness." *American Journal of Sociology* 91: 481–510.

Gutman, Herbert G. 1976. *The Black Family in Slavery and Freedom, 1750–1925.* New York: Vintage Books.

Hanifan, L. J. 1916. "The Rural School Community Center." *Annals of the American Academy of Political and Social Science* 67: 130–38.

Hare, Nathan. 1965. *The Black Anglo-Saxons.* New York: Marzani and Munsell.

Henretta, John C. 1979. "Race Differences in Middle Class Lifestyle: The Role of Home Ownership." *Social Science Research* 8: 63–78.

Henslin, James M. 1996. *Essentials of Sociology: A Down-to-Earth Approach.* Boston: Allyn and Bacon.

Hill, Mark E. 2000. "Color Differences in the Socioeconomic Status of African American Men: Results of a Longitudinal Study." *Social Forces* 78, no. 4 (June): 1437–60.

Hodge, Robert W. 1973. "Toward a Theory of Racial Differences in Employment." *Social Forces* 52, no. 1 (September): 16–31.

Hughes, Michael, and Bradley R. Hertel. 1990. "The Significance of Color Remains: A Study of Life Chances, Mate Selection, and Ethnic Consciousness among Black Americans." *Social Forces* 68, no. 4 (June): 1105–20.

Jasso, Guillermina, Mark R. Rosenzweig, and James P. Smith. 2002. "The Earnings of U.S. Immigrants: World Skill Prices, Skill Transferability and Selectivity." Unpublished manuscript, New York University.

Johnson, James W. [1930] 1958. *Black Manhattan.* New York: Knopf.

Kalmijn, Matthijs. 1996. "The Socioeconomic Assimilation of Caribbean American Blacks." *Social Forces* 74, no. 3: 911–30.

Keith, Verna M., and Cedric Herring. 1991. "Skin Tone and Stratification in the Black Community." *American Journal of Sociology* 97, no. 3 (November): 760–78.

Kessler, Denis, and André Masson. 1989. "Bequest and Wealth Accumulation: Are Some Pieces of the Puzzle Missing?" *Journal of Economic Perspectives* 3, no. 3 (summer): 141–52.

Kollehlon, Konia T., and Edward E. Eule. 2003. "The Socioeconomic Attainment Patterns of Africans in the United States." *International Migration Review* 37, no. 4 (winter): 1163–90.

Kotlikoff, Laurence, and Lawrence H. Summers. 1981. "The Role of Intergenerational Transfers in Aggregate Capital Accumulation." *Journal of Political Economy* 89, no. 4 (August): 706–32.

———. 1988. "The Contribution of Intergenerational Transfers to Total Wealth: A Reply." In *Modelling the Accumulation and Distribution of Wealth*, ed. Denis Kessler and André Masson, 53–67. Oxford: Clarendon Press.

Kposowa, Augustine. 2002. "Human Capital and the Performance of African Immigrants in the U.S. Labor Market." *Western Journal of Black Studies* 26, no. 3 (fall): 175–83.

Landry, Bart. 1987. *The New Black Middle Class*. Berkeley: University of California Press.

Levitt, Peggy, and Mary C. Waters, eds. 2002. *The Changing Face of Home: The Transnational Lives of the Second Generation*. New York: Russell Sage Foundation.

Light, Ivan H. 1972. *Ethnic Enterprise in America: Business and Welfare among Chinese, Japanese and Blacks*. Berkeley: University of California Press.

Lin, Nan. 1999. "Building a Network Theory of Social Capital." *Connections* 22, no. 1: 28–51.

———. 2001. *Social Capital: A Theory of Social Structure and Action*. Cambridge: Cambridge University Press.

Long, James E., and Steven B. Caudill. 1992. "Racial Differences in Homeownership and Housing Wealth, 1970–1986." *Economic Inquiry* 30, no. 1 (January): 83–100.

Loury, Glenn C. 1977. "A Dynamic Theory of Racial Income Differences." In *Women, Minorities, and Employment Discrimination*, ed. P. A. Wallace and A. Le Mund, 153–86. Lexington, MA: Lexington Books.

Luckett, Sandra. 2001. *Did You Know? Homes Account for 44 Percent of All Wealth: Findings from the SIPP*. U.S. Census Bureau, Current Population Reports, Household Economic Studies, Series P70–75. Washington DC: Government Printing Office.

Marger, Martin N. 1994. *Race and Ethnic Relations: American and Global Perspectives*. 3rd ed. Belmont, CA: Wadsworth Publishing.

Margo, Robert A. 1984. "Accumulation of Property by Southern Blacks before World War I: Comment and Further Evidence." *American Economic Review* 74, no. 4 (September): 768–76.

Massey, Douglas, S. Luin Goldring, and Jorge Durand. 1994. "Continuities in Transnational Migration: An Analysis of Nineteen Mexican Communities." *American Journal of Sociology* 99, no. 6 (May): 1492–1533.

McCall, Lorraine. 2001. *Measuring the Social Health of Native American Communities in New Mexico: Applying the Social Health Index to Reservations and Counties*. PhD diss., University of Southern California.

Menchik, Paul L. 1979. "Inter-generational Transmission of Inequality: An Empirical Study of Wealth Mobility." *Economica* 46, no. 184 (November): 349–62.

Menchik, Paul L., and Nancy A. Jianakoplos. 1997. "Wealth Mobility." *Review of Economics and Statistics* 79, no. 1 (February): 18–31.

Model, Suzanne. 1991. "Caribbean Immigrants: A Black Success Story?" *International Migration Review* 25, no. 2: 249–76.

———. 1995. "West Indian Prosperity: Fact or Fiction." *Social Problems* 42, no. 4 (November): 535–33.

Modigliani, Franco. 1988. "Measuring the Contribution of Intergenerational Transfers to Total Wealth: Conceptual Issues and Empirical Findings." In *Modelling the Accumulation and Distribution of Wealth*, ed. Denis Kessler and André Masson, 21–52. Oxford: Clarendon Press.

Neckerman, Kathryn, and Joleen Kirschenman. 1991. "Hiring Strategies, Racial Bias, and Inner-City Workers." *Social Problems* 38, no. 4 (November): 433–47.

O'Hare, William P. 1983. *Wealth and Economic Status: A Perspective on Racial Inequality*. Washington DC: Joint Center for Political and Economic Studies.

Oliver, Melvin. 1988. "The Urban Black Community as Network: Toward a Social Network Perspective." *Sociological Quarterly* 29, no. 4: 623–45.

Oliver, Melvin L., and Thomas M. Shapiro. 1989. "Race and Wealth." *Review of Black Political Economy* 17, no. 4 (spring): 5–25.

——. 1997. *Black Wealth, White Wealth: A New Perspective on Racial Inequality.* New York: Routledge.

——. 2001. "Wealth and Racial Stratification." In *America Becoming: Racial Trends and Their Consequences,* Vol. 2, ed. Neil J. Smelser, William Julius Wilson, and Faith Mitchell, 222–52. National Research Council. Washington DC: National Academy Press.

Orzechowski, Shawna, and Peter Sepielli. 2003. *Household Net Worth and Asset Ownership: 2003.* U.S. Census Bureau, Current Population Reports, Household Economic Studies, Series P70–88. Washington DC: Government Printing Office.

Osofsky, Gilbert. [1971] 1996. *Harlem: The Making of a Ghetto, Negro New York, 1890–1930.* 2nd ed. Chicago: Elephant Paperbacks.

Parcel, Toby. 1982. "Wealth Accumulation of Black and White Men: The Case of Housing Equity." *Social Problems* 30, no. 2 (November): 199–211.

Portes, Alejandro, ed. 1996. *The New Second Generation.* New York: Russell Sage Foundation.

——. 1998. "Social Capital: Its Origins and Applications in Modern Sociology." *Annual Review of Sociology* 24: 1–24.

——. 2003. "Conclusion: Theoretical Convergencies and Empirical Evidence in the Study of Immigrant Transnationalism." *International Migration Review* 37, no. 3 (fall): 874–982.

Portes, Alejandro, and Rubén Rumbaut. 1996. *Immigrant America: A Portrait.* Berkeley: University of California Press.

Portes, Alejandro, and Julia Sensenbrenner. 1993. "Embeddedness and Immigration: Notes on the Social Determinants of Economic Status." *American Journal of Sociology* 98: 1320–50.

Portes, Alejandro, and Min Zhou. 1993. "The New Second Generation: Segmented Assimilation and Its Variants." *Annals of the American Academy of Political and Social Science* 530 (November): 74–96.

Putnam, Robert D. 1995. "Bowling Alone: America's Declining Social Capital." *Journal of Democracy* 6: 65–78.

——. 2000. *Bowling Alone: The Collapse and Revival of American Community.* New York: Simon and Schuster.

Reid, Ira De A. 1939. *The Negro Immigrant: His Background, Characteristics and Social Adjustments, 1899–1937.* New York: Columbia University Press.

Reskin, Barbara, and Patricia Roos, eds. 1990. *Job Queues, Gender Queues.* Philadelphia: Temple University Press.

Runciman, W. G., ed. 1978. *Weber: Selections in Translation,* trans. Eric Matthews. Cambridge: Cambridge University Press.

Russell, Kathy, Midge Wilson, and Ronald Hall. 1992. *The Color Complex: The Politics of Skin Color among African Americans.* New York: Anchor Books.

Sassen, Saskia. 2000. *Cities in a World Economy.* 2nd ed. Thousand Oaks, CA: Pine Forge Press.

Schultz, Theodore W. 1961. "Investment in Human Capital." *American Economic Review* 51, no. 1 (March): 1–17.

Smelser, Neil J., William Julius Wilson, and Faith Mitchell, eds. 2001. *America Becoming: Racial Trends and Their Consequences.* Washington DC: National Academy Press.

Smith, James. 1975. "White Wealth and Black People: The Distribution of Wealth in Washington DC in 1967." In *The Personal Distribution of Income and Wealth,* ed. James D. Smith, 329–64. New York: Columbia University Press.

Soltow, Lee. 1972. "A Century of Personal Wealth Accumulation." In *The Economics of Black America,* ed. Harold G. Vatter and Thomas Palm, 80–84. New York: Harcourt Brace Jovanovich.

Sowell, Thomas. 1978. "Three Black Histories." In *Essays and Data on American Ethnic Groups*, ed. Thomas Sowell and Lynn D. Collins, 7–64. Washington DC: Urban Institute.

Straight, Ronald L. 2002. "Wealth: "Asset-Accumulation Differences by Race: SCF Data, 1995 and 1998." *American Economic Review, Papers and Proceedings of the One Hundred Fourteenth Annual Meeting of the American Economic Association* 92, no. 2 (May): 330–34.

Terrell, Henry. 1971. "Wealth Accumulation of Black and White Families: The Empirical Evidence." *Journal of Finance Papers and Proceedings of the Twenty-ninth Annual Meeting of the American Finance Association* 26, no. 2 (May): 363–77.

Thurow, Lester. 1968. *Income and Opportunity*. Washington DC: Brookings Institution.

——. 1975. *Generating Inequality: Mechanisms of Distribution in the U.S. Economy*. New York: Basic Books.

Tidwell, Billy J. 1987. *Beyond the Margin: Toward Economic Well-Being for Black Americans*. Washington DC: National Urban League.

U.S. Census Bureau. 2005. "Current Population Survey (CSP): Definitions and Explanations," available at www.census.gov/population/www/cps/cpsdef.html (last accessed March 1, 2007).

Vatter, Harold G., and Thomas Palm. 1972. *The Economics of Black America*. New York: Harcourt Brace Jovanovich.

Veblen, Thornstein. 1934. *The Theory of the Leisure Class*. New York: Viking Press.

Vickerman, Milton. 2002. "Second-Generation West Indian Transnationalism." In *The Changing Face of Home: The Transnational Lives of the Second Generation*, ed. Peggy Levitt and Mary C. Waters, 341–66. New York: Russell Sage Foundation.

Waldinger, Roger. 1996. *Still the Promised City? African-Americans and New Immigrants in Postindustrial New York*. Cambridge, MA: Harvard University Press.

Waldinger, Roger, and Michael I. Lichter. 2003. *How the Other Half Works: Immigration and the Social Organization of Labor*. Berkeley: University of California Press.

Waters, Mary C. 1999. *Black Identities: West Indian Immigrant Dreams and American Realities*. New York and Cambridge: Russell Sage Foundation and Harvard University Press.

Wilson, William J. 1980. *The Declining Significance of Race: Blacks and Changing American Institutions*. 2nd ed. Chicago: University of Chicago Press.

——. 1987. *The Truly Disadvantaged: The Inner City, the Underclass and Public Policy*. Chicago: University of Chicago Press.

Wolff, Edward N. 1991. "The Distribution of Household Wealth: Methodological Issues, Time Trends, and Cross-Sectional Comparisons." In *Economic Inequality and Poverty: International Perspectives*, ed. Lars Osberg, 92–133. Armonk, NY: M. E. Sharpe.

Wolff, Edward N., and Marcia Marley. 1987. "Introduction and Overview." In *International Comparisons of the Distribution of Household Wealth*, ed. Edward N. Wolff, 1–26. Oxford: Clarendon Press.

Zhou, Min, and Carl L. Bankston III. 1994. "Social Capital and the Adaptation of the Second Generation: The Case of Vietnamese Youth in New Orleans." Special issue, *International Migration Review* 28, no. 4 (winter): 821–45.

CHAPTER 6

Contrasting Religious Preferences between Catholic African Americans and Haitian Americans

Yanick St. Jean

Most of the Haitian priests . . . have formed their own opinion. They are very autocratic. . . . A Haitian priest is used to you only saying, "Yes, Father. No, Father. Good morning, Father. Good bye, Father." There is no talk; there is nothing. When that priest . . . has been already molded into that feudalism, or system, and he comes here and then you're saying, "Father, what you're doing, you cannot do it. Father, that's wrong." I mean they get so insulted.

— A Haitian American

The Haitian priest . . . gives you examples that you can also relate to or experience. And yeah, they speak your language, your people, you just feel comfortable with them.

— A Haitian American

All my life with . . . white priests that I thought were very . . . I won't say racist but who were not culturally indoctrinated to the African American culture. I'll say that. I won't say that they're racist. I think that would be maybe a little too strong but who truthfully have not made the transition of being white in their attitude towards African Americans. I'll put it that way. And then I've had some . . . I think, [who] made the change [cultural sensitivity] and the acceptance. . . . I've known mostly white priests.

— An African American

In my life as a sister, I have come across many black priests through different situations, at conventions, at meetings, at forums. And so, for me, I have no difficulty receiving a black priest in that sacramental role. In fact, I rejoice a little bit because it's few and far between in my times and so to hear a black priest as presider, homilist, preacher, that brings joy and pride for me. . . . I've seen it many times in my eighteen years in the order. And in fact, when I made vows, I had a black priest.

—An African American

In the United States, when one thinks of Catholicism, one immediately thinks of Catholics as Irish, Italian, and Latin Americans. Yet, for many years, black membership in U.S. Catholic churches has been increasing due especially to the influx of Haitian immigrants (Lincoln and Mamiya 1990, 342). Primarily, Catholic Haitians continue immigrating to the United States. This immigration has consequences for Catholic membership and ethnic diversity within the Catholic Church in the United States. Today, among Haitian Americans, popular Catholicism is so webbed with ethnicity that the two are not easily teased apart. For most African Americans, however, becoming Christian during colonial times meant joining the evangelical or Protestant churches—the Methodists, Presbyterians, and Baptists.

Historically, in the Protestant-influenced United States, Catholic slaves were "a minority within a minority" (Raboteau 1995). American Catholics behaved in a way that was consistent with American expectations of the era. American Catholics were unlike the French, Spanish, and Portuguese, who attempted to "save the souls of their slaves." In Maryland and Louisiana, the small percentage of slaves who had contact with Catholicism was not nurtured in the faith. For example, "baptism was rarely succeeded by instruction, [and] few slaves received the regular pastoral care or the sacraments" (Raboteau 1995, 118). American Catholic slave owners did not teach their slaves the Catholic faith. While French Catholics fulfilled the codes for baptism and instruction, American Catholics did not; hence, slaves did not learn the fundamentals of the Catholic faith. Added to the Protestant environment in which slaves lived, this lack of instruction made Catholicism foreign and distant to them. Given the exclusion of baptized slaves from Catholic practice and faith, together with segregation in religious communities, the absence of African Americans in Catholic religious communities comes as no surprise. Moreover, a

> crucial avenue to religious authority, the priesthood, remained virtually closed to black Catholics during the nineteenth century. . . . It took another century for black Catholic priests to begin pasturing their own people. The Catholic view of the priest as a sacral figure, ordained primarily to officiate at the holy sacrifice of the Mass, differed significantly from the Protestant notion of the minister as preacher of the Word. The sacral character and the necessity of meticulous training in liturgical gesture and language made it impossible for a Catholic layman to assume the role of priest, in contrast to the relative ease with which a Baptist, for example, could become a preacher. As a result, the status and the authority of the black Protestant minister were not duplicated among black Catholics. (Raboteau 1995, 122)

That African Americans were left out the Catholic priesthood is important to note. The priest is a sacral figure, necessary to the performance of sacraments, including transfiguration of the host into the body of Christ. This ritual of the Catholic Mass is most important according to the Catholic faith. Before the twentieth century, African American Catholics were nurtured by European American priests, and a nineteenth-century African American priest would be status inconsistent. Indeed, the fact that African American priests are still rare is a vestige of the past.

In Haiti, however, the melding of ethnicity and Catholicism has its roots in the baptismal rites performed at Portugal's insistence before the soon-to-be slaves left for the New World (Raboteau 1995). Slave codes also required baptism with instruction in the Catholic faith. A French colony until her defeat of Napoleon's troops, Haiti officially became the first free black republic in the world on January 1, 1804. More than half a century later, the United States recognized Haiti's independence. Today, though all Haitians speak Creole (a mixture of languages inherited from early settlers) and though the former priest and president Jean-Bertrand Aristide crowned Vodou the country's second official religion, the French language and Catholicism remain key markers of Haitian identity, which have survived the ousted colonizers. Catholicism remains the primary religion on the island.

In the United States and elsewhere, many Haitian immigrants remain close to their original culture, constructing a symbolic life and identity that involves a strong affiliation with Catholicism, and, for the most part, closeness to Haitian culture and identification as Haitian or Haitian American has persisted (cf. Waters 1990, 1999; Zéphir 1996; Woldemickael 1989; Stepick 1998). In the case of younger Haitian immigrants, such identity is likely based on parental pressure. A Haitian identity reminds these immigrants (and those with whom they interact) that they have a home, one to which they might return some day. An analogy might be musing about the rewards of life everlasting when life on earth is trying.

Once in the United States, retention of their ethnic identity—their history, language, religion, stories, folk tales, ideas about race—may distinguish Haitian immigrants from African Americans; at the same time, they may share similar experiences with African Americans in terms of racial prejudice and discrimination directed toward them by white Americans. For first-generation immigrants especially, however, symbolic closeness to their motherland, hope for return migration, and lack of familiarity with American culture keep their identities alive. Symbolic closeness guards against perceptions of American prejudice, as these immigrants, making sense of their experiences, use a remote reference group and conceptions of race foreign to the United States, where one is either black or white.

Between Haitian Americans and African Americans, interactions may often be "accidental rather than intentional" (Zéphir 1996, 74). While the struggle for social and racial justice unifies the two groups in America, these two communities differ regarding "cultural traditions and values, and language" (Zéphir 1996, 77). In terms of religious affiliation, while Haitian Americans are primarily Catholics (Pamphile 2001) and the practice of that faith is a part of their Haitian identity, African Americans only make up approximately 3 percent of the U.S. Catholic population and belong primarily to Baptist and Protestant congregations.

Religious affiliation is not the only marker of difference between the two groups: African Americans and Haitian Americans do not share each other's collections of heroes. African Americans will not likely accord the same reverence to Haitian historical figures like Toussaint

L'Ouverture (leader of the Haitian Revolution), Jean-Jacques Dessalines (founder of Haiti), Henri Christophe and Alexandre Pétion (heroes of Independence), Sanite Belair (leader of insurgents during the war of independence), Jean-Baptiste Pointe DuSable (founder of the city of Chicago), Pierre Toussaint (Haitian saint), and Elizabeth Lange (Haitian-born founder of the Oblate Sisters of Providence and candidate for sainthood).

African-American popular culture does not include (or acknowledge) giants of Haitian literature, a literature rooted in the 1804 revolution. Some of these writers include Oswald Durand, Jean Price-Mars, Massillon Coicou, Jean Brierre, René Dépestre, Émile Roumer, and Jacques Roumain. Much of this literature has not been translated from French or Haitian Creole. Likewise, few Haitian Americans have similar levels of admiration for African-American heroes and writers, except perhaps for Dr. Martin Luther King, Jr., who belongs to humanity. Haitian Americans may not know W. E. B. DuBois, Ida B. Wells, Sojourner Truth, or Harriet Tubman. If they do, these great names of American history and literature do not have the same relevance to, or impact on, Haitian lives.

Issues of concern to Haitian Americans and African Americans may also be different. For example, reading the biography of Jean-Robert Cadet and about his experience in Haiti as a *restavec* (also the title of his book) will evoke different thoughts and emotions in Haitians and African Americans. While Cadet's brutal, revolting experience would stir the emotions of any group, including Haitian Americans, for Haitians that experience is a familiar, structural déjà vu. Though the abuse described by Cadet is not always present, most Haitians of the middle class have had a *restavec* in their homes. Haitians will see the *restavec* phenomenon as providing a young child from the countryside with an opportunity to live in the city, to learn to read and to write, and to gain economic mobility. The *restavec* experience, foreign to African-American habits, would likely be understood as a form of slavery (which it is, often). But *restavec*-ness as slavery is an American interpretation, and such an interpretation is one indicator of assimilation into the host culture. The same issue is given different meanings by, and impacts, the two groups differently. Notice that the subtitle of Cadet's book, *Restavec*: *From Haitian Slave Child to Middle-Class*

American, suggests that Cadet does not see himself as African American; rather, he is an American.

As one scholar puts it, "African American support of the Haitian Revolution had by no means nullified the significant differences between Haitians and African Americans. . . . Divergent geographical settings and contrasting cultural assimilation often resulted in marked dissimilarities between these two peoples. While Haitians adopted Latin culture, African Americans embraced Anglo-Saxon trends; Haitians cultivated their French cultural affiliations, while African Americans valued English culture more" (Pamphile 2001, 23–24).

In sum, while Haitian Americans and African Americans both have African ancestry, they also have different markers—language, religion, heroes, remembrance—hence interpretations of life, which means that Haitian Americans can learn from African Americans, and vice versa.

I envision this difference as that suggested by Andrew Greeley (1989, 2000), David Tracy (1981), and others between the analogical (sacramental) and dialectical (Protestant) imaginations of Catholics and Protestants, and the possibility for each to learn from and contribute to the other, without anyone's being superior.

I reason that African American Catholics will be closer to Haitian American Catholics than non-Catholic African Americans because they participate in common religious rituals and share common beliefs in the Catholic community. At the same time, Catholicism tends to absorb the surrounding culture with its ethnic flavors; therefore, variations in worldviews would be due to factors other than religion. Irish Catholicism is different from the Italian, Polish, German, Mexican, and French versions. Local circumstances infuse each with localized sensibility. How Italians, Germans, Mexicans, French, and Tarahumara Indians practice Catholicism informs us about their ethnicities. Similarly, how Haitians and African Americans think about and practice Catholicism informs us about ethnic particularities.

This chapter therefore examines two expressions of Catholicism—the Haitian and the African American—as a way of comparing these two ethnicities. African Americans and Haitian Americans who speak in this study were interviewed for a larger project on the impact of a sacramental (Catholic) imagination on antiracism. The sacramental imagination is the idea that the divine inhabits the world. Sometimes, I refer to this imagination (or point of view) as Divine-in-the-World.

I compare the views of Catholic Haitian Americans and African Americans on the unmarked research topic of their preferences for priests. As with food, dress, music, liturgy, and church seating, the preference for priests represents an ethnoreligious, therefore cultural, habit of the community. The issue of preference for priests is one corner of research that can shed light on the larger issue of differences between Haitian Americans and African Americans and help clarify the meaning of the sacramental imagination.

To illustrate this contrast of Catholic expressions, I took excerpts from interviews with Haitian and African Americans about their discussions of the sociologically unexplored topic of preference for clergy. During the course of the interviews, I asked the respondents about the Divine-in-the-World and the sacramental imagination. In these interviews, I tried to understand the sacramental imagination and what Catholicism means to the respondents. For this analysis, I decided on clergy not only because, to the best of my knowledge, this area has not been investigated, but also to begin shifting from the "marked," or topical, areas of discourse (e.g., immigration, affirmative action, interracial marriage) to "unmarked" areas, such as cultural habits that reinforce our identities (cf. Brekhus 1998). In the study of Catholicism, preference for liturgy is one such area. To the extent that preferences for priests and the reasons behind them differ, these preferences also indicate ethnic differences. In the sociology of everyday life (Goffman 1959), the preference for priests offers a reservoir of insights about the cultural values of the community, and this contributes to sociological knowledge about these minority groups in the United States.

In this analysis, ten first-generation Haitian American Catholics and ten African American Catholics share their views of the world. The African Americans and Haitian Americans interviewed are engaged in white-collar occupations, such as engineer, college professor, college administrator, physician, high school teacher, nurse, active nun, former nun, and graduating college student. Haitian American respondents are immigrants who have lived in the United States for over two decades. All interviews took place in the Midwest and were conducted between

2003 and 2005. (Due to the small sample size and to ensure anonymity, I am not disclosing the specific cities.)

The snowball process proved slow, as most Haitian and African Americans hesitated to make recommendations, differing in this manner from the European Americans interviewed for the larger project, who were eager to provide names and contact information and who often did so without seeking prior permission. Further, individuals recommended by these European Americans usually agreed to an interview, unlike the Haitian and African American referrals.

Haitian American recommendations tended to be indirect. Three Haitian Americans gave me specific contacts. The remainder did not. Instead, one suggested I attend a club meeting scheduled for that week and attempt to recruit there, while another provided the name of a church frequented by Haitian Americans. One Haitian American wanted to ensure her identity would be masked, despite having been told about a consent form that dealt with issues of confidentiality. Evident are issues of trust. Similarly, few potential interviewees recommended by African Americans accepted my invitation to participate in the study. For example, one religious sister recommended by another left me an interesting voice mail saying the study "sounded weird," so she wished to decline participation. Here too, recruitment proved slow.

I interviewed in a number of settings, including, on occasion, the homes of respondents. One interesting difference between African Americans and Haitian Americans is this: before or during their interviews, African Americans (like European Americans) would offer the interviewer a drink of water, while Haitians usually insisted that the interviewer consume "something other than water" and eat, usually a traditional Haitian dish, as well. I would decline the invitation, claiming that eating detracts from the interview (it does). Several more offers would be made before the respondent finally acquiesced. On one occasion, as I was leaving the setting, the respondent insisted on my taking some fruits for the road. I agreed to take one piece. "Take one for each day of the week," she insisted! This show of generosity, unmatched by any other group interviewed, seems an interesting characteristic of Haitians. It is not suggested that other groups were inhospitable. In Haiti, any occasion is an occasion for sharing food. As one respondent puts it, such occasions are often created.

THE INTERVIEWS

African American Respondents Speak

An administrator, single, in her late forties, the first African American respondent describes herself as an inactive Catholic who attends Mass occasionally, primarily with African Americans. The priest is white, which is common historically in African American parishes. According to this respondent,

> A cute black priest . . . comes sometimes. . . . What a waste. Oh, gee, he shouldn't have been a priest. . . . 'Cause he's so cute, there's so few good black men. . . . I mean, I'm glad he found his calling . . . but, gee, there's so few good men . . . you hate to give 'em up.

This respondent with a healthy sense of humor does not mind an officiating African American. Yet, such a vocation is a glaring reminder of the unbalanced African American sex ratio (see Albrecht and Fossett 1997; Lichter et al. 1992). Demographics impact the marriage market and the respondent's view of who should or should not be priest. Such men have the qualities to be responsible spouses and parents; hence, any such vocation is a gain for the church but a loss for single women like herself. African American priests make up only 1 percent of all priests in the United States.[1]

For the next respondent, however, who is married, priestly vocations are only a plus:

> I have had an African American pastor for our church, and we were very excited about that. We continued to support him and attend his anniversaries. . . . You know, we try to stay abreast of what's happening with an African American Catholic community, so it's kind of exciting when someone becomes a priest.

Each vocation is a source of pride for the African American Catholic community. This view is consistent with that expressed by the next respondent, a single woman and one of the youngest people in the sample, who said, "I think it would be great [having a black priest officiate]":

> I haven't had many [black priests] at my churches before. We had two priests who happened to be black that visited our church and I enjoyed

it. . . . [O]ne was originally from . . . a country in Africa, I forget which one. But then another one was from [this city] I believe. That was years ago.

African American priests are sought by black American parishioners, and their exiguous visits prove rewarding. For this respondent, who is biracial and reports feeling neither black nor white, a visiting priest from Africa whose language and culture may be at variance with the American way of life, still offers her an important, though fleeting, encounter with part of her identity.

Yet, not everyone lacks this opportunity to meet and interact with an African American clergyman:

> In my life as a sister I have come across many black priests through different situations, at conventions, at meetings, at forums. And so for me I have no difficulty receiving a black priest in that sacramental role. . . . I've seen it many times in my eighteen years in the order. And in fact, when I made vows, I had [a] black priest.

But it takes a religious vocation to have this level of access to African American priests on a regular basis. This religious professional prefers such a priest, especially when it comes to spiritual direction, because "that priest is African American and [he] would understand African-Americans and our spirituality." One European American priest, she says, is revered in the African American community, but "that doesn't mean he understands [or] that he has the spirituality of African Americans. Now, because I would prefer [a priest who is African American] doesn't mean that I would not go [to or would] not have a white person as a spiritual director." Of course, this may be a matter of necessity over choice. This religious professional did not elaborate on the meaning of spirituality or its African American expression.

Outside the interview setting, the respondent expressed her appreciation for priests from Africa during this clergy shortage. However, in a whisper, as if to confess, she added, Africans could not take the place of African American priests because African priests do not understand African Americans.

Another respondent says,

We have a white priest. . . . [I've spent] all my life with a white priest . . .
white priests that I thought were very . . . I won't say racist, but who were
not culturally indoctrinated to the African American culture. I'll say that.
I won't say that they're racist. I think that would be maybe a little too
strong but who truthfully have not made the transition of being white in
their attitude towards African Americans. I'll put it that way. And then
I've had some . . . I think, [who] made the change [cultural sensitivity]
and the acceptance. So, I have no problem with their color. As I say, I've
known mostly white priests.

Cultural sensitivity is attitudinal, according to the following response:

It depends upon the attitude. It depends upon the individual. . . . [T]he
priest that we have at [our parish] now, I would not certainly want to
change him just for a priest who is black. And I know some black priests
that I certainly wouldn't want. . . . So, I think I would judge the attitude
of the individual.

Besides priestly attitude and understanding of African American
spirituality, there is another reason why an African American clergyman is valued. As one future priest put it,

I prefer a black priest because my mission . . . one of my goals in life is
to constantly lift the black male. . . . That's why you hear me talk so
much about it. That's one of my goals, without putting the black woman
down.

By serving as role model, an African American priest fulfills yet another community goal. For the African American male, a priestly vocation is a "lift."

In general, the preference of African American respondents for
priests rests not on color but on assumptions that such priests will be
more insightful about the African American experience and spirituality.
One respondent of mixed origins, who self-identifies as African American and attends Mass where parishioners and pastor are white, says she
is comfortable there and would also be at ease with an African or
African American celebrant. Most African American respondents are

excited about the possibility of an African American celebrant, but color in itself does not seem an issue.

Haitian American Respondents Speak

It is difficult to estimate the number of Haitian American priests in the United States because of conflicting information. A study conducted five years ago by the Center for Applied Research in the Apostolate (CARA) reported thirty active diocesan priests (either incardinated or externs) serving in ten dioceses in the United States (Froehle and Gautier 1999).[2] According to sociologist Dean Hoge (personal communication 2004), these numbers, which seem low, may be explained by the hesitation of foreign priests to interview. Indeed, while I was able to interview one African priest, Haitian priests, without ever outright declining, have not been so willing. In a recent telephone conversation, the director of the national office of the Haitian Apostolate, Monsignor Guy Sansaricq, said to me that there are one hundred Haitian American priests in the United States, and he is in contact with all of them. This number seems more reliable than CARA's.

Like the African Americans, most Haitian Americans interviewed about their clergy found skin color to be unimportant. Instead, many prioritized ethnic (national) awareness and linguistic affinity. One attorney, resident in America since his early teens, is comfortable with an activist priest regardless of ethnicity:

> I just want activist priests. I mean there's a strong white priest in the city of Chicago. . . . He has a black congregation. You should go see him. You should go interview him. . . . [He] . . . is an activist priest who stands up, fights, connects with the community, is brave. . . . His congregation is black. . . . [T]hey integrate the form of the Baptist service in terms of the choir and . . . the rhythm of the church. It's not sterile. It perpetuates the same thing . . . the rituals that perpetuate belief in things unseen. It does the same thing except [this priest] . . . is more like Jesus. . . . He's an activist. He's a fighter. He confronts the status quo. He is not fearful of it. So he's that kind of priest. So whether black or white, you know, the priests that I value are priests who stand up and fight and lead and organize. People cannot be religious and just be religious. . . . If you're religious and you're not involved in the fight for social justice, what do you do for religion, cleansing yourself all the time? For what?

Though no longer attending Mass regularly, he seeks an icon-for-Christ, one who is culturally sensitive to congregational needs specifically. In his view, a European American priest can meet the spiritual needs of non-European Americans. His early emigration and marriage to a non-Haitian, non-American speaker of English may partially account for the fact that he does not place an emphasis on linguistic affinity as a criterion for high priestly rating.

Raised Episcopalian, the next respondent grew up surrounded by Catholic relatives and friends, attended Catholic College, and in many respects considers herself Catholic. Having immigrated in her late teens, she confesses to being more comfortable with a Haitian than an African American priest:

> I have a feeling they [African American priests] just base their preaching on the Bible a lot. Because I watch them on TV, I don't know that . . . that will not attract me too much. . . . The Haitian priest relates modern life to the Bible, I find. And they give you examples that you can also relate to or experience. And yeah, they speak your language, your people, you just feel comfortable with them.

While both priests are black, there may be differences in the content of their preaching, language of pulpit, and familiarity with Haitian life and experience.

> I don't care if you're black or white. My niece . . . [is] getting married in New York and she had the option to take a priest from Haiti, a Haitian priest from Haiti, a Haitian priest here and a Caucasian priest here. . . . She picked the Caucasian. . . . Hm-hmm. . . . It's not about race; it's about understanding and culture. If the priest gets it, you know. We have a lot of white priests in Haiti from France that speak Creole and French and understand the culture. It doesn't matter to me. But I believe that if you're going to . . . preach the gospel to a certain group of people, you have to know what they are all about. You have to understand them. You have to understand their culture. . . . I am putting the focus on language and culture a lot. . . . Language is a path to understanding.

Does a priest "get it?" Black or white, does he hold insights into the culture? Priorities stressed often are cultural and communicative competence. A priest who is white and has insights into the Haitian experience is more accepted than one, regardless of color, who does not.

A frequent traveler used to attending Mass in languages other than her native tongue, the next respondent adds,

Do I prefer a Haitian priest? No not necessarily because . . . I left Haiti a long time ago, so it doesn't matter to me because I have learned to assist Mass in Spanish. The worst one . . . not the worst one but the harder one to follow, that's the Creole one. . . . Because you were used to the Latin and French, that's a condition on Creole. It's not that it's bad now, just like you didn't know English. It's not the same. Like I say, I can speak Creole. Yes, I understand what they're saying but you cannot follow . . . because you cannot read the Creole like somebody else. . . . Creole is difficult to read . . . if you did not learn it in school. We did not. My generation went to French directly.

She recalls her visit to a national church, where the songs are in Creole:

You know, they have some songs now in Creole for the church. . . . I go to the church and then they have the music in Creole. That's a different story. And then you . . . are dancing and you forget you are in a church. . . . No, it's a Catholic church, and the priests are with you.

The respondent's discomfort with the Creole Mass is related to her middle-class upbringing and current social location. An abbey where she sometimes attends Mass offers her an atmosphere of reverence that contrasts with the Creole rituals. At her Midwestern parish, she says,

We have an [African] priest now. . . . He's very nice. [Our parish] has a . . . majority of white population. . . . [This priest] has an accent, and he sometimes should speak slower so people can understand his sermons. But he takes in people. You know, he brings you in. He likes the interaction. . . . Yeah, he wants people . . . he wants interaction. He wants to interact with the congregation. He's good. . . . I've seen them greeting him outside after Mass and . . . they seem to like him. He's only been there a few months. . . . There is a Haitian priest too. . . . He stutters. Yeah, he's difficult to understand, and I know there were complaints [about] him. . . . And I went to one service there . . . I think Holy Week and he was so hard, even for myself who knows his accent, to understand.

While the African is clearly favored, in both instances, language is an issue. However, no respondent mentioned telling a priest that his speech was lacking in whatever aspect. Parishioner complaints about the stuttering Haitian were indirect. But the respondent speaks favorably of another Haitian priest:

> We have a house in [the South], and we spend time there, and we went to midnight Mass when we were there for Christmas. . . . But there's a Haitian priest there. He's very, very loved, you know, black Haitian priest. There is a large . . . Haitian population in the city too so that's probably why. [The Congregation is white]. They have Haitian families there. They have Cuban families.

While she enjoys Mass by a Haitian priest, "Haitian" is not a requisite. The mention of "black" may also be her way of stressing that his color did not impact American parishioners' reactions to this Haitian priest.

For the next respondent, too, a Haitian priest is optional:

> I prefer a Haitian priest, and we have African American priests that are very good that we enjoy. We have Haitian priests . . . that we have gone to that we enjoy. And, you know, it doesn't make any difference. They are priests and they did very well everywhere. There's a sensitivity sometimes.

Note the acknowledgment of a "sensitivity" factor, probably a cultural reference, which includes language affinity. Another respondent confessed, "I love all of them. . . . All are my brothers. All are my priests. . . . There is one [European American]. I invite him to come to eat here." There is no racial preference, and in some cases, there is no ethnic preference. This is consistent with the community orientation and openness to diversity that are characteristics of the sacramental imagination (see Greeley 2000). However, there may be variations. The increasing presence of priests from Africa in Midwestern congregations where a majority of parishioners are white provides research opportunities to refine our understanding of the preference for priests.

Married to an African American, the next respondent sketches an interesting profile of the Haitian priest not seen previously in interviews.

The black priest is a priest. It's just a priest . . . and you can find a black priest that's as committed, as caring, as ministerial as the white priest. I don't see any difference. [Haitian priest?] That's another story. . . . It seems like . . . right now they have a factory to make priests.[3] . . . Most of the Haitian priests . . . they have six, seven, eight years in the priesthood. They have formed their own opinion. They are very autocratic. They know that they are next to God, and then they are the ones who decide everything. And when a Haitian priest comes to the United States, then I have noticed that there are problems because the Haitians right now, they are more educated, they go to other churches, they see how things are being done, and they want it to be done the same way. A Haitian priest is used to you only saying, "Yes, Father. No, Father. Good morning, Father. Good bye, Father." There is no talk; there is nothing. When that priest . . . has been already molded into that feudalism, or system, and he comes here and then you're saying, "Father, what you're doing, you cannot do it. Father, that's wrong." I mean they get so insulted. . . . There is a problem. There is a clash of culture. . . . Even though they eat the same food . . . they speak the same language but there's a clash of culture. And I have noticed for the past eight years every problem that we have with priests is a clash of culture.

Such priests will not engage Haitians who have lived in the United States for many years. Tension is produced by parishioners' adoption of American traits. According to the respondent, while Haitians enjoy Mass the way that it is celebrated in Haiti, they reject this authoritative style of interaction. Being Haitian does not necessarily make a priest acceptable to Haitian Americans in the United States who, like this respondent, may have undergone assimilation.

One issue raised often in interviews with Haitians is the syncretism of religion. Haitian Catholicism was influenced by French Catholicism. But as related by some respondents, elements of vodou permeate Catholicism and produce a mix that persists after these Haitians have come to the United States. The respondents denied being well versed in this topic, but all are aware of its presence in Haitian culture. Two respondents spoke at some length about this issue:

Whether the Haitian wants to accept . . . it or not, our belief system is very strongly affected by our folklore. In fact, I was thinking about that last night. Last night, coming back from a party, I was crossing—what's the name of that street—where they have cemeteries on both sides of the street. . . . And I said to myself, "If I tell a Haitian that I was crossing that thing and I saw a dead person, a zombie, crossing the street, 60 percent of Haitians will not challenge what I say." They will accept the possibility that a zombie could be crossing the street. And the same Haitian, who is a devout Catholic . . . devout Catholic. But if I tell them that I saw a zombie crossing the street, there is something in the back of their mind that could suggest that that could be true.

The respondent continues:

Some Haitians . . . will tell you that vodou is a religion, and I believe it is. I believe vodou is a religion because it's a set of beliefs for the majority of Haitians . . . the people, the peasants, you know, the [prolétaire]. You have 75 to 80 percent or maybe more than that . . . in Haiti. And most of them believe in vodou. But is . . . superstition the backbone of vodouism or which one comes first? . . . To me, I put them in the same basket. Maybe I do that for lack of knowledge or ignorance, but to me that's the same thing. Is superstition . . . supposed to be a tenet of vodouism? . . . None of them is Catholic and that's what makes the Catholicism, as practiced by the Haitians. That makes it imperfect, somewhat adulterated, because it is tainted by that fundamental knowledge in the culture, that fundamental nature of the culture, that fundamental element. . . . I know I was joking when I say that I saw that zombie crossing the street, you know, theoretically. . . . This is a pure invention, a pure lie, but a lot of Haitians might say, "You never know." *This* is Catholic. *This* is . . . Haitian. You . . . never know because *dèyè mon, gin mon* [beyond mountains there are mountains]. That is part of the mystery of things.

No such views appear in interviews with African Americans.

CONCLUSION

This analysis used the respondents' preference for priests to examine differences between Haitian and African Americans. I discovered the following: (1) In the absence of an African-American priest, a priest familiar with that ethnic experience is rated highly and preferred by most African Americans. (2) To be accepted by Haitian-American respondents, priests need not be Haitian. However, a priest sensitive to Haitian culture and language is rated highly. A Haitian American married to an English-speaking non-Haitian put less emphasis on cultural and linguistic factors. A Haitian American whose upbringing emphasized French was not comfortable with the Creole Mass.

Linguistic differences are evident among Haitians, as for example that which appears in one discussion of the Mass in Creole. Among Haitian Americans, language is a mark of education and status. Also, in a study of the use of language in the Catholic Mass in a Brooklyn church, one social scientist found that "the conflicts and divisions inherited from the colonial slave past continue to plague Haitians in their new conditions of exile" (Buchanan 1979, 310). But these marks of social location within the Haitian group (French and Creole) are not nearly as sharp as those delineating ethnic boundaries between in- and out-groups, between Haitian Americans and African Americans. While most members of the elite and middle classes speak French, and some immigrants hang on to French to retain their status, every Haitian, elite or nonelite, knows and speaks Creole.

Most Haitian-American respondents see sensitivity to Haitian culture as having an integrative function. As one former nun put it, there is nothing like praying in your own language. Haitian bishop Monsignor Sansaricq explained,

> Language preference depends on the social class. Haitians speak Creole in Haiti. There is a percentage fluent in French. In the United States, Haitians who are better educated move into neighborhoods where there are no Haitians. In Haiti, there is a great evolution toward Creole. So Haitians who have been [in the United States] twenty years have not gone through the transition process. In every group there is a certain [segment] where some prefer to assimilate to mainstream culture. The Haitian community is not monolithic. Some people hang on to French, but the majority is the Creole. (Personal communication 2004)

The Haitian immigrants interviewed attend Mass wherever they are, in their own neighborhoods where a majority of parishioners are European Americans. They do not seek churches with a majority of Haitians. If they do, it is for a special occasion, more social and cultural than spiritual. Indeed, one business owner mentioned attending Mass in her own parish on Sunday morning and at a national church in the af-

ternoon for social reasons; however, these choices may typify this professional class.

African American respondents assume that their priests are fluent in
English. For obvious reasons, language is not an issue. Instead, cultural
sensitivity and spirituality are. According to one African American
priest researcher, spirituality means a

> [c]oncern . . . with the desire of the African American community to
> know itself and to know God in the context of African American experi-
> ence, history and culture, [a concern] as old as the first sermon preached
> by enslaved Africans and their brothers and sisters huddled together in
> some plantation swamp, and as new as the reflections of James Cone . . .
> and others beginning in the 1960s. It is a theology of, about, and by
> African Americans. And while the formal proponents of this theology
> were a group of creative Protestant scholars, African American Catholic
> thinkers have used it as a point of departure to elaborate theological re-
> flection that is both African American and Catholic. . . . The African
> American bishops, in their pastoral letter, *What We Have Seen and
> Heard*, spoke eloquently of some of the qualities of an African American
> spirituality. (Kelly 2000, 377–78)

Who, then, could be more sensitive to African American spirituality
than the African American himself? Note, too, that the idea of this spirituality is rooted in the works of "a group of creative Protestant scholars." Consequently, African American Catholic thinking, or the African
American Catholic imagination with Protestant influences, would be
different from that of the African or the Haitian. It is worth repeating
the comment by a nun that an African priest cannot replace an African
American because African priests do not understand African Americans. Thus, I suggest that among African American Catholics, a culturally sensitive European American priest might be more accepted than a
Haitian, French African, or even Anglophone African if he is not sensitive to African American culture and the Protestant-influenced notions
of African American spirituality.

Other differences between Haitian and African Americans include
priestly vocations. African American priests are rare. By contrast, a respondent describes a waiting list for a Haitian seminary currently too
small to accommodate the demand, and she suggests, jokingly, that

Haiti may be supplying the United States with priests in about seven years. While research is needed on reasons for this increase in vocations, no such surplus can be expected soon of African American priests. As Bishop Sansaricq suggested, "It is true that there are many priests in Haiti, but not enough—the same in India, Africa, Philippines or Asia. A culture of misery is more conducive to vocations than a culture of plenty. In the United States, so many avenues are open that young men tend to shy away from exigencies of the Catholic priesthood. Haitians are more used to scarcity and a situation of deprivation, so they tend to be more religious" (personal communication 2004).

These vocations may be, due to Haiti's economic scarcity, a route to social mobility. After all, Jean-Bertrand Aristide went from priest to president. One future priest, who is African American, also suggested that an African American priesthood can give a "lift" to the African American male. For the most part, African Americans did not raise the issue of syncretism in their religion and Catholicism, but among Haitian Americans, this remains a topic of debate. When I asked Bishop Sansaricq to comment, he said, "This is speculation—not scientific observation. It is based on personal observation that needs to be tested. Vodou has permeated Haitian culture to a vast degree and that is a fact, but the Church has always stressed the difference between Catholicism and vodou. In a country where education is not advanced, many marginal Catholics accept a number of the tenets of vodou religion. Well-educated Haitians have *nothing* to do with vodou" (personal communication 2004). Bishop Sansaricq is referring to "the culture of *la classe de bourgeoisie* in Haiti, where even *la Bishop petite bonne* [the little maid] was placed at the margin of vodou culture," added one Haitian American respondent, who read the bishop's comment. This issue, which can increase our understanding of the Haitian Catholic imagination, needs additional research attention.

In sum, languages spoken, content of Catholicism and priestly vocations, and perceptions of syncretism differentiate first-generation Haitian American immigrants and African Americans. But Haitian American and African American respondents also share values. While they are open to diversity, both groups prefer priests sensitive to their cultures. And because their cultures and languages are different, this value consensus also fuels their differences.

To the extent that language shapes thought and one's knowledge of the world, this analysis reveals cultural differences between African Americans and Haitian Americans. Some linguists suggest, "Bilingualism offers the only humane and ultimately hopeful way to bridge the communication gap and mitigate the curse of Babel" (Haugen 1973). I suggest a bridging of religious and metaphorical imaginations. While both groups interviewed are Catholic, their religious imaginations are divided by ethnicity.

Including other denominations of Christianity would have provided a different perspective on the issue, as would interviews with African immigrants. However, the intent of this pioneer analysis is to bring to the fore a neglected, sociologically unmarked corner of research with potential for insights into ethnic differences between Haitian Americans and African Americans in their religious communities.

NOTES

1. In 2002–2003, African Americans made up 2 percent of theologate students versus 79 percent white, 11 percent Hispanic/Latino, and 8 percent Asian seminarians (See Center for Applied Research in the Apostolate 2004).

2. Among them were three in Connecticut, eleven in New York, eight in New Jersey, four in Florida, two in Illinois, and one each in Rhode Island and Washington, D.C. There are also four Haitian priests from religious orders serving in the United States in parish ministry (Froehle and Gautier 1999).

3. The respondent is referring to a seminary in Haiti.

GLOSSARY OF TERMS

Analogical imagination: This term is used interchangeably with *Catholic imagination* and *sacramental imagination*. See sacramental imagination.

Catholic imagination: This term is used interchangeably with *analogical imagination* and *sacramental imagination*. See sacramental imagination.

Divine-in-the-World: This is the same as God-in-the-world and is a characteristic of the sacramental imagination.

Restavec: Haitian Creole from the French *rester avec* (stay with), this word has a negative connotation in Creole, indicating lower status. The *restavec* phenomenon must be differentiated from situations where a child from the countryside is entrusted to a well-to-do family to help with household chores in exchange for room, board, and schooling. *Restavec*-ness is a slavelike condition. This phenomenon is so weaved into Haitian culture that it is taken for granted and seldom, if ever, challenged by Haitians in Haiti.

Sacramental imagination: This term refers to seeing "the invisible in the visible," the sacred in the profane (or everyday). Here, the word "imagination" refers to creativity. Think of the sacramental imagination as a religious culture, a Catholic culture or point of view, a sacramental way of seeing the world.

ACKNOWLEDGMENTS

This analysis is part of a larger project on the sacramental imagination. Thanks to all who generously gave of their time to participate in the study. Without you, this work would not have been possible.

REFERENCES

Albrecht, Carol Mulford, and Mark A. Fossett. 1997. "Mate Availability, Women's Marriage Prevalence, and Husbands' Education." *Journal of Family Issues* 18, no. 4: 429–53.

Brekhus, Wayne. 1998. "A Sociology of the Unmarked: Redirecting our Focus." *Sociological Theory* 16, no. 1: 34–51.

Buchanan, Susan Huelsebusch. 1979. "Language and Identity: Haitians in New York City." *International Migration Review* 13, no. 2: 298–313.

Cadet, Jean Robert. 1998. *Restavec: From Haitian Slave Child to Middle-Class American*. Austin: University of Texas Press.

Center for Applied Research in the Apostolate (CARA). 2004. Catholic Ministry Formation Enrollments, Statistical Overview for 2003–2004 (May).

Froehle, Bryan T., and Mary L. Gautier. 1999. *Sourcebook on the Availability and Distribution of Priests in the United States*. Washington DC: Georgetown University.

Goffman, Erving. 1959. *The Presentation of Self in Everyday Life*. New York: Doubleday.

Greeley, Andrew M. 2000. *The Catholic Imagination*. Berkeley: University of California.

———. 1989. "Protestant and Catholic: Is the Analogical Imagination Extinct." *American Sociological Review* 54: 485–502.

Haugen, Einar. 1973. "The Curse of Babel." *Daedalus* 102, no. 3: 47–58.

Kelly, William S. J. 2000. *Black Catholic Theology: A Sourcebook*. New York: McGraw-Hill.

Lichter, Daniel T., George Kephart, Diane K. McLaughlin, and David Landry. 1992. "Race and the Retreat from Marriage: A Shortage of Marriageable Men?" *American Sociological Review* 57, no. 6: 781–800.

Lincoln, C. Eric, and Lawrence H. Mamiya. 1990. *The Black Church in the African American Experience*. Durham, NC: Duke University Press.

Pamphile, Leon. 2001. *Haitians and African Americans: A Heritage of Tragedy and Hope*. Gainesville: University Press of Florida.

Raboteau, Albert. 1995. *A Fire in the Bones: Reflections on African American Religious History*. Boston: Beacon Press.

Stepick, Alex. 1998. *Pride against Prejudice: Haitians in the United States*. Boston: Allyn and Bacon.

Tracy, David. 1981. *The Analogical Imagination: Christian Theology and the Culture of Pluralism*. New York: Crossroad Publishing Company.

Waters, Mary C. 1990. *Ethnic Options: Choosing Identities in America*. Berkeley: University of California Press.

———. 1999. *Black Identities: West Indian Immigrant Dreams and American Realities*. New York and Cambridge: Russell Sage Foundation and Harvard University Press.

Woldemikael, Tekle Mariam. 1989. *Becoming Black American: Immigrant Communities and Ethnic Minorities in the United States and Canada*. New York: AMS Press.

Zéphir, Flore. 1996. *Haitian Immigrants in Black America: A Sociological and Sociolinguistic Portrait*. Westport, CT: Bergin and Garvey.

CHAPTER 7

Becoming American and Maintaining an Ethnic Identity: The Case of Dominican Americans

Ana S. Q. Liberato and Joe R. Feagin

[White Americans] think we are all black. They all have the idea that Dominicans are black and treat us poorly, just the same way they treat black Americans. (Luisa, forty-five, sales representative)

One never forgets the original culture. For example, I do not feel a hundred percent integrated into U.S. society, even when I have been here for ten years. I love Santo Domingo, and I love New York because it has given me many opportunities, but I still feel as if I am not from Santo Domingo anymore—but not from New York either. (Maria, forty-four, beautician)

The traditional image of the United States as a great land of immigrants remains as true today as it ever was. Earlier immigrations made the United States the strong and vital country it is, albeit at the great expense of indigenous peoples of color. Today, continuing immigrations provide many new people, both workers and families, that keep the country strong and dynamic, even as European countries are in demographic and, at least potentially, socioeconomic decline. Sadly, the hostility of many native-born Americans toward recent immigrant groups, which has gotten much media attention, is also part of a continuing tradition of nativism historically directed toward each new group of immigrants.

Over the last four decades, many new immigrants from the Caribbean, Latin America, and Asia have entered the United States, not only providing the dynamism of new workers and mostly younger families but also altering the nation's demographic makeup in the direction of a more racially and ethnically diverse society. Over the next few decades, whites will become a statistical minority in most U.S. cities and numerous major states. Whites are already a minority in many of the country's larger cities in California, Texas, New Mexico, and Hawaii. By about 2050, demographers estimate, African Americans, Latinos, Asian Americans, and Native Americans will be the statistical majority in the United States (Feagin 2006, 307–308).

Dominican immigrants and their children are an important part of this demographic trend. According to the 2000 U.S. census, there are just over one million non-U.S.-born Dominican immigrants in the United States, with the number of U.S.-born Dominicans at nearly four hundred thousand. Most Dominican Americans live on the East Coast, in the states of New York, New Jersey, Florida, and Massachusetts (Hernández and Rivera-Batiz 2003).

Because of their relatively recent immigration to the United States, Dominican Americans still constitute a distinctive ethnic group, but they are a part of the larger African American or Latino racial groups. They are almost always considered by outsiders, especially powerful whites, as African Americans or, less often, as Hispanics. Most still maintain a distinctive ethnic identity in the form of their culture and language. In the U.S. setting, they generally view themselves as part of a distinctive Caribbean nationality group and recognize the traditions, values, and attitudes that they collectively share (Harrison 1995).

In this chapter, we assess the significance of these historical and contemporary realities, as well as the emotional attachment that most Dominicans feel toward their common cultural heritage. We examine the racial-ethnic identity of first- and second-generation[1] Dominican Americans and describe how they perceive, define, and evaluate their Dominicanness, as well as how they think they are perceived by significant outsiders, especially whites. We find out how they come to define what it means to be a Dominican immigrant in the United States, as they transplant their Dominican identity, try to assimilate into the new culture, and negotiate and adapt to the white-maintained racial hierarchy of U.S. society. In doing this, we explore Dominican immigrants' interactions with the U.S. system of racial categorization and stratification, paying close attention to the ways in which they may or may not challenge traditional discourses of racial-ethnic identity learned in their homeland and the United States.

DEMOGRAPHIC BACKGROUND

Dominicans have been defined as "one of the most transnational people in Latin America with over a million of them being transnational migrants" (Sagás and Molina 2004, 10). Today, most maintain strong ties both to the home country and to their new host country. Dominicans started migrating to the United States in large numbers after the 1965 U.S. military intervention in the Dominican Republic. The U.S. government accepted Dominican migration as one means to alleviate political tensions on the island (Itzigsohn and Dore-Cabral 2000). Early immigrants were mostly urban, lower-middle-class people, but since the decline of the Dominican economy in the 1980s, migration has been an option chosen by Dominicans of various class backgrounds (Hernández 2002).

According to the Inter-American Development Bank, Dominicans living in New York alone now send about $1 billion a year in remittances to the Dominican Republic. Dominican immigrants sent an estimated $2.7 billion in remittances in 2004. These remittances make the Dominican Republic the fourth largest remittance market (Green 2004).

U.S. census data show that Dominicans tend to be younger than other groups of color, such as African Americans, Asian Americans, Native Americans, and non-Dominican Latinos. Fertility rates are high among Dominican women (Hernández 2002). In general, Dominicans have lower levels of educational attainment than the U.S. population as a whole, as reported in table 7.1. The educational situation varies noticeably when immigrant status is taken into consideration (Hernández and Rivera-Batiz 2003). This low educational attainment often has an impact on job prospects (Hernández 2002).

The limited English skills of the Dominican American population as a whole represent a challenge in a society where many members of the dominant group are often obsessed with "English as the official language." For example, in 1990, some 52 percent declared that they spoke English "not well." This seems to have hurt their socioeconomic mobility. Indeed, in that year, those who spoke "poor" English earned an average of $6,846 less than those who spoke "strong" English (Hernández 2002). In addition, Dominicans who speak "poor,"

Table 7.1.   Educational Attainment by Gender for Dominican Americans and U.S. Population Age Twenty-five and Older

Educational Attainment	Dominican Americans		U.S. Population	
	Female (%)	Male (%)	Female (%)	Male (%)
No schooling completed	6.3	2.4	1.4	1.5
High school graduate*	19.9	20.7	29.6	27.6
Associate's degree	5.5	4.1	6.8	5.8
Bachelor's degree	7.0	6.5	15	16.1
Master's degree	1.8	1.7	5.8	6.0
Professional degree	1.9	2.3	1.4	2.5
Doctoral degree	0.3	0.4	0.5	1.4
Other**	57.3	61.9	40.0	40.5

Source: U.S. Census Bureau 2000.
*Includes equivalency.
**Includes nursery school to twelfth grade, some college, or no degree.

"moderate," or "strong" English still earned less than Puerto Ricans, non-Hispanic blacks, and whites.

Among selected ethnic minorities, Dominican Americans have the lowest median household income ($29,099), just below that of African Americans as a group, and well below the national figure of $41,994 shown in table 7.2. Dominican Americans also have the largest concentration of people below the poverty line, a proportion more than double that for the country as a whole.

Despite having the highest rate of participation in manufacturing jobs in 1991 as compared to other Hispanic groups (25.7 percent for Dominicans versus 18.6 percent for other Hispanics), Dominicans struggled to find or keep high-paying jobs and still earned lower wages than African Americans, Native Americans, Asians, and other non-Dominican Hispanic Americans (Torres Saillant and Hernández 1998). As we see in table 7.3, most Dominican Americans in the labor force worked in service jobs, manufacturing, construction, and retail trade; Dominican Americans were about half as likely as the general population to be in managerial-type jobs. Among all male groups in New York City, Dominican men have exhibited the highest unemployment rates (Hernández 2002).

Despite facing these major socioeconomic challenges, there is room for hope for Dominican mobility based on the improvement in educational attainment for the second generation. For instance, the school en-

**Table 7.2.   Median Household Income and Proportion
of Population below Poverty for Selected Groups**

Group	Median Household Income ($)	Percentage below Poverty Line
Dominicans	29,099	27.0
Puerto Ricans	30,644	25.8
Cubans	36,671	14.6
Other Hispanics or Latinos	34,651	20.7
African Americans	29,423	24.9
White Americans	44,687	9.1
U.S	41,994	12.4

Source: U.S. Census Bureau 2000.

rollment rate of Dominicans in New York City public schools is higher
than that of other children of color, while the proportion of second-
generation Dominican Americans who have attained some college education has risen significantly as well (Hernández and Rivera-Batiz
2003).

In spite of many economic difficulties and the trials of racial discrimination, most Dominican immigrants have been able to create relatively stable lives in the United States. At the same time, most have
maintained familial, cultural, political, and economic ties with the
homeland and fellow immigrants (Torres Saillant and Hernández
1998). The maintenance of these important social ties has made possible the exchange of cultural and political customs and information.
These contacts have allowed many immigrants to become bicultural
and have made Dominican Americans much more aware of global
processes (Sagás and Molina 2004, 8). These ties have also helped second-generation Dominican Americans to develop emotional attachments to the Dominican Republic and a sense of pride in their origins.

Table 7.3.   Percentage of Employed Civilian Population Age Sixteen and Older

Profession	Dominican Americans	U.S. Population
Management	17.0	33.6
Service	24.6	14.9
Sales	27.2	26.7
Farming, fishing, and forestry	0.3	0.7
Construction, extraction, and maintenance	7.5	9.4
Production, transportation, and material moving	23.3	14.6

Source: U.S. Census Bureau 2000.

The consequences of these practices and attachments can be narrow or broad, depending on the character, intensity, and systematicity of the activities in which Dominican immigrants and their descendants engage (Itzigsohn et al. 1999) and on the favorable (or unfavorable) conditions that their living environment offers for the development and consolidation of transnational practices (Sagás and Molina 2004). We now explore these issues in much greater detail, using field research that we have conducted.

THE EXPERIENCES AND VIEWS OF DOMINICANS IN THE UNITED STATES: OUR INTERVIEWS

Much of the data in the following sections come from forty semistructured interviews with Dominican Americans that Ana Liberato conducted in New York and Florida in 2004 and 2005 (fully reported in Liberato 2005).[2] Our data collection process also involved participant observation during 2004 and 2005 at family and community events, such as birthday parties (*quinceañera*), Christmas parties (*fiesta de año nuevo* and *nochebuena*), Mass (Pentecostal Church), political rallies (Dominican Revolutionary Party), family gatherings (to welcome a visiting relative, to pray for someone's health, to celebrate a Dominican holiday), and visits to the political headquarters of three major Dominican political parties in New York. These events took place at different times. Although, this study is based on the interviews, the data collected at these events were important because they enabled us to link some aspects of people's narratives with their individual behavior.

TRANSNATIONALIZING BUSINESS AND POLITICS

The development of transnational practices among Dominicans has been a far-reaching process (Sagás and Molina 2004). For instance, the rise of an entrepreneurial class in New York City has a lot to do with the existence of successful transnational ties (Portes and Guarnizo 1991). Dominican-American entrepreneurs utilize diverse social networks to conduct business operations between the United States and the Dominican Republic. Examples of Dominican-owned firms are remittance companies, small-loan and investment firms, grocery stores, car-repair shops, and car wash businesses (Portes and Guarnizo 1991). With the help of these ties, Dominicans now own about twenty thousand businesses in New York City alone (Portes and Guarnizo 1991).

Dominicans from the homeland have benefited from transnationalism (Itzigsohn et al. 1999). Poor Dominicans there have gained access to goods and services otherwise inaccessible, which enhance their standard of living (Itzigsohn et al. 1999). In this way, poor Dominicans feel more compelled to migrate as they recognize the economic benefits of migration for individuals, households, and communities.

Transnationalism increasingly involves the internationalization of economic opportunity and social mobility in the Dominican context. The reality of transnationalism has been deepened by government and private initiatives broadening the economic opportunities of migrant Dominicans and their relatives on the island. There are now more home-ownership opportunities for Dominicans living overseas, especially for those living in the United States, Italy, and Spain (Mejía 2006). Many housing projects in Santo Domingo and other cities have developed exclusively for the returning and transient immigrant market, offering low mortgages and attractive payment plans (Mejía 2006). A survey in New York in 2003 by Horwath Consulting indicated that 93 percent of Dominican Americans desire to purchase a house some day in the Dominican Republic, 37.7 percent of those interviewed declared that they already owned a house on the island, and 87.3 percent declared their desire to buy property other than a house (*DiarioDigital RD* 2006).

For Dominican Americans, such homeownership in the Dominican Republic may signify several aspirations. On the one hand, owning a house may be considered the realization of an important dream, which, in return, enhances their wealth and that of relatives. On the other hand, home ownership may constitute an investment in retirement. For relatives back home, this ownership often translates into direct or indirect economic benefit (e.g., saving rent money by moving into and taking care of the newly purchased house, enhancing their social status by being in charge of property and handling remittances).

Transnationalism has involved the circulation of remittances to political groups (Levitt 2001). Dominicans abroad are often involved in the political life of their home country. Jose Itzigsohn (1995) indicates that these Dominicans are an important source of financial support for Dominican political parties. Party membership and activism are also important features of this political transnationalism (Levitt 2001). The two largest Dominican political parties have offices in New York City and Providence, Rhode Island.

Island political circles value the political opinions of Dominican immigrants in the United States highly because their views are believed to influence the political preferences of Dominicans at home. As a result, the political importance of Dominicans abroad has strengthened (Levitt 2001). This political importance is manifested in the passing of new laws that protect the dual-citizenship rights of Dominican immigrants (Itzigsohn et al. 1999).[3]

RACIAL IDENTITY IN THE DOMINICAN REPUBLIC

The formation of racial-ethnic identities in the Dominican Republic is the product of complex and oppressive historical processes. These racial-ethnic identities have been constructed based on how Dominicans see themselves in contrast to Haitians and based on how Dominicans perceive themselves as being seen by people, especially whites, in other countries (Torres Saillant 1995). Ginetta Candelario (2000), among others, has linked the development of this complex identity to both European colonialism and U.S. imperialism and the colonizers' deeply racist portrayal of all the peoples of color whom they encountered. After colonization, many people of color came to see themselves in the same negative terms as the white colonizers saw them. Thus, the white racist framing of people of color is especially problematical for the mental health of those oppressed. In situations of white-imposed oppression, it is relatively "normal" for those trying to reduce the levels of racial discrimination and related oppression to try to please whites as much as they can. Such attempts to suit and conform to whites and whiteness lead not only to whiteness worship and servile assimilation, but also to various forms of self-hate and internal group discrimination favoring lighter-skinned members of the oppressed group.

In terms of racial definition, the racial categories in the Dominican Republic contrast with those of the United States. On the island, the racial categories are based on a combination of color and physical features. There is an explicit emphasis on phenotypic features that distinguish "black" from "white" (Candelario 2000).

On the island, the Spanish terms *negro, prieto*, and *mulatto* are often used to distinguish between the favored Dominicans and despised Haitians (Sagás 2000). The term *negro* is used much less often for Dominicans than for Haitians because it can be viewed as an insult. It is much more common to hear Dominicans use *negro* when referring to Haitians (Sagás 2000). In certain intimate contexts of Dominican family and friends, however, variations on the term *negro* can signify appreciation and care (e.g., *mi negra, mi negro*, or *negrita*).

For the most part, Dominicans downplay their African origins and blackness and, concomitantly, overemphasize their whiteness and Hispanic-Catholic heritage (Torres Saillant 1998; Sagás 2000). This identification is strongly manifested in Dominicans' sentiments and behaviors toward Haitians (whose country makes up about one-third of Hispaniola), who are considered the "real black ones." Strong differentiation from Haitians becomes a very important feature of Dominican racial identity. Haitians are placed into a separate category because of their negatively viewed color, hair, language, and thus "race" (Torres Saillant 1998; Sagás 2000; Hansen 2001).

Researchers have shown that there is an association in the Dominican Republic between skin color and class. Robert Toplin (1971) noted that "a clearly disproportionate number of black [Dominicans] . . . find themselves in a culture of poverty" (139). Nancy Denton and Douglas Massey (1989) found that there is "an affiliation between race and class in the Dominican Republic, Puerto Rico and Cuba" (792). Seda Bonilla (1961) found race to be a barrier to higher class status in those countries. Denton and Massey (1989) write,

> The upper classes have traditionally emphasized whiteness and pay careful attention to ancestry. They can identify people who have colored ancestors, even when the people are apparently white. Those of the darker color also have a difficulty achieving political office. As a result of these subtle prejudices, the proportion of blacks has declined in subsequent censuses, reflecting the social pressure to identify as white whenever possible. (792)

These findings are also supported by the work of many scholars, including Marianne Masferrer and Carmelo Mesa-Lago (1974), Bonilla (1961), Diógenes Céspedes (1997), Meindert Fennema and Troetje Loewenthal (1987), James Ferguson (1993), Franklin Franco (1977, 1997), Ernesto Sagás (2000), Carlos Persinal (1997), and Norman Whitten and Arlene Torres (1998).

TRANSNATIONAL IDENTITY: DOMINICANS IN THE UNITED STATES

There is an association between the way Dominicans define their identity in the United States and the dominant racial ideology that operates in the Dominican Republic (Torres Saillant 1998). This is so because immigrants transplant their social and political knowledge into the new society. The white-imposed system of racial categorization that Dominican immigrants encounter in U.S. society affects the formation of their racial identity. There are two realities when it comes to the issue of racial identity in the United States. Generally speaking, whites, especially powerful whites in key institutions, impose and control the racial identities of all groups of Americans, especially when they are outside their homes in the public sphere. These imposed racial identities are difficult to counter, although immigrants resist using them.

The U.S. system of more or less rigid racial categorization sharply contrasts with the more flexible system of racial categorization in the Dominican Republic and much of Latin America. As a consequence, once in the United States, many Dominicans who have considered themselves "white" have had to accept the identity of "black," "Hispanic," or "person of color," the racialized labels imposed on them by dominant whites and others in the United States (Levitt 2001; Torres Saillant 1998).

Peggy Levitt's 2001 study of Dominicans in Boston illustrates how the U.S. system of racial classification troubles many Dominicans:

Mirafloreños take racial distinctions seriously. They are proud of their ancestral ties to the Canary Islands. They admire those with "good hair" and "good skin"—people with the physical characteristics associated with whiteness. Banilejos, in general, are known throughout the country for their feelings of racial superiority. What a shock it is for Mirafloreños

to go to the United States, thinking of themselves as white, only to realize that they are considered people of color. From the point of view of
Bostonians, they belong to the very racial category they reject so
adamantly at home. (108)

Levitt (2001) argues that Dominicans have struggled with different
strategies to fit within the new racial tableau in the United States. She
identifies the following strategy, among others: differentiating themselves from other African Americans and assertively learning white
Anglo-Saxon values.

Additionally, Jorge Duany (1998) reports that Dominican migrants
have not only created such coping strategies but have also tried to redefine their racial identity altogether. Since most Americans, especially
whites, consider and name Dominicans as blacks or colored, Dominican Americans are forced to undergo a drastic transformation in their
understanding of racial-ethnic groups. The transformation of their
racial ideology leads them to reconsider the use of Dominican and U.S.
racial categories. Because of this, Dominicans who identify themselves
as black in New York would likely call themselves *indios* or *trigueño*
(that is, not negro) in their home country (Duany 1998, 165).

Silvio Torres Saillant (1998) calls attention to how age and generational membership shape these processes of identity negotiation and
definition. Dominican youngsters who have resided longer in the
United States are more likely to accept the white-imposed "black"
identity. They are more likely to emphasize their Afro-Caribbean ancestry within the imposed racial identity that they also accept. Torres
Saillant believes this to be because younger Dominicans become aware
during the process of socialization of the struggles for equality of black
Americans and other people of color. This knowledge promotes in them
feelings of empathy, empowerment, and pride in their African roots and
leads them to defy dominant racial ideologies (Torres Saillant 1998).
Yet, this acceptance can also be seen as a *realistic* reaction to the omni-
present racism they face.

Candelario (2000) has found that many Dominican Americans, particularly in New York City, prefer to use the term *Hispanic* in self-
defining their racial-ethnic identity. Dominicans who use that term may
be in search of a cultural connection with Spanish-European roots

highly regarded in the Dominican Republic. More likely, however, this is a way of trying to say, especially to whites, that Dominicans do not wish to be seen as "black." In any event, the use of the term *Hispanic* is ineffective for Dominicans because most whites associate this term with a negative minority status rather than with a positive image of Western culture (Candelario 2000). Indeed, most whites would likely categorize Dominicans not only as "not white" but also as "black." Recent research shows that few whites today see any of the Caribbean, Latino, African, Native, or Asian American groups as "white," no matter how some or many members of these groups may wish to identify as white (Feagin 2006, 291).

The aforementioned differences, tensions, and ambiguities occur in an increasingly transnational context. Transnationalization generates or forces a renegotiation of ethnoracial identities and has the potential to enhance the emergence of alternative ethnoracial identities in the Dominican Republic and the United States. Frank Moya Pons (1981) has argued that Dominican Americans' social and cultural experiences with whiteness in the United States increase their awareness of their blackness.

Torres Saillant and Ramona Hernández (1998) have argued that the dynamics of transnationalization have failed to create a full reevaluation of Dominican racial awareness on the island and in the United States. David Howard (2001) maintains that "the very success of the Dominican social and cultural regenerative experience has reproduced racial norms, rather than dispelled them" (113). Accordingly, many Dominicans still tend to deny their Africanness and strongly emphasize their difference from Haitians and African Americans, in spite of their being treated by white Americans as African Americans. Dominican Americans even tend to hold the negative stereotypes created by whites for other U.S. groups of color, despite their own recurring encounters with U.S. racism. They often buy into a white racial framing of society and thus tend to see whites as the genuine Americans and African Americans as inferior and second-class citizens (Howard 2001).

COLLECTIVE REMEMBERING AND MAINTAINING RACIAL-ETHNIC IDENTITY

The formation of racial and ethnic identities is linked with processes of *collective remembering*, or the recollection of shared representations of the past in a society, group, organization, or institution (Kansteiner 2002). According to Maurice Halbwachs (1980), individual and group experiences are often intertwined with historical and political factors in the creation of representations of the past available to members of a particular group. The availability of these representations in the social space helps individuals to link their personal experiences with group experiences, group consciousness, and events involving other people (Kansteiner 2002). Therefore, what is in people's heads is often only meaningful in reference to the collective memory and is only consequential if the group itself survives (Schuman and Corning 2000). The act of recollection is much more than just "retrieving information"; indeed, it is a process of uncovering knowledge that has been produced within group life (Schwartz 1982; Halbwachs 1980).

For Halbwachs, the past is a functional byproduct with its own "geography" and "morphology." Memory is an object, "a thing"[4] with a specific social location. Memory can be "localized" in the "practices and institutions of social or psychic life" (Kansteiner 2002, 188; Schwartz 1991), as well as in the social experiences produced and consumed by families, political groups, ethnic groups, and nations (Kansteiner 2002). Thus, collective memories exist on the level of gender, class, ethnic, and immigrant groups. They exist on the level of nations, generations, the public and private spheres, and professions (Schwartz 2000). Books, speeches, films, monuments, commemorations, songs, pictures, buildings, holidays, letters, narratives, newspapers, magazines, rites, speeches, discourse, and so on, are all repositories of memory.

Dominican immigrants in the United States are both consumers and producers of collective memory. These collective memories feature cultural meanings and their perceptions of themselves and others, events, characters, behaviors, and institutions (Rothstein 2000). They use this knowledge to guide their social interactions and in solving dilemmas in the new social context (Rothstein 2000). For example, first-generation Dominican Americans tend to perceive Dominican culture in a more positive light, making them more likely to want to preserve it.[5]

The commitment to the preservation of Dominican culture manifests itself in the private and group practices of many immigrants. For instance, we participated in different activities in which elements of

Dominican culture served as an organizing theme for the events: a Christmas party (*Nochebuena*), a New Year's party, a house party, a gathering to play dominos, a graduation celebration, a baptism, a reunion to watch a baseball game, and an *hora santa* (religious rite) on behalf of a sick person. Dominican cuisine, music videos, TV shows, family photographs, postcards, flags, clothing, and kitchen supplies were common repositories of memory utilized by Dominican immigrants in "performing their nationality."

Public sites of memory are instrumental in achieving certain performances of Dominican nationality. Examples of these sites are the streets, businesses, and schools that feature the names of historical Dominican personalities, events such as the Dominican Republican Day Parade celebrated each summer in New York City, Dominican newspapers that circulate in the city, and commercial and political billboards placed in different locations in New York City. These sites and the discourses that accompany them are part of the shared cultural system (Irwin-Zarecka 1994; Schwartz 2000) that informs the collective consciousness of Dominican immigrants. They are significant in shaping the form of, and struggle over, identities within the group and are also central to the maintenance of the transnational community.

RACE AND ETHNIC TALK OF IMMIGRANTS: FIRST- AND SECOND-GENERATION DOMINICANS IN AMERICA DEFINE THE MEANING OF THEIR IDENTITY

The celebration of Dominican culture is very important to first- and second-generation Dominican immigrants. For both groups, Dominicanness is something they practice in everyday life through the display of symbols, through their particular lifestyles, and through the use of nonmaterial culture in orienting behavior. We identified multiple ways in which second-generation Dominicans do their ethnicity: making the "right" choice of attire (Dominican style) for the high school prom, using Dominican cultural symbols in tattoo designs (the Dominican flag), accepting the importance of and celebrating the fifteenth birthday as opposed to the sixteenth, and joining Dominican-centered student organizations. The first generation does ethnicity by watching Dominican television shows, such as *Sábado de Corporán*, *9X9 Roberto*, or *Nuria en el 9* on Direct TV. One respondent, Mercedes, a forty-nine-year-old service worker, maintains her cultural roots through *Café con Bolero* (Coffee with Bolero), a meeting with friends on Sunday mornings to play Latin American music, drink strong coffee, talk about immigrant life, remember life back in the Dominican Republic, and discuss issues affecting the Dominican people.

In many cases, such activities have a strong gendered component, thereby constituting a form of gendered identity. For instance, we identified Dominicanized concepts of beauty and womanhood being used in the personal care and dating practices adopted by our female respondents. Many respondents expressed pride in the view that Dominican beauticians are especially good at dealing with Dominican women's hair. Many Dominican women have formal and informal business ties with hair salons in the areas they live. These salons provide the desired (Dominicanized) hair care that immigrant women are looking for, such as straightening. In New York City, Dominican beauty salons most often provide such services; in smaller communities, beauticians use friendship and familial ties to develop the necessary beauty services.

Another gendered reality can be seen in the women who prepare Dominican foods to be sold to the community on important occasions, such as weddings, graduation parties, baptisms, and birthdays. First- and second-generation Dominicans consider the flavor of these foods to be more authentic compared to those purchased at local stores or prepared at home with seasonings not considered genuinely Dominican. These female-centered networks arise because some women's culinary and hair skills become common knowledge within the group, enabling them to develop a network of customers.

Dominican immigrants often engage in activities in which they express their national identity in reference to space, with a sense of spatial demarcation or control. Examples are painting the Dominican flag on walls, playing Dominican music in public places, and giving Dominican names to streets, businesses (*tenares*), and popular products (phone cards such as Enrriquillo, Mi Quisqueya, and Plátano). These practices reveal a territorialized sense of strong national identity that is experienced in relation to physical and cultural spaces.

This is also manifested in language. Many respondents in New York City use the words *allá abajo* (downtown) to refer to places and events in the downtown area. When talking about race relations in the city, many respondents use these words to refer to life in the white upper-class areas of the city. *Allá abajo* seems to signify more than just an attempt by immigrants to do a translation of the word "downtown" into Spanish. *Allá abajo* means non-Dominican. Everything that happens *allá abajo* has to do with whites and wealthy New Yorkers, not with Dominicans and other people of color. *Allá abajo* refers to things non-Dominican in a geographic, socioeconomic, and cultural sense.

All of these examples suggest that many migrant Dominican and their descendants keep, in different ways and at different levels, emotional and psychological ties with the Dominican Republic. Remaining Dominican, or trying to do so, gives them the sense of community, pride, and empowerment that is so important for survival in the highly racist U.S. context. The development of a territorialized identity may be seen as a form of resistance to racial-class hierarchies, but it is also an attempt to claim power, at least in the form of certain cultural and geographic spaces.

The First-Generation

In our interviews, first-generation Dominicans in America consistently talked about the mixture of racial groups, individual and collective struggles, and pain, sacrifice, and empowerment when defining what it means to be a Dominican immigrant in the United States. Those interviewed consistently mentioned the "special" racial mixture of the Dominican people, which in their view makes them more open-minded and adaptable to new circumstances, less prejudiced, more likeable, more beautiful, unique, and better workers, lovers, and baseball players.

They often mentioned the struggles that characterize the lives of Dominican people in the Dominican Republic and the United States. The struggles have economic roots: "We are economic refugees," said a fifty-two-year-old truck driver from New York City. The struggle can be of emotional character as well: "I have felt so much loneliness in this big city," said a fifty-one-year-old female Dominican homemaker. Their struggles are often framed in terms of both how hard it is for Dominicans to have a decent life in the Dominican Republic because of poverty and the lack of opportunities and how challenging it is to fight for a better life once in the United States.

The experience of being a Dominican immigrant was linked to ideas of personal pain. The painful circumstances narrated by respondents are legion. They include feelings of being "neither from here nor from there," personal suffering after leaving loved ones behind, dealing with snow, and coping with stress and insecurity over poor language skills, their own or their families' often problematic legal status, and their difficulties adapting to the U.S. lifestyle. They also cited the inability to get decent jobs and to practice former careers, trouble building close personal relationships in neighborhoods, feelings of rejection from white Americans, and a sense that they could never fully assimilate into U.S. society. Adrian, a fifty-seven-year-old entrepreneur, and Marino, a fifty-two-year-old truck driver, in New York City particularly emphasized the issue of isolation and lack of adaptation:

> Here in New York we are merely holding up and learning to survive, but we never adapt to this type of life. We cannot adapt to life in the United States. We are survivors here. . . . We Dominicans are country people— we love the rivers, we love to be outside—but here in New York you are locked up in your apartment.

> I have suffered a lot because this country [the United States] is made for young people, not for old guys like me. Everything is so different here. I do not have close friends anymore. I left my family and friends behind. I prepared myself mentally before leaving the Dominican Republic to come here. I made myself believe that I had left no one or anything behind, so I could stay here working instead of going back, forced by the sadness of missing home. I would not stay a month here if I had not prepared myself mentally.

Maria, a forty-four-year-old beautician, also mentioned problems with adapting to U.S. society:

> One never forgets the original culture. For example, I do not feel a hundred percent integrated into U.S. society even when I have been here for ten years. I love Santo Domingo, and I love New York because it has given me many opportunities, but I still feel as if I am not from Santo Domingo anymore—but not from New York either. I think the language

barrier has a lot to do with it. The problem is that by not speaking the
[English] language, we stay more focused on our Dominican culture.

The first respondent revealed a strong sense of involuntary cultural
disconnect with the host society and presented U.S. culture as an obstacle to the everyday life of Dominican immigrants and as being very
different from his previous cultural universe. Because the difference is
acute, it is very difficult for Dominicans to adapt. The second and third
respondents showed how emotions dominate in narratives of migration
and identity. Accordingly, part of being a Dominican immigrant in the
United States has to do with managing strong emotions like loneliness,
fear, anxiety, and frustration. It also greatly involves dealing with the
ambiguity of not being fully Dominican any more, yet not being fully
integrated into U.S. society either.

Our respondents defined Dominicanness in terms of the "sacrificed"
life that they live in the United States. To be a Dominican American
means giving up many personal dreams, relationships, and lifestyles in
order to create the material conditions necessary to help relatives and
acquire property in the Dominican Republic. The idea of returning
home someday and buying a house is central to the notion of sacrifice
conveyed in the narratives of the first generation. Arelis, a fifty-one-
year-old service worker, put it this way:

> Many of us are here working to send remittances to the Dominican Re-
> public. We live very limited lives here in order to save money and send
> it to our families back home. The hope is that we someday will be able
> to go back for good, but to go back to live under much better conditions
> than those we lived under before migrating. I am afraid we remain too
> focused on finding ways to help those back home, failing to focus on our
> new lives here in the United States.

Arelis's account suggests that first-generation Dominicans in America
live in a particular state of mind in which the desire to return to the Dominican Republic drives actions and plans. He suggests that creating
the foundations for a better life in the Dominican Republic is more important to Dominican immigrants than any other thing. Achieving this
constitutes the "Dominican American dream," as one respondent posi-
tively and assertively put it. On the other hand, one second-generation

Dominican called this the "Dominican syndrome," a sort of cultural illness that prevents the first generation from focusing on their present
and future life in the United States.

Many respondents mentioned strength, resilience, and empowerment when defining what it means to be a Dominican immigrant.
While they experience loneliness, economic hardship, and discrimination, most still manage to succeed to some degree. The large number of Dominican-owned small businesses in New York City was
noted as an example of their success and modest empowerment. The
success of some Dominican politicians was also interpreted as part of
the empowerment:

> We already have Dominicans as public servants in Brooklyn and Queens.
> In uptown Manhattan about 80 percent of small businesses are owned by
> Dominicans. The taxi drivers are Dominicans and so are the restaurants
> and bodegueros. We Dominicans are active people. We are even getting
> to Harlem, and there are many African Americans who see us as a threat.
> We are really advancing everywhere we are. (Pedro, fifty-five, a New
> York market employee)
>
> We have made the effort to improve ourselves. Nobody has helped us.
> We have done it in our own terms. Our activists have fought hard for us.
> We are growing and becoming more powerful and more important.
> (Luisa, forty-five, sales representative)

In these narratives, Dominicanness is associated with positive
qualities, such as strength, dedication, and success. Dominicans are
depicted as determined, progressive, and willing to assimilate. This
emphasis on how the community rises, despite facing serious obsta-
cles, conveys a very positive picture of Dominican Americans. Other
respondents affirmed these positive conceptions with expressions
such as the following: "Dominicans are positive people who come to
this country to work." "We Dominicans are intelligent people who
care about the future." "Dominicans are strong people who do not allow anybody to humiliate them." "Dominicans earn the respect and
love of others because we are very hard working people." Respondents also made the following comments: "Dominicans care about
their relatives back home." "Dominicans are looking for a better future." "Dominicans keep their pride up." "Dominicans were able to

take control of Washington Heights, a territory previously dominated by well-to-do Jewish people."

At the same time, Dominicanness is associated with qualities such as individualism and internal division. Dominicans in the United States are sometimes portrayed as divided and unwilling to support each other in times of need. Many respondents mentioned the Jewish and Cuban peoples as examples of cohesive and united communities that represent the opposite of what the Dominican community often is. Cubans and Jews have supposedly remained "united" and therefore have been able to excel. The words of Jose, a fifty-nine-year-old political activist from New York City, and Mateo, a forty-seven-year-old private employee from New York City, illustrate this view:

> The biggest problem is that we Dominicans are not united at all as a people. I say that with a lot of sorrow. We are absolutely divided as people. Just think about the Jewish people and the way they treat each other. A Jew would not do anything that could hurt another Jew, even if that means to sacrifice his personal interest. Dominicans would have a much better life in this country if we were like the Jews. We would have a higher economic status if we were more united.
>
> Dominicans are with no doubt very progressive people. They may not read or write in English but still are able to own a bodega or a supermarket. This happens because we have the spirit of entrepreneurship. This is very important for any community. However, we have a big problem: we envy each other. You see, if you are a doctor your fellow Dominicans are bothered by it as opposed to being proud of it. We forget that when one Dominican succeeds, the whole community succeeds. We even allow party politics to get in the way. We allow our political preferences to divide us.

Mateo and Jose suggest that Dominicans lack what Cubans and Jews possess: an integrated and united community. They, like many other respondents, exaggerate Cubans' and Jews' reputation for not discriminating against their own people, for favoring their people over others when it comes to employment, for not envying the progress of fellow Cubans and Jews, and for not allowing partisan politics to divide them. They also feel that Cubans and Jews put the interests of the community over individual interests, have strong advocacy groups, and help those in need within the community. Frustration with Dominican individualism and lack of solidarity is reflected in expressions like *el dominicano es malo* (Dominicans are bad), *el dominicano no es facil* (Dominicans are difficult people), *el dominicano sufre el progeso del otro dominicano* (Dominicans envy each other), and *el dominicano es muy individualista*, (Dominicans are selfish people).

The Second-Generation

The accounts of the first and second generations differ from each other in certain important ways. Second-generation Dominican Americans often talked about different issues in descriptions of being in the United States. Second-generation Dominican Americans mentioned cultural matters and tended to define Dominicanness in terms of practices associated with Dominican culture and having ties to the Dominican Republic (e.g., listening to merengue and *bachata* music, eating Dominican food, enjoying baseball, dancing, reading Dominican newspapers, speaking Spanish, traveling to the Dominican Republic, having a permanent home to stay in when visiting the Dominican Republic, caring about relatives in the Dominican Republic, and maintaining communication with kin). The understanding is that one can be a Dominican as long as one speaks Spanish or identifies with Dominican culture, maintains family ties with relatives, and practices certain Dominican traditions. The following accounts illustrate this point:

> Speaking Spanish always reminds me that I am Dominican. If I did not speak Spanish, I would not feel that connection. It is the language, dancing, and listening to Dominican music that gives you the feeling. The language and the music create a connection among all of us. (Tina, twenty, retail employee)
>
> I do not need to try hard to do things the Dominican way. It just happens because of my family and the way I was raised, and all the influence makes me do things different from, let's say, blacks or whites. Being Dominican makes you different. We have our own language, our own culture and traditions, our own worldview. I grew up around all this stuff and my Dominican side comes natural. (Luisa, nineteen, college student)
>
> My family is Dominican. Everybody is Dominican. I have no other part of anything else. Both of my parents are Dominican. They speak

Spanish all the time. We cook Dominican food. We visit the DR, celebrate Dominican holidays, and follow baseball. Dominican culture is
pretty much alive around me. (Julio, nineteen, college student)

Tina, Luisa, and Julio conceptualize Dominicanness in terms of the
cultural repertoire they have and perform in everyday life. Other
second-generation Dominican Americans associated their Dominicanness with qualities like "having the ability to relax and enjoy life," "being family-oriented happy people," and "being strong and in search of
a better life." Being able to relax and being happy and family-oriented
were considered qualities lacking in U.S. society. Their Dominican
background gives these respondents access to these positive qualities.
Victor, a twenty-year-old college student, said, "[F]rom Dominican
culture I get the emotional stuff and from American culture I get the
material stuff."

However, second-generation Dominican Americans also highlighted
the differences between "American culture" and Dominican values and
customs, frequently stressing that Dominicans come from a very "different world" as compared to other Americans. Many respondents used
these differences to convey the idea that they had gone through a specific set of life experiences by having a Dominican background. The
following quotes illustrate this:

Being the children of Dominican immigrants means that you will see
your parents struggling trying to adapt to American culture. They do not
understand or agree with the norms of U.S. society. This makes it difficult for you sometimes because you live a Dominican life at home, but
when you go outside, you encounter American culture and that is the culture you grow up with at school. . . . I remember my favorite teacher
telling me that I could be anything I wanted to be in the world. Being a
girl was not supposed to stop me from becoming successful and achieving my dreams. But then, in my house, I was taught that a woman is the
one who cleans, cooks, takes care of the kids. . . . You know . . . that kind
of stuff. This is what happens when you come from two very different
cultures. (Sonia, twenty-two, college student)

   Being the children of Dominican immigrants is a very interesting
thing. . . . [L]ike my father . . . he holds on to Dominican culture. He does
politics here for the Dominican Republic. I tell him, "Dad, you don't live

there anymore," but sometimes I understand that that is the one thing he can do to remain connected to the Dominican Republic . . . like the little string that he has. . . . And raising their children in a Dominican way here, that, too, is a way to remain connected. I can see that. (Rosa, twenty-two, college student)

Let me tell you that my uncle here is working with Leonel Fernandez's campaign in Miami. At first, I did not know that he was so involved in Dominican politics. My mom's side of the family is very tied to the Dominican Republic and to the culture. My uncles are all very politically inclined. They want everybody to vote during the Dominican elections. They want me to become a Dominican citizen so I could vote. But this is great for them but not for me. I am not interested in voting there. I can see, however, that this is part of the experience of having a Dominican background. (Lourdes, twenty-one, college student)

Being the child of Dominican parents is not necessarily a special situation. It does give you the advantage of being bilingual. . . . I also remember that my parents could not help much with my homework because their English was not very good. I remember that they did not know what to do or where to go to get me registered in sport teams. I also remember that my friends could not figure out my dad. They could not understand his behaviors, his manners, his English. They just could not figure him out. (Alex, eighteen, student)

For these respondents, their Dominican background gives them access to unique experiences, which puts them in contact with different gender messages, political practices, and parenting styles. These experiences are seen here as being part of a Dominican cultural repertoire of which they are cognizant. However, these experiences were also seen as placing second-generation Dominican Americans in a different situation from their parents and as a disadvantage, as is illustrated in the last account.

RACIAL-ETHNIC LABELS: SELF-IDENTIFICATION

First-generation Dominicans in America used several classifications to identify themselves racially. When asked how they would define themselves racially, first-generation Dominicans used categories such as *mestizo, dominicano, latinoamericano, mezclado, hispano, caribeño, latino*, *mulata*, *trigueña*, *blanco*, and *india*. Some respondents used two labels to specify their identity (e.g., Dominican and Hispanic, Latino and Hispanic, *trigueña* and Latina, white and Latino). The labels emphasize racial characteristics (e.g., *blanco*, *mezclado*, and *mestizo*) or racial-ethnic characteristics (Hispanic, Latino, Dominican).

To identify themselves racially, second-generation Dominican Americans used terms such as *Hispanic*, *Dominican*, *black*, *Dominican American*, and *Latino*. It was common to find respondents specifying their identity as being Dominican and Hispanic or just Dominican. It was interesting to realize that many of those who identified themselves as just Dominicans did not speak much Spanish and, in some cases, had not been to the Dominican Republic more than twice or had not visited the country in a long time.

The Meaning of Racial-Ethnic Labels: *Mezclado*, Mestizo, Indio, Black, Hispanic, Latino, and Dominican

The occasionally used label *mezclado* refers to the mixture between Africans and Spaniards ("we are the descendants of the black slave and the Spanish"). It also refers to the mixture between Africans and indigenous people ("I am mezclado because I have black blood and Indian blood"). Some respondents categorized themselves as *mestizo* and defined the label as signifying the combination of indigenous people (Indians) and Spanish people.

The categories Hispanic and Latino were used in diverse ways by first- and second-generation Dominican Americans. Respondents often used these categories interchangeably. Being Hispanic or Latino means that one speaks Spanish, comes from a Latin American country, and shares similar cultural traits (e.g., religion). Being Hispanic also means that one has similar life experiences in the United States. Examples of these life experiences are having left the Dominican Republic for economic or political reasons, being culturally different from other Americans, being discriminated against, having an accent, and searching desperately for better opportunities.

The category *Dominican* had different meanings for different respondents. According to Manuel, a fifty-nine-year-old, first-generation Dominican from New York, being of the *raza dominicana* means that one has no specific race or that one sees no color in oneself or other people: "I am Dominican and we Dominicans do not distinguish people by color. We are all Dominicans. We have no problems with color there. It does not matter if you are Chinese, Turkish, Jewish, or whatever. We are all Dominicans. We do not classify people by color," Manuel added somewhat naively.

The category *Dominican* also signified the national origin of the respondent, the place where one grew up, the birthplace of one's parents, and the place where many relatives and friends still live. "I am one hundred percent Dominican. My parents are Dominican. My siblings are all Dominican. All my family is Dominican. I still have uncles, aunts, and lots of cousins in the Dominican Republic. My family visits the DR and keeps contact with our relatives," said Miguelina, an eighteen-year-old college student from New York. Miguelina has been in the Dominican Republic once on a summer visit. Her parents came to New York when teenagers and, according to her, are more "Americanized" than many other Dominicans she knows. Still, Miguelina identifies herself as Dominican, thereby showing that she gives a lot of importance to familial and transnational ties in defining her identity. Miguelina stressed the fact that she needs to state her Dominican identity but not her American identity, which is clear to everybody because she speaks and acts "like an American."

The very few who used the category *black* mentioned the physical traits they share with other African Americans. Being black meant having very dark skin and other African features. Some respondents indicated that especially whites view them as African Americans. It is often their accent that helps people, especially whites, realize that they are not native-born African Americans. "Look at me! I am a brother! I am a black man. Everybody would think I am black if I would not have this accent," said thirty-three-year-old first-generation Agustin.

The first-generation Dominicans in America that used the category *india* also talked about being of mixed race. They mentioned how the Spanish colonials mixed with "everybody," creating a special race of people. Yoselyn, a thirty-year-old housekeeper defined what it is to be *india* this way: "I am not too dark. I have long thin hair and do not have big lips or a big nose." Yoselyn also said that Dominicans can be "black-looking white people" or "white-looking black people," meaning that you can find very dark-skinned Dominicans having very salient "European features," and you can also find very light-skinned Dominicans having very accentuated "African features." Using the category *india* allowed Yoselyn to claim her mixed background without having to pick a black or a European identity.

The Racial Looking Glass Self: Dominicans in White Minds

Charles Horton Cooley (1902) coined the term "looking glass self" to explain how people use other people's views of themselves in forming self-concepts. Our analysis indicates that Dominicans in America see themselves in a very poor light when they see themselves through the eyes of the dominant racial group in the United States.

First-generation Dominicans in America regularly mentioned white Americans' negative images or misconceptions about them:

White Americans think we are an obstacle, a problem. They think we are their slaves and that we are here to clean their homes. (Jose, forty-seven, political activist)

Many whites think we are drug dealers. They think we are here taking advantage of the system. (Rafaela, forty-nine, NGO staff member)

Whites see us the same way we see Haitians in the Dominican Republic. They think we are invading them. They are in a defensive type of attitude all the time. (Angelo, forty-five, teacher)

White Americans think we are uneducated and with a very low coefficient of intelligence. They get surprised when I tell them that I am a professional. They just cannot believe it. But why is it that they cannot believe it? (Lucia, fifty, housekeeper)

They think we are all black. They all have the idea that Dominicans are black and treat us poorly, just the same way they treat black Americans. (Luisa, forty-five, sales representative)

The very negative stereotypes that these Dominican Americans described dealt with Dominicans' personalities, their socioeconomic status, their racial character, their occupations, and their very worth as a people. The narratives indicate that the respondents believe that white Americans see them as outsiders in U.S. society. In this, they are correct, for they have encountered the four-hundred-year-old white racial framing of society that was first developed by early European Americans seeking to explain, to themselves and others, how they as good Christians could enslave many Africans and African Americans from the mid-1600s to the mid-1800s. This white racial framing has continued from the era of vigorous legal segregation to the present day.

When immigrant groups who are dark skinned or have some African ancestry enter the United States, whites usually view them in terms of this traditional racist framing. Indeed, in the quotes above, the respondents cite white images of them that are essentially the same as the images whites have held for centuries in regard to people of African descent.

Second-generation Dominican Americans mentioned similar negative stereotypes held by whites, including the images of criminality, poverty, and lack of education. In addition, they emphasized how these racist stereotypes and attitudes made the process of becoming assimilated to the core culture and society much more difficult. They did not speak very often about how these stereotypes involved white evaluations of their character, worth, and potential as a group:

The most difficult thing is that whites believe that you are not a real American. Yes, my parents are Dominicans. Yes, I identify myself as Dominican American. I was raised in a Dominican home, but I live in U.S. society, and I am also an American citizen. I embrace my Dominican side, but I also embrace my American side. I would see more problem in calling myself Dominican only, like if I were from there, lived there, grew up there, whatever. The truth is that I did not. (Carmen, twenty-two, student)

Whites do not see you as a typical American girl. They see you as a Hispanic girl, a minority. . . . [T]hat is annoying, but anyways . . . [it's] fine; you try to fit in. That is the hardest part because then you never know what to consider yourself. . . . For a long time then I wanted to be . . . I was like the wannabe American girl. I really shadowed my Dominican culture. I never understood why so much tribulation. . . . Things changed a bit when I started college and started participating in the Dominican Student Association. Now, I feel as if I have rediscovered Dominican culture. (Julissa, twenty-one, student)

There is a skit on *Saturday Night Live* of a guy who actually imitates Dominicans, called Dominican Lou. But Dominicans are not yet very visible in the minds of white Americans in general. The people of New York are the ones who see them everyday and interact with them. They may have the image of Dominican Lou who is loud, ignorant, and dumb. That is a terrible image. (Teresa, twenty-two, student)

Well, in general, I mean, we are different. They see us different. White Americans look at us different because we are Hispanics. But I think there are a lot of good Dominicans out there, people who want to do the right thing. Just because some members of the community are involved in bad things does not mean we are all bad. In NYC, in the news, you see Dominicans going to jail for selling drugs, and that is why Dominicans got that bad image. They take those people as reference and then think that Dominicans are all drug dealers. Not even 5 percent of Dominicans are doing that. There are a lot of Dominicans working in factories, grocery stores, and trying to achieve something in this country. Those stereotypes are very harmful. (Tomas, twenty-four, student)

In other accounts, oddly enough, whites were absolved from responsibility in the creation and circulation of the negative stereotypes. Apologies for whites are likely part of an attempt to please whites, consciously or unconsciously, in the process of one-way adaptation to a white-controlled culture and society. One argument was that these stereotypes exist because Dominicans have failed to understand white culture and insist on behaving in ways that whites consider strange or annoying. Here are the words of Rafael, a forty-nine-year-old from New York City, who also seems to equate Americanness with whiteness:

We Dominicans have been in this country for a relative short period of time. We need to understand that Americans are very different from us. White people have very different lifestyles. They do not like loud music. They do not like to have a lot people gathering in their backyards. Americans go walking quietly; they do things quietly. But we are not like that. We like noise. We listen to loud music; we like to gather in large groups and start a party. This is not normal to them. They do not like that. That is why they think we are loud, and that is why they think we are ruining their lives. Maybe they do not want to discriminate. They may indeed fall in love with us by seeing how hard we work and how much we struggle to keep up living.

As in most accounts, the word "Americans" here refers to whites, in spite of the fact that 30 percent of Americans and most New Yorkers are not white. The sense of dominance of white power is palpable in most of these interviews.

Another line of argument was that racial stereotyping is natural. Here are the words of Carmelo, a fifty-seven-year-old man from Florida:

> White people think we are coming to this country to invade them and take their jobs. They feel we want to take their resources and change their culture. It is natural they see us that way. We are the ones coming to their land. They will see us as invaders and as a threat. That's just the way it is. If you think about it, they have taken us as their guests in their society. They have opened their country to us. And, here, we have enjoyed a lot of opportunities.

Of course, all the whites to whom he refers are also the descendants of immigrants, who long ago invaded the lands of the indigenous people of color in North America, to whom more Dominicans have ancestral linkages than do whites.

Another argument was that Dominicans are partly responsible for the existence of these stereotypes because they are not taking advantage of the opportunities offered by U.S. society:

> We are just another group here. If you come to do the right thing, you are welcome. I have always thought that if you do the right thing, you are going to be treated well in this country. If Dominicans act well, blacks act well, Mexicans act well, they're not going to be discriminated against. I do not feel discriminated against. I feel being a Hispanic means you have a different culture and are different from every culture. But there are a few of us involved in bad business and that speaks bad of the community. We create the bad press. (Juan, twenty-four, student)

Rafael, Juan, and Carmelo justified the discriminatory actions of many whites. They seem to recognize that Dominicans hold a lower racial status as compared to whites, but they do not problematize this racialized power hierarchy or the system of racism that surrounds it. On the contrary, they give whites license to stereotype others racially and to exercise their racialized power freely when needed. Accordingly,

Americans of color must conform to white expectations of appropriate behavior in order to succeed and have a good life. These respondents seem to believe that Americans of color need to learn how to win the acceptance of racist whites. They can win it by doing hard work, doing the right thing, and taking advantage of the opportunities that are offered in society. Yet, previous groups of color, especially African Americans who have been in North America for four painful centuries, can easily demonstrate that such strategies often do not work.

CONCLUSION

One goal of this chapter has been to examine the racial-ethnic identity imposed by the white-dominated society on first- and second-generation Dominicans in America and also to describe how they define and evaluate their own identities, their Dominicanness.

The data show that first-generation Dominicans in America place a lot of value in their experiences of migration and adaptation to the host society. The circumstances of migration and the tribulations of adaptation are central to their definitions of what constitutes a Dominican immigrant in the United States. Second-generation Dominican Americans place a greater value on Dominican culture when thinking about themselves, the Dominican community, and U.S. society. They express a lot of pride in their Dominican roots and, at the same time, assert their U.S. citizenship. Their accounts suggest that they feel the need to perform their Dominican identity in order to maintain it. They achieve this through the use of the Spanish language, celebrating Dominican holidays, maintaining strong family relationships, and doing things "the Dominican way."

Members of the first generation transplant their preexisting racial knowledge into a new society, then learn and incorporate the racist categorizations that are imposed in U.S. society in trying to define their racial-ethnic identity. Grappling with imposed racial identities, they often create in their own minds new racial-ethnic terms by combining knowledge and views from the homeland and the host society. For instance, first-generation respondents used racial categories that are commonly used in the Dominican Republic. Examples of these categories are *indio, mulatto, trigueño, dominicano,* and *mestizo.* They used dual categories in stating their identity: "I am trigueña and Latina," "I am Dominican and Hispanic," "I am white and Latino."

Many first-generation respondents used the label *dominicano* in tandem with an accentuated (fictional) color blindness ("I am dominicano. I do not have race"). The use of the category *dominicano* helped some avoid talking about themselves in racial terms. Other first-generation respondents used the label *mezclado* in order to emphasize their mixed racial background. The use of the category *mezclado* allowed them to create racial ambiguity and may have functioned as a way to protect themselves from undesirable, imposed identities or to challenge the dominant racial classifications in the United States. Since the systemic racism in which they interact allows no space for racial ambiguities (Feagin 2000, 2006; Bonilla Silva and Embrick 2006), they face daunting challenges in developing new racial-ethnic identities on a permanent basis.

Further, unlike first-generation respondents, the second-generation did not use categories such as *indio, mulatto,* or *trigueño.* They preferred categories such as *Hispanic, Latino, Hispanic American,* and *Dominican.* Many expressed "having no problem" with using the category *Dominican American* but stated that this would not be the category they would use if asked about their racial-ethnic identity. Others rejected the use of this category because they saw no need to specify what they considered to be their self-evident Americanness.

The analysis showed that first-generation respondents share their cultural knowledge with the second-generation. This explains in part the fact that both generational groups reproduce important aspects of the dominant racial ideologies that operate in Dominican society. As Candelario (2000) and Torres Saillant (1998) report, despite interacting in transnationalized environments and having undergone processes of racial resocialization, first- and second-generation Dominicans tend to downplay their African and Afro-Caribbean ancestry and to associate whiteness with preferred goals and "authentic" U.S. citizenship. They continue to embrace racialized labels that signify racial mixture, color blindness, having a distinct culture, or having a European ancestry, but not having a black or Afro-Caribbean identity. The suppression and invisibility of their blackness should be interpreted in light of the workings of white-oriented racism in both Dominican and American societies.

Internal Dominican Racism

The beginning of the twenty-first century finds dark-skinned Dominican and Haitian Americans affected by discriminatory practices, attitudes, and ideas of white Americans that deny them significant privileges and recognition, as well as many economic, political, and cultural resources. In this, their situation is similar to that of other African Americans.

Even worse perhaps, most Dominican community institutions and much of the Dominican population have not openly recognized, or organized to attack, this reality of white-racist prejudice and discrimination targeting dark-skinned Dominican and Haitian Americans. Nor have they recognized and worked against that prejudice and discrimination in their own communities.

The Dominican Republic itself has a long and sordid history of racial prejudice and discrimination against darker-skinned Dominicans and against Haitians. For example, in 1930, Raphael Trujillo took over absolute control and set up a U.S.-supported dictatorship in the Dominican Republic, with a vast network of spies to purge potential antagonists. Trujillo assembled a racist and nationalist plan by exiling dark-skinned Haitians and tightening patrols of the border with Haiti (Wucker 1999). In 1937, as many as seventeen thousand unarmed Haitian men, women, and children were slaughtered in a bloodbath of violence.

Joaquín Balaguer was elected president in 1966 and reelected in 1970 and 1974, lost the 1978 elections, and returned to power in 1982. Balaguer continued the authoritarian legacy of Trujillo, restricting popular participation; elections were not free (Sagás 2000). U.S. immigration laws assisted him by allowing migration of dissidents to the United States, which reduced political dissent on the island after the American intervention of 1965. Balaguer extended Trujillo's racist policies. Balaguer wrote *The Island Turned on Its Head: Haiti and Dominican Destiny*, in which he stated that Dominicans are Hispanic, white, and Christian. He further demonstrated his racist ideology by attributing to Haitians the responsibility for the "progressive ethnic decadence" of the Dominican nation (Sagás 2000). This racist mythology has been buttressed now for decades by many means, as Sagás (2000) notes:

An analysis of Dominican history textbooks from the early 20th century to the present reveals a number of flagrant errors, romantic myths, and plenty of antihaitianismo. One of the most common myths is that of messiahnism. Juan Pablo Duarte, the nation's leading hero and intellectual author of Dominican independence, is glorified to extremes. Joaquín Balaguer even compares him to Jesus Christ. (87)

This racial mythologizing continues. Candelario (2000) notes, "Trujillo's legacy continues to be institutionalized in the permanent display of El Museo del Hombre Dominicano. An exemplary ideological state apparatus, the museo is a state-funded institution that displays and propagates a heavily indigenist Dominican national identity at the expense of a sorely needed full historicization and exploration of the African roots of the nation" (402). Today, most Dominican social and political institutions reinforce anti-Haitian ideology and downplay Dominicans' very substantial African ancestry.

Memory, Ethnic Identity, and Transnationalism

Clearly, the first- and second-generation immigrants we interviewed preserved important aspects of their Dominican racial knowledge. Both groups drew on their island heritage and went beyond the dichotomous white-black model of racial categorization that whites have historically made dominant in U.S. society to create their own sometimes distinctive racial-ethnic labels (Baily 2006). Yet, there are important differences in their discourses on racial identity. When talking about the Dominican experience in the United States, first-generation Dominicans consistently talked about resistance and individual and collective struggles. First-generation respondents defined Dominicanness in terms of experiences of pain, sacrifice, and empowerment. Combining and isolating these concepts, they constructed at least three different types of Dominican immigrants: *el sufrido* (the struggler), *el luchador* (the fighter), *el sacrificado* (the martyr).

In contrast, second-generation respondents consistently talked about Dominican cultural issues in describing what it means to be Dominican in the United States. They stressed the significance of listening to merengue and *bachata*, eating Dominican food, maintaining ties with kin, dancing, and caring for relatives. Their descriptions emphasize activities Dominicans engage in because of their cultural and historical background rather than the kind of experiences that result from migration.

Further, the data show that both generations share a knowledge of Dominican culture. Both integrate personal and familial experiences into narratives of identity and give importance to their Dominican background. Some gave coherence to their talk about whites' negative racial attitudes toward them by referring to the tense relations between the Dominican Republic and Haiti, to the low socioeconomic status of many Dominican immigrants, to the poverty that affects many Dominicans back home, to the failures of Dominican politicians, and to the social and economic crisis affecting the country. They also referred to characteristics of family relationships in the Dominican Republic to make sense of the state of their own primary relationships. These are examples of how people register everyday life events in their consciousness and use their memory of these events to create their own narratives and justify the perspectives they take in creating such narratives.

These are also concrete examples of cultural knowledge being replicated in the transnational context as a form of cultural remittance from one generation to the next (Levitt 2001). Explaining how collective memory and cultural remittance are transmitted transnationally by Dominicans of different ages, social classes, education levels, and generational backgrounds is beyond the scope of this study but constitutes an important topic for future research.

Dominicans, Transnationalism, and Continuing White Racism

In the context of an enduring global racist order long ago created and still maintained by Europeans and European Americans, one can predict that, in the short run, there will be little change in the white-generated racist ideology targeting, and often participated in by, Dominican immigrants. Transnationalism and experience with white discrimination have the potential to awaken a critical racial awareness, but it seems unlikely that a full embrace of blackness by Dominicans will be an outcome of this process. Dominican immigrants' success in attempting to create new racial-ethnic identities between white and black and their modest challenging of elements of the dominant racist ideology both depend on the weakening of the racist institutions of U.S. society. Immigrants' attempts to create alternative identities emerge under the constraints that emanate from the ideological and institutional apparatuses that have long sustained racial hierarchies in the United States (Feagin 2006; Feagin, Vera, and Batur 2001). In the United States, the processes of negotiation of racial-ethnic identity by immigrants generally operate within the context of systemic racism and alienated racial relations—which often successfully silence and neutralize immigrants' subversive attempts at change.

The accounts of respondents like Carmen, Julissa, Teresa, and Tomas illustrate the difficulties immigrants of color and their descendants face when trying to create their own racial-ethnic definitions. These respondents showed a desire to assimilate into U.S. society and asserted their U.S. birth and citizenship, but they faced difficulties when trying to define their racial-ethnic identities in their own terms. Regardless of how they see themselves, they struggle with the fact that, in the end, their racial identity will be imposed on them, that is, defined by how powerful whites view them. They are, as members of the second-generation, becoming Americans, and as the data show, they are mostly asserting not a black but a Dominican identity. Clearly, they are, like numerous other recent immigrants of color, caught in the vice of white-imposed antiblack racism, which presses them to be as "white" as they can be in dress, language, thought, and values. Yet, no amount of conformity to this image of whiteness will make them white and allow them to assimilate fully into a dominant culture that will likely view them as black and undesirable for the foreseeable future.

Yet, as we suggested in the opening, the situation of racial oppression and enforced white assimilation in the United States seems likely to change, albeit perhaps slowly, in coming decades, as Americans of African, Latin American, Caribbean, and Asian descent come to dominate the U.S. population, at first in major cities and states, and eventually in much of the country. One issue we cannot deal with here is the type of white response. Certainly, whites today are becoming aware of these demographic changes, as evidenced by anti-immigrant protests. Most whites today seem to fear the more multiracial future, where they will be a statistical minority of people, voters, and, probably, political officials (Feagin 2006, 307). As of today, most whites seem quite un-prepared to live in a country that actually mimics the old image of a highly diverse country of immigrants.

NOTES

1. The second generation includes those who are U.S.-born or came to the United States before the age of nine.

2. Ana Liberato conducted and transcribed all the interviews. A grounded-theory approach was used to analyze the data. Research participants were contacted in a snowball fashion using contacts in local organizations and personal contacts. We are indebted to Belio Martinez and the Dominican Students Association at the University of Florida for their help. In the case of New York, most interviews took place at respondents' homes in an environment of hospitality and flexibility. In the case of Florida, the respondents were interviewed in either their place of residence or at a local university campus. Most frequently, the semi-structured interviews began with a brief conversation about the economic crisis currently affecting the Dominican Republic, the causes driving Dominican migration to the United States, and Dominican culture. The interviews also involved standard question-answer format. The sample includes twenty-five first-generation respondents (twelve female and thirteen male) and fifteen second-generation respondents (nine female and six male). The first-generation sample ranged in age from thirty-eight to seventy-nine, while the second-generation sample ranged in age from seventeen to thirty-four. Time of residence in the United States ranged from ten to thirty-three years. Interviews with first-generation respondents were carried out in Spanish, while interviews with the second generation were done in English. The size of the New York sample was twenty-one, while the size of the Florida sample was nineteen.

3. In 1994, the Dominican state granted the right to double citizenship for Dominicans abroad, assuring their political rights and enhancing their presence in the life of the nation (Itzigsohn et al. 1999; Portes 1996).

4. The notion of memory as a "thing" has been widely criticized by sociologists who prefer to define memory as a process.

5. We would expect willingness to preserve Dominican culture to be lower if people's evaluations and recollections of Dominican culture featured negative themes.

REFERENCES

Baily, Benjamin. 2006. "Black and Latino: Dominican Americans Negotiate Racial Worlds." In *Mixed Messages: Multiracial Identities in the "Color-Blind" Era*, ed. David Brunsma, 285–301. Boulder, CO: Lynne Rienner Publishers.

Bonilla, Seda E. 1961. "Social Structure and Race Relations." *Social Forces* 40, no. 2: 141–48.

Bonilla Silva, Eduardo, and David G. Embrick. 2006. "Black, Honorary White, White: The Future of Race in the United States?" In *Mixed Messages: Multiracial Identities in the "Color-Blind" Era*, ed. David Brunsma, 33–49. Boulder, CO: Lynne Rienner Publishers.

Candelario, Ginetta. 2000. *Situating Ambiguity: Dominican Identity Formations*. PhD diss., City University of New York.

Céspedes, Diógenes. 1997. *Contra la ideología racista en Santo Domingo.* (Dos campañas por Peña Gomez). Santo Domingo, Dominican Republic: Editora de Colores, S.A.

Cooley, Charles Horton. 1902. *Human Nature and the Social Order.* New York: C. Scribner's Sons.

Denton, Nancy A., and Douglas S. Massey. 1989. "Racial Identity amongst Caribbean Hispanics: The Effect of Double Minority Status on Residential Segregation." *American Sociological Review* 54, no. 5: 790–808.

DiarioDigital RD. 2006. "Estudio revela criollos ausentes prefieren inmuebles en RD," available at www.diariodigitalrd.com/?module=displaystory&story_id=2439&format=html (last accessed March 11, 2007).

Duany, Jorge. 1998. "Reconstructing Racial Identity: Ethnicity, Color and Class among Dominicans in the United States and Puerto Rico." *Latin American Perspectives* 25, no. 3: 147–72.

Feagin, Joe R. 2000. *Racist America: Roots, Current Realities, and Future Reparations.* New York: Routledge.

——. 2006. *Systemic Racism: A Theory of Oppression.* New York: Routledge.

Feagin, Joe R., Hernan Vera, and Pinar Batur. 2001. *White Racism: The Basics.* 2nd ed. New York: Routledge.

Fennema, Meindert, and Troetje Loewenthal. 1987. *Construccion de raza y nacion República Dominicana.* Santo Domingo, Dominican Republic: Editoria Univisitaria–UASD.

Ferguson, James. 1993. *Beyond the Lighthouse.* London: Latin America Bureau.

Franco, Franklin J. 1977. *Los negros, los mulattos y la nacion Dominicana.* Santo Domingo, Dominican Republic: Editoria Nacional.

——. 1997. *Sobre racismo y antihationismo (y otros ensayos).* Santo Domingo, Dominican Republic: Imprisora Vidal.

Green, Eric. 2004. "Dominican Republic Rated Fourth-Largest Remittance Market in the Americas," available at http://usinfo.state.gov/wh/Archive/2004/Nov/23-326710.html (last accessed March 11, 2007).

Halbwachs, Maurice. 1980. *The Collective Memory.* New York: Harper Colophon Books.

Hansen, Christian K. 2001. "A Tomb for Columbus in Santo Domingo: Political Cosmology, Population and Racial Frontiers." *Social Anthropology* 9, no. 2: 165–92.

Harrison, Faye V. 1995. "The Persistence of Power of '"Race"' in the Cultural and Political Economy of Racism." *Annual Review Anthropology* 24: 47–74.

Hernández, Ramona. 2002. *The Mobility of Workers under Advanced Capitalism: Dominican Migration to the United States.* New York: Columbia University Press.

Hernández, Ramona, and Francisco L. Rivera-Batiz. 2003. *Dominican in the United States: A Socioeconomic Profile.* Dominican Research Monographs. New York: CUNY Dominican Studies Institute.

Howard, David. 2001. *Coloring the Nation: Race and Ethnicity in the Dominican Republic.* Boulder, CO: Lynne Rienner Publishers.

Irwin-Zarecka, Iwona. 1994. *Frames of Remembrance: The Dynamics of Collective Memory.* New Brunswick, NJ: Transaction Publishers.

Itzigsohn, Jose. 1995. "Migrant Remittances, Labor Markets, and Household Strategies: A Comparative Study of the Low Income Household Strategies in the Caribbean Basin." *Social Forces* 74, no. 2: 633–55.

Itzigsohn, Jose, and Carol Dore-Cabral. 2000. "Competing Identities? Race, Ethnicity and Panethnicity among Dominicans in the United States." *Sociological Forum* 15, no. 2: 225–47.

Itzigsohn, Jose, Carol Dore-Cabral, Esther Hernández Medina, and Obed Vazquez. 1999. "Mapping Dominican Transnationalization: Narrow and Broad Transnational Practices." *Ethnic and Racial Studies* 22, no. 2: 316–39.

Kansteiner, Wulf. 2002. "Finding Meaning in Memory: A Methodological Critique of Collective Memory Studies." *History and Theory* 41 (May): 179–97.

Levitt, Peggy. 2001. *The Transnational Villagers*. Berkeley: University of California Press.

Liberato, Ana Q. 2005. *The Collective Memory of Anti-Democratic Regimes: Joaquin Balaguer and the Development of Political Trust in the Dominican Republic*. PhD diss., University of Florida.

Masferrer, Marianne, and Carmelo Mesa-Lago. 1974. "The Gradual Integration of the Black in Cuba: Under the Colony, the Republic, and the Revolution." In *Slavery and Race Relations in Latin America*, ed. Robert B. Toplin, 348–84. Westport, CT: Greenwood Press.

Mejia Odalis. 2006. "El BNV promueve financiamiento a 14.5%," available at www.alide.org.pe/download/E-Banca/E-Banca-N34.pdf (last accessed March 11, 2007).

Moya Pons, Frank. 1981. *Dominican National Identity and Return Migration*. Occasional Paper 1, Center for Latin American Studies, University of Florida.

Persinal, Carlos A. 1997. *La presencia negra en Santo Domingo*. Santo Domingo, Dominican Republic: Imprisora Búho.

Portes, Alejandro. 1996. "Transnational Communities: Their Emergence and Significance in the Contemporary World System." In *Latin America in the World Economy*, ed. Roberto P. Korzeniewicz and William C. Smith, 151–68. Westport, CT: Greenwood Press.

Portes, Alejandro, and Luis E. Guarnizo. 1991. "Tropical Capitalist: U.S.-Bound Immigration and Small Enterprise Development in the Dominican Republic." In *Migration, Remittances, and Small Business Development: Mexico and Caribbean Basin Countries*, ed. Sergio Diaz-Briquets and Sidney Weintraub, 109–38. Boulder, CO: Westview Press.

Rothstein, Bo. 2000. "Trust, Social Dilemmas and Collective Memories." *Journal of Theoretical Politics* 12, no. 4: 477–501.

Sagás, Ernesto. 2000. *Race and Politics in the Dominican Republic*. Gainesville: University Press of Florida.

Sagás, Ernesto, and Sintia E. Molina, eds. 2004. *Dominican Migration: Transnational Perspectives*. New World Diasporas Series. Gainesville: University Press of Florida.

Schuman, Howard, and Amy Corning. 2000. "Collective Knowledge of Public Events: The Soviet Era from the Great Purge to Glasnost." *American Journal of Sociology* 105, no. 4: 913–56.

Schwartz, Barry. 1982. "The Social Context of Commemoration: A Study in Collective Memory." *Social Forces* 61, no. 2: 374–402.

———. 1991. "Social Change and Collective Memory: The Democratization of George Washington." *American Sociological Review* 56, no. 2: 21–236.

———. 2000. *Abraham Lincoln and the Forge of National Memory*. Chicago: Chicago University Press.

Toplin, Robert B. 1971. "Reinterpreting Comparative Race Relations—the United States and Brazil." *Journal of Black Studies* 2, no. 2: 135–55.

Torres Saillant, Silvio. 1995. "The Dominican Republic." In *No Longer Invisible: Afro-Latin Americans Today*, ed. Miles Litvinoff, 109–38. London: Minority Rights Group.

———. 1998. "The Tribulations of Racial Identity: Black Consciousness in Dominican Racial Identity." *Latin American Perspectives* 25, no. 3: 126–46.

Torres Saillant, Silvio, and Ramona Hernández. 1998. *The New Americans: Dominican Americans*. Westport, CT: Greenwood Press.

U.S. Census Bureau. 2000. "American FactFinder," available at http://factfinder.census.gov/home/saff/main.html?_lang=en (last accessed March 11, 2007).

Whitten, Norman E., Jr., and Arlene Torres, eds. 1998. *Blackness in Latin America and the Caribbean: Social Dynamics and Cultural Transformations*. Vol. 1. Bloomington: Indiana University Press.

Wucker, Michele. 1999. *Why the Cocks Fight: Dominicans, Haitians and the Struggle for Hispaniola*. New York: Hill and Wang.

CHAPTER 8

Beyond Social Distancing:
Intermarriage and Ethnic Boundaries
among Black Americans in Boston

Regine O. Jackson

In April 2002, the *Orlando Sentinel* (Hunt 2002) ran a story in the local section of their Sunday paper titled "Black Immigrants Feel No Racial Kinship in U.S." The article described the growth of central Florida's black immigrant population in the 1990s. Featured on the front page, the *Sentinel* offered readers nearly twelve hundred words of text, complete with photographs, interviews with representative "new blacks," and demographic data tables. Such extensive coverage is welcome attention for populations that have remained largely invisible to the majority of Americans for decades. However, not long after the presentation of the statistics, a menacing leitmotif becomes apparent. Boldface subheadings throughout the article announce the central message: "Distrust, Stereotypes," "Divisions May Endure," "Separate Heritage." Here, as in many other stories that appeared across the country after the public release of the 2000 census data, an emphasis on conflict, competition, or antagonism between immigrant blacks and native black Americans[1] is the recurring theme; see for instance, "Black vs. Black: The New New Yorkers" (Gordy 1994), "A Diverse—and Divided—Black Community" (Fears 2002), "'African-American' Becomes a Term for Debate" (Swarns 2004), "Immigrants Reshaping Black Experience" (Rodriguez 2001), "Caribbean Americans Form Own Caucus" (Charles 2003), "A Battle over Race, Nationality, and Control at a Black University" (Wilson 2001).

Even a passing review of these newspaper articles reveals a striking bias. Immigrant blacks are frequently quoted as spewing pejorative stereotypes of native blacks and dissociating themselves from the native black American community. For example, the author of a *Boston*

Globe piece writes, "Even though most Haitians, Jamaicans, Nigerians and Somalis consider themselves black, that doesn't mean they automatically connect with African Americans. Some of them view American blacks as lacking a strong work ethic" (Rodriguez 2001). A few paragraphs later, the reporter cautions readers that "the resentment is real," and she quotes a Jamaican immigrant: "This black lady was telling my sister the other day, 'Go back home to your country.' She told her, 'You go back to your Section 8!'"

The antipathy, we are told, goes both ways. Native blacks see the newcomers as competition for jobs and other resources, resent their willingness to acquiesce to whites, and view them with suspicion. The following are but a few examples: A journalist with the *New York Newsday* reports that the director of a Haitian service organization receives periodic visits and phone calls from native black Americans who say, "You black Jews should go back to where you come from" (Gordy 1994). In a *New York Times* feature, Alan Keyes is said to "represent a number of native blacks" in asserting that his Democratic challenger for the Senate seat in Illinois—whose father is a Kenyan—is not "*really* African American": "Barack Obama and I have the same race—that is physical characteristics. We are not from the same heritage."[2] The *Los Angeles Times* printed a misguided rant about the numbers of black immigrants by linguist John McWhorther (2004). The editorial concluded that the term *black* should be used in lieu of *African American* when referring to blacks born in America: "My roots trace back to working class Black people—*Americans, not foreigners*—and I'm proud of that. . . . They and their dearest are the heritage that I can feel in my heart, and they knew the sidewalks of Philadelphia and Atlanta, not Sierra Leone"(McWhorther 2004, A1, emphasis added).

This attention to mutual hostility and division is not limited to newspaper writing. Television, Hollywood movies, popular fiction, and even social science have all participated in constructing the image of discordant, intraracial relations among black Americans. Toni Morrison (1993) refers to this rhetoric as a particular brand of "race talk":

Popular culture, shaped by film, theater, advertising, the press, television and literature, is heavily engaged in race talk. It participates freely in this most enduring and efficient rite of passage into American culture: negative appraisals of the native-born black population. Only when the lesson of racial estrangement is learned is assimilation complete. Whatever the lived experience of immigrants with African Americans—pleasant, beneficial or bruising—the rhetorical experience renders blacks as noncitizens, already discredited outlaws. . . . It doesn't matter anymore what shade the newcomer's skin is. A hostile posture toward resident blacks must be struck at the Americanizing door before it will open. The public is asked to accept American blacks as the common denominator in each conflict between an immigrant and a job or between a wannabe and status. It hardly matters what complexities, contexts and misinformation accompany these conflicts. They can all be subsumed as the equation of brand X vs. blacks. (57)

Social science research, in particular, has gone from representing black Americans as culturally, socially, and economically homogenous to presuming pervasive social division and conflict in intraracial relations. In fact, the arguments popularized by journalists and television are often founded on the social science literature.

The hostility between immigrant blacks and native black Americans is neither entirely constructed nor surprising. Immigrants and native-born Americans—of all races—tend to clash at first; and there is considerable evidence of both intraracial hostility among other groups and older immigrants expressing resentment toward newer arrivals (see Halter 1993; Nagel 1994; Pyke and Dang 2003; Wong 1987). However, the tendency in the reporting on African and Caribbean black Americans toward erasing moments of cooperation and amity in favor of sensationalist rhetoric about conflict and cultural differences is remarkable. While many accounts argue that residential segregation and racism will eventually compel black Americans to come together, the literature ignores the way immigrant blacks and native blacks affirm and negotiate cultural differences in their neighborhoods, their workplaces, and even in their own families.

In an extension of the stereotype of the dysfunctional black family, the overemphasis on social divisions suggests dysfunctional black communities. Not only do black Americans appear unique in their inability to get along, also such coverage conveys the impression that black Americans are incapable of functioning in a multicultural society. While everyone else is celebrating the new diversity, native black

Americans are characterized as longing for the "good old days" when they were the only minorities. At the same time, the constant high-lighting of distrust reinforces notions of many of the immigrant send-ing countries as "uncivilized," disorganized, and backward: it is no wonder that African countries are ravaged by civil wars or that Haiti is "the poorest country in the Western Hemisphere." The unflattering rep-resentations, in other words, are constructed through a generalized no-tion of black inferiority and do not bode well for any blacks, regardless of nativity (see Pierre 2004).

Moreover, with all the focus on social distancing and conflict, the complexity of immigrant black/native black American relations is over-looked, and other interpretations of their respective positionings are not taken into account. (Notably, "individualism" and "patriotism," valued American characteristics, are never invoked to explain the behavior of African or Caribbean blacks seeking to define themselves or native black Americans' insistence on an American identity and way of life.)

More important than how these groups are represented in the media, however, is what intraracial diversity suggests about the future of black American communities and race relations in this country. Will ethnic boundaries among black Americans prove to be as porous in the twenty-first century as they were among whites in the twentieth? Or will a pattern of divided minority communities develop as the country becomes more diverse? The picture from the majority of the coverage suggests that black immigrants are using whatever symbolic resources they have (conceptual distinctions, interpretive strategies, cultural tra-ditions) to create and maintain social boundaries between themselves and native black Americans. And yet, the social context does not seem conducive to such stable patterns of ethnic segregation (see Waters 1999).

This chapter shifts attention away from conflict and competition to describe a neglected outcome of intraracial relations and diversity among black Americans: ethnic intermarriage. My research suggests that (1) the pronounced ethnic boundaries that divide black Americans are permeable, and (2) interethnic familial and friendship relations, as well as more amiable secondary public interactions, are a very real part of the daily lives of immigrant blacks and their descendants living in

American cities. By looking beyond social distancing, we can consider how black Americans from diverse backgrounds understand and perform their similarities and differences, as well as the reasons why some African or Caribbean black Americans position themselves as part of, and others as apart from, the native black American community. Most importantly, this work suggests that, instead of distancing, immigrants' self-conscious efforts to differentiate themselves can be read as endeavoring to reconstruct the meaning of blackness and to highlight cultural diversity within the black American experience.

Data for this chapter come from a case study of intermarried Haitians in the Boston area conducted between 1998 and 2000 (fully reported in Ostine 2001). Unlike most work on intermarriage, which is concerned exclusively with marriage across racial lines, I was also interested in ethnic intermarriage *among* blacks. Furthermore, I focused on what happens after intermarriage: the process of ethnic blending that takes place within ethnically mixed black households. These data show the possibilities, as well as the challenges, of diverse and distinctive understandings of self among blacks and how those understandings are managed in the most intimate of all contexts. Given the importance of the family as a principal agent of culture, the focus on intermarriage is not a turn away from a social problem to individual situations. Rather, intermarriage has potentially profound implications for the familial and, more broadly, the social contexts urban blacks inhabit. The family becomes a place, a domain of life, where even latent ethnicity is activated, and in this context, ideas, assumptions, and expectations of familial behavior, picked up during childhood and often taken for granted, resurface.

The main goal of this chapter, then, is to describe the kinds of negotiations of ethnic difference—what I refer to as boundary work—that take place among blacks in ethnically mixed marriages. I argue that these boundary transactions reflect a more accurate continuum of social relations and accommodation than is represented in the media or the majority of scholarship on black immigrants, which focuses on distancing and conflict alone. A brief discussion of the social science literature with regard to relationships between Caribbean or African and native black Americans follows.

"WE ARE A HOUSE DIVIDED"[3]

As has been previously noted (see chapter 1), research on black immigrants in the United States begins with Ira Reid's pioneering 1939 work *The Negro Immigrant: His Background, Characteristics and Social Adjustments, 1899–1937*. Among its other attributes, *The Negro Immigrant* is notable for its detailed outline of the tensions between immigrant blacks and native black Americans. Reid argued that, with other parts of the city closed to them in the 1920s and 1930s, foreign-born blacks lived in native black American areas, especially Harlem. "Residential propinquity," however, was not an indication of group unity; foreign-born black Harlemites put "social distance" between themselves and native black Americans. Reid (1939) characterizes the impact of black immigrants on these communities as largely disruptive:

> Moving into a few centers of Negro population in large numbers, threatening the existing order of Negro adjustments he brings the bases for intra-racial conflict. . . . This group that comes over for economic and utilitarian purposes soon seeks status, recognition, position and prestige within the existing political and moral order. This struggle is at the root of such conflict as exists between the native and foreign-born Negro. (215)[4]

Gilbert Osofsky's *Harlem: The Making of a Ghetto* painted a similar picture. Osofsky (1971) maintained that "most Negro immigrants . . . demonstrated an 'exaggerated' nationalism in America" (131–35), which increased intraethnic strife.

Many believe that the early relationships documented by these scholars (see also Domingo 1925) lay the foundation for the strained intraracial relationships observed today. However, I would add that the early scholarship has been influential in determining the themes of later work. In other words, the authority of Reid's work makes certain aspects of the black immigrant experience leap out as significant, while others go unremarked.

After the publication of *The Negro Immigrant*, the study of foreign-born blacks lay dormant for almost three decades. Roy Bryce-Laporte revived the field with his seminal 1972 article on the invisibility of black immigrants. Yet, Bryce-Laporte failed to acknowledge native black Americans' familiarity with black immigrants. His argument that black immigrants were invisible belies the fact that immigrant blacks and native black Americans have shared neighborhoods, classrooms, workplaces, and even homes in places like Harlem, Brooklyn, Boston, and Chicago since the end of World War II, as well as that the descendants of the first wave of black immigrants were more dependent on native black Americans (see Greenbaum 2002; Johnson 2000; Marshall 1959; Watkins-Owens 1996; Woldemikael 1989).

Likewise, the vast majority of the research on Caribbean and African immigrants and their descendants over the last fifteen years suggests that intraracial diversity negatively influences intraracial relations. The finding that intraracial tensions and social distance pervade relations between communities of foreign- and native-born black Americans is the consensus among scholars. Philip Kasinitz (1992) writes, "West Indians appear to have been less than enamored of African Americans. Many seem to have resisted incorporation into black America, maintaining and perhaps exaggerating their separateness" (47). In *Haitian Immigrants in Black America,* Flore Zephir (1996) argues that Haitians attempt to convince whites that they are a different kind of "black" by vociferously clamoring their ethnicity: "The affirmation of Haitian ethnicity frequently manifests itself in a certain distancing from other groups occupying the same subordinate position, particularly from native Black Americans" (70). Carolle Charles (1990) makes a similar claim: "Haitians tend to develop forms of identity with a marked pattern toward disaffiliation from the black American population" (257). This tendency surfaces in the Haitian saying "I don't want to be black twice." Likewise, Tekle Woldemikael (1989) writes, "Haitians in Evanston see black Americans as having little to offer them. In fact association with, and identification as, black Americans actually has disadvantages from the Haitian perspective" (39). In perhaps the most quoted piece of scholarly work on black immigrants, Mary Waters (1999) maintains that her West Indian respondents "exhibited a great deal of tension and distancing from American blacks." She elaborates, "While the middle class respondents sometimes tempered their descriptions of problems with native black Americans by stating that they wished it weren't so, or they thought the two groups *should* come together, their degree of disdain and psychological distance was very strong, as strong in most cases as that of the working-class respondents" (188).

Notably, most of these scholars report a reluctance among their respondents to marry native black Americans, or they fail to consider the possibility at all. Percy Hintzen (2001) is an exception; he devotes a chapter to intermarriage in *West Indians in the West* but focuses on hostility and tension in the relationships. He argues that the identities of middle-class West Indian immigrants in the San Francisco Bay area and native black Americans' "xenophobic" rejection of foreigners "become the basis for the hostile relationship between the West Indian middle class and African Americans" (Hintzen 2001, 88). As one of only three case studies of intermarriage discussed, he describes the marriage of a Guyanese immigrant named George Bryan, who is currently serving a life sentence for the murder of his native black American wife, her mother, and her sister (see Hintzen 2001, 93–98). Based on this sensational example, Hintzen concludes that interethnic black relationships can have violent outcomes!

Milton Vickerman provides perhaps the most sophisticated discussion of social distancing in "The Response of West Indians toward African-Americans" (1994) and *Crosscurrents: West Indian Immigrants and Race* (1999). He argues that "West Indians' relationship with African-Americans revolves around the process of distancing and identification, sometimes leading to a synthesis of the two" (Vickerman 1999, 139). The desire to distance themselves from some native black Americans revolves primarily around the issues of work, achievement, and culture. The fear is that blacks, in general, are being stereotyped as lazy; therefore, immigrants seek to put as much distance between themselves and the stigma of welfare as possible. However, Vickerman cautions, "West Indians' reluctance to assimilate into the larger African-American community can easily be misinterpreted as a wholesale rejection of the latter group. In reality, it stems from an attempt to avoid the imposition of a more restrictive identity than that to which they are accustomed. Or to put it another way: they are attempting to preserve the broader identity options inherent within West Indian culture" (139).

While the literature on African immigrants is less abundant, distancing and conflict are prominent here as well. Marilyn Halter (1993) finds that Cape Verdeans in Massachusetts accommodated to their new situation by setting themselves apart from the native black American community: "They established their own parallel social and religious groups, maintained their *Crioulo* traditions, spoke their own language, clustered in the same neighborhoods and were essentially endogamous" (94). As one of her respondents expressed it, "The South End was the Cape Verdean ghetto but it has to be noted that in New Bedford [Massachusetts] you had the West End, which was another ghetto, these were African-Americans, for the most part, slaves who had migrated north from the south, after the Civil War and there was *no* intermingling, there was no mixture, there was nothing. . . . God forbid you married *American d'cor* [pejorative term for African American]" (165–69).

Based on a study of one hundred African college students at the University of California, Los Angeles, in 1967 and 1968, Tamar Becker (1973) reports that the overwhelming majority of her interviewees found it easier to communicate with whites than with native black Americans: "There is a basic incompatibility between Africans and black Americans that leads to mutual rejection. Almost unanimously, Africans perceived the relation between themselves and black Americans as negative and used characterizations ranging from 'misunderstanding' to 'hatred'" (177). Similarly, Isaacs (1961, 135) thought that African students were perceived by native black Americans as "barbarians, or ex-barbarians who had become snobbish Europeans" (quoted in Apraku 1996, 113).

John Arthur's *Invisible Sojourners: African Immigrant Diaspora in the United States* (2001) similarly indicates that the cultural, political, and economic affinity between African immigrants and their native black American counterparts is not as strong as it should be, considering the "historical cord that ties them together. . . . The survey data reveal that although African immigrants in the United States have much to offer and gain from interactions with American-born blacks and whites, the social world of the immigrants is largely limited to intra-African immigrant circles. African immigrants tend to form much closer relationships with black immigrants of the African diaspora (mainly from other developing nations such as Jamaica, Trinidad, the Bahamas, Guyana and Haiti) than they establish with the native-born black American population" (80). Arthur continues,

Sometimes, this uneasiness is given a political dimension in the form of statements, allegedly made to African blacks by black American youths, that the Africans did nothing to stop the slave trade and that the Africans are partly to blame for selling the African-Americans' ancestors to the white man hundreds of years ago. (83)

More recently, Monica McDermott (2003) has found that African and native-born blacks have had numerous "conflictual" encounters: "In Atlanta, several native-born blacks were careful to distance themselves from an identification with an African American identity, preferring instead to be called black" (2). She explains in a footnote that at her research site, she was repeatedly corrected for referring to native black Americans as "African Americans" because they did not want to be affiliated with African immigrants.

The repetition in the quotes selected from the aforementioned studies is intentional. It demonstrates how common these themes have become. Over and over again, we are told that, despite contextual, structural, or individual variables that might suggest otherwise, social relations between immigrant blacks and native black Americans are mired in conflict. Choosing to maintain an ethnic or national identity as "Jamaican-American" or "African" or "Nigerian American" is portrayed as a lack of identification with native black Americans, another indication of disaffection, like forming distinct social and political groups or ethnic enclaves within black neighborhoods. In fact, any expression of ethnic identity among black immigrants is read as distancing. And cooperative interpersonal relations are either insignificant or are represented as examples of segmented assimilation (see Portes and Zhou 1994). Other studies echo similar sentiments (see Grenier and Perez 1996; Johnson 2000; Ho 1991; Nesbitt 2003; Sutton and Makiesky-Brown 1987; Waters 1994).

A few examples, however, do stand out in their emphasis on cooperation and identification. In her history of Harlem, *Blood Relations: Caribbean Immigrants and the Harlem Community, 1900–1930*, Irma Watkins-Owens (1996) does not ignore the controversies and conflict evident in the interaction between black immigrants and native black Americans, "but these are placed in the larger context of a community's coming of age between 1900–1930" (1). She argues that "community

development in Harlem—which is exemplified by the formation of social networks in voluntary associations, political movements, churches,
and other organizations—was often the result of cooperation between
Caribbean immigrants and native blacks" (6).

Similarly, Reuel Rogers (2001) argues that the prevailing assumption
that black immigrants only identify with native black Americans because of the racial constraints of American life misses the affirmative
dimensions of the immigrants' racial identification with their native-
born counterparts. Rogers maintains that many of his respondents
spoke admiringly of native black Americans' long history of resistance
to racism and their struggles for civil rights. When asked if he felt close
to native black Americans, one respondent reportedly replied, "Oh yes.
. . . Our histories are similar. It just so happens that some got dropped
off here, and some in the West Indies" (Rogers 2001, 187). In fact,
Rogers finds that "some Afro-Caribbean immigrants feel a measure of
proud racial group solidarity with African Americans, notwithstanding
the differences in their histories and cultures" (187).

Finally, Susan Greenbaum's 2002 study of Afro-Cubans in Tampa,
Florida, shows that historically black colleges and universities, among
other native black American institutions, "helped support the adjustment of Afro-Cubans growing up in Tampa during the 1930s and
1940s" (230). Greenbaum continues, "It is difficult to imagine how
Afro-Cuban families and individuals would have survived without
reaching out to African-Americans during this period" (230).

In a nutshell, Watkins-Owens (1996), Rogers (2001), and Greenbaum (2002) show, as I will below, that mixing is happening in neighborhoods, workplaces, schools, and bedrooms.

JUMPIN' THE BROOM

Everything we know about immigrant adaptation suggests that immigrant blacks and native black Americans will intermarry. Peter Blau
and his colleagues clearly demonstrated the impact of structural forces,
such as group size and heterogeneity, on intermarriage rates. They
found that small groups have a smaller pool of potential partners than
larger population groups and that diversity (population heterogeneity

and inequality) leads to a higher rate of intergroup interaction and thus to higher levels of intermarriage (Blau, Blum, and Schwartz 1982; Blau, Beeker, and Fitzpatrick 1984; Blau and Schwartz 1984). Given that black immigrants and their descendants make up 20 percent or more of the African-American population in cities like New York, Boston, and Miami (see chapter 2), but a considerably smaller share of the total population in these places, the propensity for intermarriage is high.

These premises were the starting points for my study of intermarriage among Haitians in Boston.[5] Following early studies of European immigrants (Kennedy 1944; Herberg 1960), intermarriage was broadly defined to include intraracial, ethnic marriages. Specifically, intermarriage refers to a legal marriage in which only one spouse was born in Haiti (or has at least one parent who was born in Haiti). In all, thirty couples participated in the study:[6] five interracial (black-white) couples, twenty-three interethnic couples (where both spouses are black but differ in ethnic background), and three double minority couples (where the non-Haitian spouses also belong to a minority group).[7] The present discussion is based on the twenty-three black interethnic couples. Among the non-Haitian spouses, eight are native black Americans, nine are sub-Saharan African, two are Jamaican, two are Cape Verdean, one is Trinidadian, and one is Puerto Rican.[8] For each case, data were collected from the intermarried couple as a unit and the Haitian spouse individually. The couple interviews had a varied format; we began with a narrative task, followed by a standard question-response format and a hypothetical exercise (see Ostine 2001, 32).

The concepts of boundaries, boundary markers, and boundary transactions are central in my analysis of intermarriage, in part because I am interested in probing beyond an assimilationist narrative of ethnic adaptation. Anthropologist Fredrick Barth and his colleagues are largely responsible for ushering in an awareness among social scientists that culture is a changing, variable, and contingent property of interpersonal interactions, rather than an entity "above" the fray of daily life that somehow produces behavior. Unlike scholars who saw ethnicity as primordial or inherent, Barth maintained that the boundary itself is a social product.

Likewise, I proceed from the position that ethnic groups are not adequately defined by cultural items. Some cultural features signal be-

longing, others are ignored, and in some relationships, radical differences are played down and denied. Even the characteristics and attributes that signal group membership are variable: language, music, beliefs, symbols, and customs vary among ethnic group members, can be
learned by outsiders, and can change over time or in different contexts
without any impact on the salience of ethnicity the future of the ethnic
group. In other words, these criteria are dynamic and complex, thus
problematic. The only feature of ethnicity that tells us anything about
its stability is the dichotomization between insiders and
outsiders—the ethnic boundaries. A discussion cast in terms of ethnic
boundary transactions, then, allows us to recognize the broad expanse
of arrangements between intermarried couples and provides some indication about how boundaries might be drawn, adjusted, or erased.

Following Barth (1969), I define ethnic boundaries as the dividing
lines between "us" and "them." They differentiate in-group members
from outsiders and are observable in patterns of social behavior.
Boundaries between social groups and the identities they mark are produced, shifted, dissolved, and challenged in interaction. Boundary
transactions, then, are the interpersonal interactions that lead to negotiation, revision, or fortification of ethnic divisions. In this study, the expression and affirmation of boundaries is exemplified in statements like
"*We* don't do things like that . . ." "In *my* family . . ." "The way *I* was
raised . . ." These remarks represent self-conscious efforts by intermarried spouses to heighten awareness of, and sensitivity to, their ethnic identity. Finally, I treat intermarriage as a transactional social field,
a microcosm of the larger social context where important boundary-
related transactions take place between ethnic groups. These transactions impact not only how ethnic dilemmas are resolved in intermarried
households but also what those resolutions mean to individuals and the
groups with which they identify.

For the purpose of this discussion, in which it is essential to specify
the various types and forms of social relations, I present several ideal
typical cases[9] of ethnic accommodation among intermarried blacks and
the larger intergroup boundary transactions that they signal. The three
kinds of boundary transactions evidenced in my data are boundary-
crossing, boundary-blurring, and boundary-shifting (Zolberg and Long
1999).

1. Boundary-crossing involves an individual change in identification, without any real change to the boundary itself. This is the common practice of acquiring some of the attributes of another group. Examples include replacing native language and religious conversion. The most extreme example of boundary-crossing is the phenomenon of fair-skinned black Americans "passing" for white.
2. Boundary-blurring, on the other hand, implies that the social profile of a group becomes less distinct or that the clarity of the social distinction involved becomes clouded. In other words, there is a degree of ethnic blending among the previously discrete groups, rendering immigrant blacks less distinctive and the meaning of their ethnicity less clear.
3. Finally, the process of boundary-shifting involves the relocation of a boundary so that populations that once lay on one side are now included on the other: those who were once outsiders are thereby transformed into insiders. This process in some cases involves a radical redefinition of what it means to be black.

These are ideal types and are difficult to operationalize. However, in my study there were observable strategies of ethnic accommodation that offer clues as to which of the above boundary-related processes we might expect to observe between immigrant blacks and native black Americans.

FRANCINE AND TYRONE

Francine grew up in the predominantly Haitian neighborhood of Mattapan (in the city of Boston). She describes her childhood home as "working class"; her Haitian immigrant parents did not speak much English, ate rice and beans everyday, and worked "all the time":

"They went to work, came home, and went to work again. They worked two jobs, and they came home and cooked, like, for the week or whatever.
    Q: Did both your parents work when you were growing up?

A: Yes, my Dad worked at this iron place, Ironworks in Hyde Park, near Dedham, and my Mom worked for this big laundry place.

Q: So, is that what they're doing now?

A: Basically, yes, that's what they did until they retired."

Francine, however, considers herself a Bostonian. Aside from a year spent in Haiti as a young child, she has never visited the island homeland her parents left in 1971, a year before she was born at Boston City Hospital. Her husband, Tyrone, volunteered the couple for the study, and Francine was clearly reluctant to participate. On the day we met, she told me she wasn't a "typical Haitian"; she didn't speak *Kreyol* and had "never even been to Haiti."

When Francine met Tyrone, she was working as an office assistant in Cambridge and living with her parents. Tyrone, an Amherst College graduate, had just returned to Boston after three years at the University of Virginia Law School. He was working for his father's law firm and living in the Back Bay area of Boston. They describe their fortuitous meeting as "fate" since neither of them ever thought a serious relationship could begin at a nightclub.

They moved in together a few short months later. Tyrone remembered how small the apartment was. However, Francine recalled the location:

It was so wonderful—it was in the Back Bay! We could walk everywhere to everything, you know. It was home. We liked it, but we didn't stay there very long.

Many of Francine's anecdotes about the early stages of her relationship with Tyrone spoke to the social class differences between their families. For example, she recalled the afternoon they announced their engagement to her parents:

So, when we told my mother, she started yelling and screaming like [speaking in a mock Haitian accent], "Oh, congratulations! We should offer you Manishewitz [wine]." No—my father offered you Cold Duck. He had a bottle of Cold Duck! I was shaking my head. I was like: "Oh, I've got to get him out of here." And we didn't have anything. We just left.

She compared this to the champagne and the forty-five-year-old silver goblets they received from Tyrone's parents to toast their engagement.

Tyrone's family is at the center of much of the couple's married social life. They have Sunday dinner at least twice a month with his parents and his elderly grandmother. They vacation as a family on Martha's Vineyard at his parent's cottage. And they worship regularly at the Episcopal Church that Tyrone attended as a child. Francine was raised as a Seventh Day Adventist, so I asked how they chose which religion they would practice as a couple. Francine's response suggested that she didn't think of it as a decision, per se; rather, it "just made sense" since they were married in that church.

> We got married in an Episcopal church. We decided to do that because of Tyrone's parents. There is a family tradition of marrying at St. Phillip's Church. . . . But when you think of a wedding, you always think of a wedding occurring at a large church, at the bride's home church. And just the fact that it was at their church. . . . Some people may not have done that but . . . I stopped really going to church with Seventh Day Adventists right after high school. I had my own ideals, and when I started going to church with Ty and his family, it just—I started listening instead of talking at church. . . . And my parents were okay with it. My dad was fine.

Significantly, Francine's family is not as involved in the couple's life. Although her parents still live in Mattapan, about fifteen miles from Francine's home in Brookline, they phone more often than they visit. None of Francine's sisters is married—one has relocated to Miami—and many of the Haitian friends she spent time with in her "clubbing days" are still dating. So, her circle of women friends includes the wives and significant others of Tyrone's fraternity brothers and her female in-laws. The couple reports that although they haven't missed a wedding, graduation, or baby shower in Tyrone's family, they rarely accept similar invitations when Francine's family is concerned because they feel like they don't belong.

> "Q: So has living near your families been a good thing?
> Francine: Yes.
> Tyrone: Yes, very much so for me. I know that it has been—because, I always talk to my father about—how did you do it for forty years? I

mean, how do you maintain that? And he will give some good pointers which have been helpful to me.

Francine: We have a great, great time. Our family is very important to us. Every summer we're on the Cape, having over people — a house full of people."

For Francine, marriage to Tyrone has been a passport into the black middle class. The experiences she's had and the lifestyle she enjoys were very much outside her reach until they married. She interpreted many of the ideas about family life that she brought to the marriage as working-class norms that she was willing to forego in her new middle-class life. Because of this, she reasoned that she was not giving anything up by taking on Tyrone's African-American culture. I asked how Tyrone's family responded to her and especially how they felt about her working-class, immigrant background.

But they've been very accepting. . . . You know, I don't know, maybe if I was white it would be different. . . . It seems very normal to me. Very normal, nothing mixed about it. It's really strange. . . . I'm, like, so comfortable. . . . I've actually really enjoyed learning about African American culture through Ty's family. Just being with them and reading books they have or going to art exhibits or learning about jazz! I always loved history in school; I've always loved learning. So, this . . . it's an amazing experience.

Q: Is Tyrone interested in learning about Haiti? Haitian culture?

Francine: My parents never taught me about Haiti. They were from Haiti; I was from Haiti; and we lived in a home that may have been located in Boston but that was from Haiti, too. You know what I mean? Everything I learned came from just being Haitian. I never thought about having to teach my family how to be Haitian."

This couple, especially Francine, has made a conscious decision to allow one spouse's ethnic background to mark their married life. Tyrone's social network and institutional affiliations have replaced Francine's and have considerable bearing on the couple's everyday behavior and even their relationships to extended family. Additionally, patterns of behavior and ways of being associated with Haitians are abandoned.

This strategy was most common when the Haitian spouses had weak ethnic attachments and were not interested in assuming the roles that they defined as Haitian. For instance, the following respondent relies on the gender inequity that she witnessed in her family growing up to explain not just the way she has approached married life but her perception of the difference between herself and "Haitian women" in general.

> I think my mother put up with too much crap! You know, my mother put up with too much with my father. And I couldn't see myself doing that. Haitian women, in particular the ones that are from Haiti, I guess they were brought up to stick it out, stick it out, stick it out. Hang in there, and you know, accept this, forgive that. And I'm just—I can't see myself doing that as a Haitian.

Notably, the kind of ethnic repositioning evident in Francine and Tyrone's marriage can operate in either direction. There were numerous cases where the non-Haitian spouses willingly went along with ethnically defined role behavior and became "honorary Haitians."

PAULETTE AND PETER

Paulette was relatively new to Boston—she arrived in the 1980s during Boston's immigrant boom years. The Haitian population in Boston doubled in size during that decade, and Paulette and her seven younger siblings were part of that wave. After brief sojourns in other places, the entire family has reassembled in Boston. She was instrumental in assisting other members of her family migrate to the United States.

Her husband, Peter, owns a small, convenience store near the Mattapan Square trolley station. Commuters often stop in to get change or cigarettes or chewing gum as they wait for the trolley. Over the years, he has gotten to know the mostly Haitian and other West Indian patrons quite well. He always greets them with an energetic *Sak pase!* when they enter the door of his cramped, overstocked, 8 feet by 16 feet market. He describes the day he met Paulette:

> She came in and she started speaking to me in Creole really fast and laughing. I was nodding because I didn't want her to stop, but after a few minutes she realized that I didn't know what she was saying. That was it! I was hooked from that minute. It was like music to me. . . .

> Paulette: I heard him say hello to people before and everyone talks to him all the time. I thought he could speak Kreyol!

Paulette and Peter had been married less than a year at the time of the interview. Although this was not her first marriage—she was a widow when she left Haiti—family members came from Miami and Canada to attend the wedding: "a big, backyard wedding at our house in Randolph."

> Well, we did that because Peter wanted to have Haitian food at the wedding—a buffet. And so many places want you to use their food. . . . And we listen to Haitian music. . . . He loves Haitian music. If you see Peter dancing to Haitian music, you are not going to know that he is not Haitian!

Peter is proud of his knowledge of *Kompa* and popular Haitian music, as well as of the couple's Haitian art collection prominently displayed throughout their home. In the few hours I was there, the phone rang three times—each time, a sibling or cousin of Paulette's.

Peter describes his own family as close, but small. His parents are now deceased; both were only children, so he never had cousins around growing up. He has two brothers who are married with children, "but everyone pretty much does their own thing." By contrast, Peter likened Paulette's relatives to a clan:

> When you join a Haitian family, it's like joining a clan! And everybody hovers around you and takes care of you. And people come up [from Haiti] and give you gifts. People you don't even know, you've never heard of, but they are related to so and so's, so and so's distant cousin. And you become part of a whole. It's—I don't know, maybe this comes out of the heritage, the political heritage of Haiti.

The couple acknowledged that Paulette's culture has a disproportionate influence on their lifestyle, but they maintain that there was never any pressure from Paulette or her family. Peter said,

> I want her to remain in her culture. That's the beauty that she brings to the marriage.

He went on to say that he finds Haitian culture and history attractive.

Another couple, a Haitian/Trinidadian pair, also mentioned history as an important factor in shaping their relationship and their families' responses to their marriage. The Trinidadian wife, Bonnie, said,

> My aunt—as I said earlier, she loved Pierre. But more than that, she brought a historical perspective to our relationship. . . . She felt admiration for his country. And what she said to me, she said, "Well, you know"—she would say to me: "You know, the Haitian people, they're the only people to free themselves, you know, as black people. You remember that. Everybody else was given their freedom in the Caribbean. But them freed themselves." . . . So, all of that added to the kind of respect in the family for Haitians. So, there was a respect for the people of Haiti. And the feeling that this was a good marriage, not only because we loved each other, but because you're marrying into a people you can be proud to be associated with, you see.
>
> Before I went to Haiti, I read as much as I could about the country. . . . One of my favorite books to this day is *Gouverneurs de la Rosée* by Jacques Roumain. It's a very strong book, but its, oh, it's one of the greatest, one of the most beautiful books I've ever read in my life. So, when I went to Haiti, I was anxious to see the country, to see what I had read about in *Black Jacobins*, to see the places where the revolution had taken place and where the slaves had risen. So, it was for me a pilgrimage.

I expected this pattern of "ethnic repositioning" to be most common in the intermarriages involving a native-born American, white or black. What emerged as the most important variable, however, was whether one spouse had clear, cultural leverage with regard to his or her environment. Social milieu is significant in all the scenarios in that the role norms are visible, other relationships are modeled, and the ethnic roles are reinforced. Yet, this mode of accommodation was particularly associated with the social milieu in which the couple lived. For example, if one spouse's family was closer geographically or affectively to the couple, the immediate interaction context was even more important than the larger societal frame of reference. Explaining why she thinks there was not more of a Trinidadian cultural influence in their household, the following respondent suggested,

> You see, what happened was, my mother died. And I think that's the reason. If she had been alive, maybe things would be different.

MIRIAM AND MATTHEW

Miriam's family has lived in Cambridge, Massachusetts, since 1955. Her mother migrated from Haiti after marrying a physician who was an occasional tourist to the island. The couple moved back and forth from Jacmel to Cambridge for almost twenty years before the political situation made it too difficult. As a result, Miriam lived in Haiti for the first ten years of her life, even though she was born in the United States.

Miriam and Matthew met at work; she is a nurse at the Boston Medical Center and Mathew works in the Human Resources office. Miriam began working at the hospital as an interpreter and had recently finished her nursing degree at Laboure College. After repeated accidental encounters with Matthew in Human Resources, she began to notice him in the cafeteria or at the Dunkin' Donuts in the lobby.

> After a while, I just began going there when I knew he would be there. One day, he sat next to me and we started talking. I was glad; I didn't want to have to take the first step.

Miriam recalled that on their second date, they discovered that Matthew's grandfather may have had some connection to Haiti in his youth. Unable to find any factual information to fill in the details, the couple has invented a story that connects their families historically. Their musings involve an African-American church volunteer in Haiti during the American occupation who helped Haitian families migrate to the United States. The couple rationalized that their imaginary story could have happened since blacks in the United States and the West Indies have so many connections. Matthew said,

> Fredrick Douglas was an ambassador to Haiti. And Haitians fought in the Revolutionary War. So our story . . . it could happen!

Miriam and Matthew recently bought a two-family house in a "transitioning" Dorchester neighborhood. They reported that they spend most of their time these days concentrating on career advancement and maintaining their home. The couple described their approach to managing the cultural differences they bring to the marriage as "effortless." Miriam maintained that since the things people usually fight about—race, religion, and politics—were not an issue, nothing else seemed to matter:

> What is amazing for me is that we have so much in common—that it works so easily. It was no real struggle because we wanted the same things. I see us all as black people.

For Miriam and Matthew, marriage did not demand that they compromise their values. Rather, Miriam suggested that over time she had come to see values and beliefs that she had once previously ascribed exclusively to Haitians as more common values that she shared with her spouse and Matthew's family.

> In my family, your name is everything to you. You have to carry yourself in a certain way, like you know who you are and who your family is. And in his family, it's the same, you know. It's not said, it's not verbalized, but it's understood, you know.

For another couple, a Haitian/Jamaican pair, the search for "common ground" led them to have their wedding in New York City:

> We were married in New York City—in Harlem. That meant something to me. It was so symbolic to bring our families together there. . . . And it was a coming together of both families. It was a beautiful wedding. Yes. It was a beautiful, beautiful wedding.

This same couple recently adopted a Liberian orphan. The significance for them, in terms of what it signaled about their identities is illustrated in the following quote:

> We were very—I hope we still are—very idealistic and very, very concerned about the world and world issues and about what our contribution is. And we felt that, okay . . . so we've miscarried twice. So, maybe we should adopt a child. There's so many children who need homes. So, we decided what should we do. Should we go to Haiti? Should we go to Jamaica? And again, whether this is right or wrong I don't know . . . but we decided it would be an act of showing allegiance to Africa if we took from the poor who are there rather than only going back to Jamaica or going back to Haiti. So, we said we would adopt as an act of our own part of showing connectedness to African society.

Respondents like these tended to minimize ethnic differences, arguing that their spouses' values, role expectations, and behaviors were similar to their own. These couples were more likely than the others to describe their experience of ethnic accommodation as "seamless" and their sense of identity as uncompromised by their intermarriage. Some blended ethnic traditions and customs, for instance serving both *sup jumou* (squash soup) and hoppin' john (black eyed peas with rice) on New Year's Day. Others saw them as interchangeable: "It doesn't matter if we have callaloo or collards. . . . They're all greens!" Given the common racial identity or the shared immigrant experience connecting the spouses, this is not surprising. However, it is important to note that this same ethnic difference is often elaborated on and embellished to maintain the authentic distinctiveness of their ethnic groups in other circumstances.

NANCY AND FRANK

Nancy is a second-generation Haitian immigrant. Her parents migrated to Boston via New York in the early 1970s; they separated a decade later and then divorced. That was when Nancy and her mother moved to the mostly black American neighborhood of Roxbury, between the Grove Hall and Dudley Station sections. Nancy explained that her mother was determined to keep her kids out of trouble, despite the economic necessity of working overtime following the divorce:

> Lots of rules—can't do this, can't do that. . . . But there were fun times, too. We were in a lot of stuff with the Haitian community—when I was younger, we were very involved! It was a Haitian, um—what was that? A Haitian multi-cultural center or something like that for the young—a Haitian youth group. I used to be in that for a long time. I think since— I think from age seven 'til about thirteen, I was in it. And I used to dance and sing, and we did things for Mother's Day—we performed for Mother's Day—for the Haitian Mother's Day on May 30 or the last Sunday of the month. Um, and my father played in a band. . . . At one point, he didn't want me playing with the American kids. I remember that specifically. He didn't want us playing with the American kids across the street. He only wanted us to play with Haitian kids.

Nancy also recalled that religion was important in the household. "Every Sunday at 1 p.m." they went to St. Leo's, a Catholic church in Dorchester/Roxbury that conducted services in *Kreyol*. She remembers her mother being committed to the church in part because of all they did to assist Haitian families.

Nancy is married to Frank. They were introduced in 1995 by a mutual friend from Nancy's communications class at Roxbury Community College, a member of the Nation of Islam who also introduced her to the Muslim Temple No. 11. Frank had been attending the mosque for almost a year when they met. His family didn't go to church much when he was growing up—"sometimes on Easter or Christmas"—but they participated in events organized by the Nation of Islam in Roxbury. In the 1960s, the Nation of Islam mosque took over a wood-frame structure near an old brick synagogue on Washington Street; a Muslim restaurant and school soon followed. Founded by Malcolm X, the mosque was the center of social-justice and neighborhood-improvement activities. The institution had a strong influence on the Grove Hall area.

The two dated for less than a year before they married, and their involvement with the Nation of Islam intensified almost at the same rate as their relationship. They regularly worshipped at the Mosque and both worked to arrange buses to Washington, D.C., for the Million Man March. Frank proposed to Nancy the night he returned from the march. When I queried whether it was Louis Farrakhan's speech that motivated him to propose, Nancy replied,

> Actually, he had been planning the proposal for a while. In September, Frank went home by himself and told his parents that he was going to ask me to marry him. Then, that Sunday, he went and asked my mother and my dad for my hand. The way he asked my father . . . you could see that my father was very, very happy. Very pleased.

For her parents, Frank's gesture was reassuring. Although she could not be sure whether her father was pleased by Frank's seeking his permission to propose or by the promise of marriage at a time when most young couples opt for cohabitation, "but after that," Nancy said, "they seemed much more comfortable. It let them see that he had respect."

I asked how Nancy's family felt about her connection to the Nation of Islam.

> Some people feel that a Haitian can't be a Muslim, but I don't see a contradiction between my lifestyle as a Muslim and my identity as a Haitian. Those who can't see the obvious parallels between the two have a narrow view of both Haitians and black Muslims.

Nancy went on to say that because of both her Haitian background and her Muslim faith, she would have never dreamed of living with Frank before they were married or of getting married outside of the mosque. She likened her devotion to Islam to her mother's devotion to Catholicism, arguing that she probably wouldn't be so committed to the mosque if she wasn't Haitian. With no recognition of the irony, she referred to Islam as "a black man's religion," which made sense for her coming from a nation founded by black men. When I asked about the gender politics of Islam, she replied,

> A lot of females have problems with the role of women in the Nation of Islam. It's never been a big deal for me, maybe because a lot of women in my family believe the same way—that's how they act. When you think about it, it's really not that different.

At the time of the interview, the couple was expecting their first child, a boy they planned to name Toussaint. Nancy commented that she hoped his name would both connect him to Haiti and help him "be a good Muslim."

Nancy and Frank represent one of the most creative strategies of ethnic accommodation in my sample. Rather than one spouse's switching to the other's ethnic way of being, in these marriages the need to assert an identity leads to a redefinition or reconstruction of ethnic identity itself. Here, the Haitian spouse challenges commonly held Haitian norms and expectations, not in defiance of them (as evidenced by Frank's seeking permission from Nancy's parents to propose marriage) but in their expansion of the range of acceptable behaviors and forms. In the context of their family lives, the idea of what it is to be Haitian is remade to include a broader range of attributes, behaviors, and experiences. Another respondent, Danielle, who proposes a redefinition of James Davis's (1991) "one-drop rule," illustrates this well:

> There is nothing about my children that negates the fact that they are Haitian. I believe in that—what's it called?—the one-drop rule. One drop of Haitian blood is all it takes! [Laughs]

In this scenario, the role norms are often loose, amorphous, and emergent. The couples who adopted this strategy tended to talk about the inadequacy of available models or the lack of role norms altogether. These couples were more inclined to make their own judgments about what is appropriate for them (both as members of their respective ethnic groups and as individuals), which afforded them more flexibility in their behavior. The techniques involved in this mode of ethnic accommodation appear to be a means of rendering strange practices into a familiar, therefore acceptable, form. Nancy used food as an example of how her Haitian background features in her married life and her and Frank's lacto-vegetarian lifestyle:

> My husband is a vegan, so now when I make *diri kole* [rice and beans], it's with brown rice and peas, and I eat tofu and seitan instead of *griyo* [fried pork] and *boulet* [beef meatballs]. It's still Haitian food; I just use vegan substitutes. [Laughs.] You should see what I can do with some collard greens!

Among respondents in this study, this kind of ethnic reorganization sometimes led to new definitions of Haitianness; other times, it led to a redefinition of blackness itself. Consider the final example before I conclude.

EDOUARD AND CARMEN

Edouard was born in Haiti almost twenty years before Francois Duvalier was elected president. He came to the United States to live with his godparents after he finished high school. He met his wife, Carmen, at New York University in 1958. Carmen said,

> I would see this fellow looking at me and smiling. He would just look at me and smile and I would say, "Who is this?" . . . So, I asked this Ja-

maican friend, whom I knew, because all of the Caribbean students hung out together. I asked him, "Who is this fellow?" And he told me. Then I wanted to know where he was. He hung a lot with the Cuban guys. And there were a lot of Cubans there at that time. . . . I hadn't met too many Haitians then, but I liked him right off. I just felt he was such a sweet person. His English was minimal, to begin with. And I took it upon myself—being an English major—I told him, I said I'm going to help him in English. The next thing, I fall in love with him.

The couple told me that they each felt like outsiders at NYU, Carmen because she is biracial and Edouard because he is a foreigner. Moreover, they both were the first in their families to attend University. Edouard said,

I remember the day they came and told me that I got—what was it . . . that I had been elected to Phi Beta Kappa. I remember saying, "Oh, no thank you. I don't want to join a fraternity." [He laughs.] Because I had never heard of it.

Shortly after they were married, the couple moved to Los Alamos, New Mexico, for graduate work. Their social network there was diverse, but they were often the only blacks in many social situations. They described that context as somewhat liberating:

When we lived in New York City in an apartment, we had my mother coming over all the time to cook. . . . But we were by ourselves over there [in Los Alamos]. So, we had to really deal with our own lives and build friends and new relationships. . . . We were not living under any cultural pressure to do things in a particular way. Even though we carried our culture with us, we did things our way. And I think that was great, because we—our life made it. And our values really began to fuse and create our own standards.

While touring their home, I noticed a collection of classical sheet music. I inadvertently asked whether it was in New Mexico that they started listening to classical music. Carmen told me,

We'd go to New York to visit family, and Eduoard would take me to concerts where Leonard Bernstein was directing. And when we didn't have money to go to the concert, he would take me to the final rehearsal. All of our friends would say, "How come you like classical music? You're not supposed to . . . " Edouard would say, "Why not? It's an . . . music is an expression."

Like Nancy who felt that her membership in the Nation of Islam was a natural extension of being Haitian, Edouard described his affinity for classical music as part of his identity:

I think that's part of what Haiti gave me. You see. We listen to classical music. I understand it. I respond to it. I like pop music; I like to rock — I can boogie, as they say. But, classical music. . . . But, this is what the Haitian culture gave me — the love of music.

Today the couple lives in a wealthy, all-white suburb of Boston. Their children have gone through the public school system there — their son played lacrosse, then went on to an Ivy League university. They enjoy much of the intellectual and cultural life that Boston is known for — attending lectures, concerts, and eclectic restaurants with a multiracial circle of friends. When asked if they ever felt uncomfortable living outside "the black community," Edouard and Carmen said they have no regrets:

We've made some — we made some good friends. One of them — he's Czech, his wife is French and they had a child [back in 1974]. And they asked me to be the godfather of their child. . . . In a couple of weeks, we're going to France. He's in France on sabbatical. So, we're going to spend some time with him in France.

They explained that they've connected with people in multiple ways that have nothing to do with race or ethnicity — this includes relationships with colleagues at work, fellow churchgoers, or individuals involved with the organizations to which they belong. Edouard reasoned, "The Haitian culture doesn't teach you racism. We don't see things in black and white. You see people." Moreover, the couple explained that they have reached a point in their lives when they feel they are moving "beyond race." Carmen said,

As you grow older you care less about what the tribe thinks or whether the tribe approves. You become more internal, I think, and more willing to step out. That's one of the joys of getting older. You can step out and you see that what people say to you is more a signal of where they are at than where you are. And so it frees you.

BOUNDARY WORK

To summarize, I found four patterns of ethnic accommodation among the ethnically mixed black couples in my study. Some couples displayed an unadulterated adherence to ethnically defined standards of behavior. In these instances, one spouse dominated the marriage, ethnically speaking, and the intermarried households were organized in ways that differed little from what you would expect if both spouses shared an ethnic background. Whichever spouse's ethnicity dominated, this approach required unidirectional conformity to an established set of ethnic role norms. Others combined their ethnic traditions, so that what each spouse considered crucial to his or her ethnicity was not necessarily sacrificed but neither was it dominant in the household. In these marriages, ethnic accommodation entailed more than unidirectional conformity; rather, the couples emphasized shared traits while retaining some characteristics of their individual backgrounds. Finally, some respondents redefined the limits of ethnically acceptable conduct to include or account for the accommodations they had made in their married lives. For these couples, family roles were based on norms arising from the conditions of their specific circumstances. The fourth pattern is not described here. However, there were also couples who refused to relinquish their ethnically based ideas about what marriage and family life should be and thus adopted a separatist approach. Hintzen (2001) reports a similar pattern, describing respondents who remained "uncompromisingly West Indian" after intermarriage.

Although each intermarriage in the study tells a unique story about the negotiation of ethnic identity in a heterogeneous context, what these data demonstrate is not in the outcome itself—that is, in what religion respondents practice or what language they speak at home or where they live—but in what they suggest about boundaries between the groups the spouses represent. The behavioral choices made here have implications beyond the individuals because subjective processes of ethnic self-identification are connected to group-level behavior. In some cases, what appeared to be an abandonment of ethnic background was actually a creative attempt at accommodation that in fact allowed respondents to maintain their unique subjectivities.

Boundary-Crossing

Francine and Tyrone and Paulette and Peter are examples of couples whose accommodation of ethnic differences has little impact on the boundaries between black immigrant and native black American groups. Ethnic outsiders are converted into insiders, but there is no change to the perceived distinction that the boundary demarcates. One spouse (Francine and Peter, in the cases described above) simply repositions him- or herself, thereby erasing the cultural differences within the marriage. The activities and role norms that (ideologically) define their families culturally or make one group unlike the other remain intact. Whether or not repositioning requires an unlearning of one's original ethnicity, this strategy entails a great deal of familiarity with the culture and the role expectations the spouse brings to the marriage. Moreover, it requires that the learned ethnicity be performed in ways that signal the differences between groups (note, for example, the rhetorical strategies Francine uses to signal difference from Haitians).

Boundary-Blurring

In this scenario, neither spouse is required to relinquish his or her ethnic sense of self because the different norms are compatible. Some of these respondents, like Miriam and Matthew, emphasized the similarities in their cultural backgrounds and the overlapping nature of their histories. Others exhibited relatively novel responses to family life representing amalgams of elements from their different ethnic role models. This sort of ethnic blending was the most common pattern in the ethnically mixed, intraracial unions. Importantly, one way these couples exhibited a tendency toward blurring group boundaries involved emphasizing racial identity over ethnic variations. These couples saw what is commonly perceived as manifest ethnic differences *across* boundaries as overlapping ethnic variations *within* a racially bounded identity.

Boundary-Shifting

Nancy and Frank and Eduoard and Carmen represent couples who redefine the limits of ethnically acceptable conduct in ways that account for the accommodations they have made in their married lives. Whether it is around the issue of religion or the decision of where to live, they tend to understand their behavior as somehow reflecting their ethnicity and thereby validating their ethnic identities. For instance, the task of having to bridge the cultural differences between their families of origin and their families of choice is constructed as an ethnically defined role that resonates with other intermarried Haitians. For these couples, intermarriage is potentially a site of new identities as people use the experience to define and redefine what being ethnic, in this case Haitian, means to them. For Nancy and Frank (as well as Francine, for that matter), becoming middle class was more important than "becoming black" or "staying Haitian." Similarly, Edouard and Carmen expressed an interest in transcending race altogether.

This strategy of ethnic accommodation also occurs via the adoption of cultural or structural forms that are transformed and fundamentally reconstituted with ethnic meaning (Cohen 1985, 46). In this way, cultural forms or structures imported from across the boundary (music, food, history, organizations) provide new media for the expression of ethnic values. The members of an ethnic group take an "alien" social form (a lacto-vegetarian lifestyle, for instance) and basically make it over symbolically so that it represents their own sense of collective self. In these marriages, the location and meaning of Haitian ethnic group boundaries and identity are negotiated, revised, and revitalized.

To sum up, I am suggesting that the pattern of ethnic repositioning seems to be the most remarkable strategy of ethnic accommodation (at least, it is the pattern that has been of most interest to social scientists). It suggests that perceived boundaries between groups are permeable and that the differentiating characteristics can be learned. Blending, on the other hand, threatens the distinctions between black immigrants and native black Americans. This blurring of ethnic differences implies for the future that immigrant blacks may begin to see themselves as part of the larger pan-ethnic black (middle-class) community. Continued blending of ethnic differences on the individual level may eventually lead to the eradication of ethnic boundaries between certain groups, and postimmigrant identity formation will be based on a less particular definition of "we" that includes former ethnic outsiders. Finally, ethnic reorganization also challenges group boundaries, but in a significantly different way. Rather than blurring the boundaries between groups, ethnic reorganization restricts or expands the definition of who belongs and what behaviors are appropriate for group members; importantly, however, the boundary itself remains significant. In this case, identity formation will continue to involve making a distinction between insiders and outsiders, albeit based on an expanded notion of "we."

CONCLUSION

I am not arguing that intraracial relations among black Americans in Boston are conflict-free. They are not—and when we consider the restricted space for the construction of black identities, some degree of conflict is understandable. Moreover, additional data are necessary before these findings can be applied to other groups in other contexts. We should remember, however, that black communities are not hermetically sealed off from each another. Black Americans from various backgrounds interact voluntarily and amicably in neighborhoods, workplaces, social situations, and schools. And my data show that Haitians in Boston are marrying outside their ethnic group; many are coupling with native black Americans. Despite all the signifying captured and reported by the media, symbolic boundaries between black immigrants and native black Americans have not become social boundaries. In other words, the distinct ways of seeing things and ways of being that black Americans struggle over have not hardened into meaningful patterns of social exclusion (see Lamont 1992, and Lamont and Molnar 2002 for more on the distinction).

In addition, this chapter has attempted to show that distancing or conflict is only one facet of the interactions between black immigrants and native black Americans. Individuals are crossing boundaries by adopting some characteristics of ethnic outsiders, blurring boundaries by recognizing that black Americans have multiple and varied subjectivities, and shifting boundaries that separate black ethnic groups in favor of a more inclusive black American community.

Given the contemporary social context in which black immigrant/ black American relations exist (especially the mainstream tendencies either to deny diverse black subjectivities or to accentuate cultural differences and deny racism), complete assimilation into the native black American community is unlikely. At the same time, extreme separation is equally unlikely. As Zolberg and Long (1999) argue,

> Fraught with tensions, sometimes generating confrontations, and occasionally provoking adverse reactions, these negotiations are nevertheless likely to result in the institutionalization of new relations. (29)

Finally, I hope to have shown that it is possible to consider boundaries as a means of communication as opposed to division. Boundaries are essential to diffusion (of ideas, people, resources, norms, and so forth) across communities. Beyond separation, beyond social distancing, boundaries create the conditions for meaningful connections, exchange, bridging, and inclusion. Rather than marking distance and disidentification, the symbolic boundaries that black immigrants perform in the process of negotiating belonging in America should be understood as an attempt to contest and reframe the meaning of social boundaries between blacks and nonblacks.

NOTES

1. See chapter 1 of this volume for a note on terminology.

2. Alan Keyes quoted in "'African-American' Becomes a Term for Debate" *New York Times*, August 29, 2004).

3. These are the words of an African immigrant from Senegal who has lived in the United States for about thirty years (quoted in Arthur 2001, 81).

4. It is important to note that Reid's analysis was heavily influenced by the work of Robert Park, whose race relations cycle saw conflict as an inevitable part of a social process that ended with assimilation. Given that these ideas governed most of the thinking about immigrants at the time, it is not surprising that Reid's analysis puts such an emphasis on conflict.

5. Boston is home to the third largest community of Haitian immigrants in the country. Although the 2000 census counted less than fifty thousand Haitians in the state of Massachusetts, consulate officials and community leaders maintain that approximately eighty thousand Haitians live in the Greater Boston area, mostly in the neighborhoods of Mattapan, Dorchester, and Hyde Park. According to these estimates, nearly one out of every four black Americans in Boston is of Haitian descent.

6. A combination of advertisements for volunteers, snowballing, and theoretical sampling was used to obtain interview respondents. From the pool of volunteers and referrals, theoretical sampling was used to guide the selection of the respondents for this study (see Strauss 1987; also referred to as "purposeful sampling" by Patton 1990 or "criterion-based sampling" by LeCompte and Preissle 1993). This is a strategy in which particular settings, people, or events are selected deliberately (and in some cases recruited into the study) in order to provide important information that cannot be acquired as well from other methods, such as convenience or probability sampling (Maxwell 1996). For instance, I sought to interview equal numbers of intermarried Haitian men and Haitian women; I also wanted to include intermarried Haitians who lived outside the areas of concentration. Thirteen of the participants responded to printed advertisements posted at various Haitian and Caribbean businesses, such as restaurants, markets and bakeries, community organizations, and large employers of Haitians, namely, Boston area hospitals, hotels, and nursing homes. I also handed out flyers and business cards at a range of events, such as the "Migrating Colors" art exhibit opening at the Boston Center for the Arts (January 1999) and the annual Caribbean carnival held in Boston every August. The remaining seventeen participants were recruited into the sample based on references from contacts in the field and the social networks of previously interviewed couples. These techniques served to balance the sample between eager volunteers and individuals who saw themselves as central to the Haitian community and those who were a bit more withdrawn.

7. All three non-Haitian spouses in the double minority couples were of Hispanic origin, but one identified as black American.

8. It is important to note that the study was designed as an investigation of ethnicity among intermarried Haitians. As such, there are no African/native black American or other Caribbean/native black American couples represented here. However, the cultural characteristics these groups share increase the propensity for intermarriage and ethnic blending. Anglophone Caribbean and African immigrants share a common language with native black Americans; among many native black Americans, there is a symbolic connection to Africa (and things African); and West Indian culture, reggae music, for instance, is becoming part of the popular culture of native black America, especially in places like New York City. Therefore, despite the limitations of the case study, I believe that the processes described here are significant beyond the case of Haitians in Boston.

9. Ideal types are hypothetical constructions (see Shils and Finch, *Max Weber on the Methodology of the Social Sciences*, 1949). This method was selected to illuminate important variations in forms of ethnic accommodation. I selected the defining characteristics of each type of accommodation observable in my sample and built on these to form a coherent analytic framework. Notably, not all the characteristics attributed to each type were present in any one actual case, but because they were derived from actual cases, they have explanatory value. In addition, specific place names and other identifiable information have been changed to protect the anonymity of my respondents.

REFERENCES

Apraku, Kofi. 1996. *Outside Looking In: An African Perspective on American Pluralistic Society.* Westport, CT: Praeger.

Arthur, John. 2001. *Invisible Sojourners: African Immigrant Diaspora in the United States.* Westport, CT: Praeger.

Barth, Fredrick, ed. 1969. *Ethnic Groups and Boundaries: The Social Organization of Cultural Difference*. Long Grove, IL: Waveland Press.

Becker, Tamar. 1973. "Black Africans and Black Americans on an American Campus: The African View" *Sociology and Social Research* 57, no. 2: 168–81.

Blau, Peter, Carolyn Beeker, and Kevin M. Fitzpatrick. 1984. "Intersecting Social Affiliations and Intermarriage." *Social Forces* 62: 585–605.

Blau, Peter, Terry C. Blum, and Joseph E. Schwartz. 1982. "Heterogeneity and Intermarriage" *American Sociological Review* 47: 45–62.

Blau, Peter, and Joseph E. Schwartz. 1984. *Crosscutting Social Circles: Testing a Theory of Intergroup Relations*. Orlando, FL: Academic Press.

Bryce-Laporte, Roy S. 1972. "Black Immigrants: The Experience of Invisibility and Inequality." *Journal of Black Studies* 3, no. 1: 29–56.

Charles, Carolle. 1990. "Different Meanings of Blackness: Patterns of Identity among Haitian Migrants in New York City." *Cimarron* 3 (winter): 129–39.

Charles, Jacqueline. 2003. "Caribbean Americans Form Own Caucus." *Miami Herald*, April 9, A1.

Cohen, Anthony P. 1985. *The Symbolic Construction of Community*. New York: Routledge.

Davis, F. James. 1991. *Who Is Black? One Nation's Definition*. University Park: Pennsylvania State Press.

Domingo, W. A. 1925. "The Tropics in New York." *Survey Graphic* (March): 648–50.

Fears, Darryl. 2002. "A Diverse and Divided Black Community." *Washington Post*, February 14, A1.

Gordy, Molly. 1994. "Black vs. Black: Roots of Rage out of Africa? Haitians See It Differently Series. The New New Yorkers." *New York Newsday*, April 4, A15.

Greenbaum, Susan D. 2002. *More Than Black: Afro-Cubans in Tampa*. Gainesville: University Press of Florida.

Grenier, Guillermo, and Lisandro Perez. 1996. "Miami Spice: The Ethnic Cauldron Sizzles." In *Origins and Destinies: Immigration, Race and Ethnicity in America*, ed. S. Pedraza and R. Rumbaut. Belmont, CA: Wadsworth.

Halter, Marilyn. 1993. *Between Race and Ethnicity: Cape Verdean American Immigrants, 1860–1965*. Urbana: University of Illinois Press.

Herberg, Will. 1960. *Protestant-Catholic-Jew*. New York: Anchor Books.

Hintzen, Percy. 2001. *West Indians in the West: Self-Representations in an Immigrant Community*. New York: New York University Press.

Ho, Christine. 1991. *Saltwater Trinnies: Afro-Trinidadian Networks and Non-assimilation in Los Angeles*. New York: AMS Press.

Hunt, April. 2002. "Black Immigrants Feel No Racial Kinship." *Orlando Sentinel*, April 28, B1.

Johnson, Violet. 2000. "Black Immigrants in the United States." In *We Are a People: Narrative and Multiplicity in Constructing Ethnic Identity*, ed. P. Spickard and W. Burroughs. Philadelphia: Temple University Press.

Kasinitz, Philip. 1992. *Caribbean New York: Black Immigrants and the Politics of Race*. Ithaca, NY: Cornell University Press.

Kennedy, Ruby Jo Reeves. 1944. "Single or Triple Melting Pot? Intermarriage Trends in New Haven, 1870–1940." *American Journal of Sociology* 49: 331–39.

Lamont, Michèle. 1992. *Money, Morals and Manners: The Culture of the French and American Upper-Middle Class*. Chicago: University of Chicago Press.

Lamont, Michèle, and Virág Molnár. 2002. "The Study of Boundaries in the Social Sciences." *Annual Review of Sociology* 28: 167–95.

LeCompte, M. D., and J. Preissle. 1993. *Ethnography and Qualitative Design in Educational Research*. 2nd ed. San Diego, CA: Academic Press.

Marshall, Paule. 1959. *Brown Girl, Brownstones*. New York: Feminist Press at the City University of New York.

Maxwell, Joseph A. 1996. *Qualitative Research Design: An Interactive Approach*. Thousand Oaks, CA: Sage Publications.

McDermott, Monica. 2003. "Black like Who? African and Haitian Immigrants and Urban American Conceptions of Race." Paper presented at the annual meeting of the American Sociological Association, Atlanta, GA.

McWhorther, John. 2004. "Why I'm Black, Not African American." *Los Angeles Times*, September 8, B11.

Morrison, Toni. 1993. "On the Backs of Blacks." *Time Magazine*, December 2, 57.

Nagel, Joanne. 1994. "Constructing Ethnicity: Creating and Recreating Ethnic Identity and Culture." *Social Problems* 41: 152–76.

Nesbitt, Francis Njubi. 2003. "African Intellectuals in the Belly of the Beast: Migration, Identity and the Politics of African Intellectuals in the North." *Critical Arts Journal* 17, nos. 1–2: 17–35.

Osofsky, Gilbert. [1971] 1996. *Harlem: The Making of a Ghetto, Negro New York, 1890–1930*. 2nd ed. Chicago: Elephant Paperbacks.

Ostine, Regine. 2001. *After Intermarriage: Ethnicity and Identity among Haitians in Boston*. PhD diss., University of Michigan.

Patton, M. Q. 1990. *Qualitative Evaluation and Research Methods*. 2nd ed. Newbury Park, CA: Sage.

Pierre, Jemima. 2004. "Black Immigrants in the United States and the '"Cultural Narratives'" of Ethnicity." *Identities* 11: 141–70.

Portes, Alejandro, and Min Zhou. 1994. "Should Immigrants Assimilate?" *Public Interest* 116: 18–33.

Pyke, Karen, and Tran Dang. 2003. "'FOB' and 'Whitewashed': Identity and Internalized Racism among Second Generation Asian Americans." *Qualitative Sociology* 26, no. 2: 147–72.

Reid, Ira. 1939. *The Negro Immigrant: His Background Characteristics and Social Adjustment, 1899–1937*. New York: Columbia University Press.

Rodriguez, Cindy. 2001. "Immigrants Reshaping Black Experience." *Boston Globe*, August 15, A1.

Rogers, Reuel. 2001. "Black Like Who?" In *Islands in the City: West Indian Migration to New York*, ed. Nancy Foner. Berkeley: University of California Press.

Shils, Edward A., and Henry A. Finch, eds. 1949. *Max Weber on the Methodology of the Social Sciences*. New York: Free Press.

Strauss, Anselm. 1987. *Qualitative Analysis for Social Scientists*. Cambridge: Cambridge University Press.

Sutton, Constance R., and Susan R. Makiesky-Barrow. 1987. "Migration and West Indian Racial and Ethnic Consciousness." In *Caribbean Life in New York: Sociocultural Dimensions*, ed. C. Sutton and E. Chaney. New York: Center for Migration Studies.

Swarns, Rachel, L. 2004. "'African-American' Becomes a Term for Debate." *New York Times*, August 29, A1.

Vickerman, Milton. 1994. "The Response of West Indians toward African-Americans: Distancing and Identification." In *Research in Race and Ethnic Relations 7*, ed. R. Dennis, 83–128. Greenwich, CT: JAI Press.

———. 1999. *Crosscurrents: West Indian Immigrants and Race.* New York: Oxford University Press.

Waters, Mary C. 1994. "Ethnic and Racial Identities of Second-Generation Black Immigrants in New York City." *International Migration Review* 28: 795–820.

———. 1999. *Black Identities: West Indian Immigrant Dreams and American Realities.* Cambridge, MA: Harvard University Press.

Watkins-Owens, Irma. 1996. *Blood Relations: Caribbean Immigrants and the Harlem Community, 1900–1930.* Bloomington: Indiana University Press.

Wilson, Robin. 2001. "A Battle over Race, Nationality and Control at a Black University." *Chronicle of Higher Education*, July 27, A8.

Woldemikael, Tekle. 1989. *Becoming Black American: Haitians and American Institutions in Evanston, Illinois.* New York: AMS Press.

Wong, Bernard. 1987. "The Chinese: New Immigrants in New York's Chinatown." In *New Immigrants in New York*, ed. Nancy Foner. New York: Columbia University Press.

Zolberg, Aristide, and Litt Woon Long. 1999. "Why Islam is like Spanish: Cultural Incorporation in Europe and the United States" *Politics and Society* 27, no. 1: 5–38.

Zephir, Flore. 1996. *Haitian Immigrants in Black America: A Sociological and Socio-linguistic Portrait.* Westport, CT: Bergin and Garvey.

CHAPTER 9

The Stress of Migration and the Mental Health of African Immigrants

Hugo Kamya

When my mother and I walked into the doctor's examining room, I did not know what to expect. My mother, seventy, had been unwell with age-related illnesses. She had been diagnosed with macular degeneration. She had diabetes and suffered from ulcers and high blood pressure. Our visit with the doctor at one of the country's first-class hospitals promised all one could hope for. My mother, too, was very impressed right from the time we were received in the waiting room. Even the number of forms we had to fill out did not turn her off. Instead, she seemed to marvel at her son's ability to negotiate this new world for her. She also seemed to enjoy looking around as more people filed in and out of the doctor's office. She worried that she would forget and give the wrong details about her medical history. Not until we entered the doctor's office and the questions became more pointed did she begin to have doubts. The doctor wanted to know all about her medical history, including her sexual history and private life. Her mind went "blank," as she later explained to a woman friend. "How could I begin to tell my son my life?" I had been asked to become the interpreter of the most intimate details of her life. My mother's story, as she sought treatment at one of this country's prestigious medical institutions, reveals a poignant experience in this new place of settlement. Although older Africans are less likely to migrate and become first-generation immigrants in the United States, more young Africans who migrate are filing visa petitions for their older parents (as well as extended kin) to be legally admitted into the country.

Mot's immigrant experience is starkly different. Mot is a seventeen-year-old, dark-skinned immigrant from Sudan who was airlifted from the refugee camps of Kakuma in Kenya. After a few months in Boston, Mot ventured out in the workforce. He applied for several service jobs, but no one would hire him. He was told he did not have any skills. Depressed and angry, he turned his fury against himself and others. He started drinking, watching violent movies, and assaulting kids his own age. When he finally showed up in my clinical practice, he looked disheveled and upset with this new world of opportunity. He lamented that he had no place he could call home. He wished to return, but there was no place he could go back to. He thought about the killing fields he had escaped. He said the one thing he had hoped for was to get a job. Together, we spent several sessions exploring and examining his abilities. He showed me the application he made out to a local grocery store. He stated he had laboriously worked on it but had received no call back from the employer. On close examination, I observed that Mot's attempts to present his best, honest self were backfiring on him. One of the questions on these applications asked about his skills, and Mot honestly reported that he had no skills. We examined what Mot had gone through in his short seventeen-year life: the wars and conflicts in his native Sudan, his narrow escapes and near death experiences, and his tremendous swimming ability as he crossed several rivers to escape crocodiles and warring groups. We identified that he had crisis-management skills, which he subsequently was able to put down on his application. Shortly thereafter, Mot was hired for a job of his liking. As a young immigrant, Mot's story underscores immigrants' tremendous will to survive against all odds in their new home as they seek to enter into mainstream America. In the main, these immigrants come searching for better educational and economic opportunities (Takyi 2002; Apraku 1991; Djamba 1999; Kamya 1997; Berger 2004; Drachman and Shen-Ryan 1991; Glassman and Skolnik 1984). Kofi Apraku (1991) also notes family and cultural pressures as contributing to decisions to emigrate.

In this chapter, I use the backdrop of these experiences to focus our attention on the mental health of African immigrants. I first review past and recent studies on immigration as they relate to the stress of the acculturation experience and examine coping routines associated with premigration, migration, and postmigration. The chapter concludes by offering suggestions about providing culturally competent services in addressing the mental well-being of African immigrants. I also draw attention to the paucity of data on these populations.

THE IMMIGRANT EXPERIENCE

The stories of Mot, my mother, and other contemporary Africans show that the immigration experience can be a stressful one because of the profound change that it entails, whether migration is voluntary or involuntary. Ultimately, the migration process for African immigrants involves primarily a change in their life's circumstances (Cervantes and Castro 1985) mediated by the interaction between the individual's internal resources, the support resources available to them and their communities, and the reception or behavior of the host population, which may "range from acceptance, tolerance, and encouragement to disdain, ridicule, or hostility toward immigrants' efforts to learn the new language, norms, and values" (Shuval 1993, 648). The changes wrought by the immigrant experience involve stressor events associated with different phases, including the separation from people, places, and possessions during the *departure* phase, the possibility of prolonged transition periods during the *transit* phase, and the need to build a new life and a new identity amid a different culture in the *resettlement* phase (Garza-Guerrero 1974; Stewart 1986; Akhtar 1999; Coll and Magnuson 1997). Thus, all migrants separate from a familiar network of social relations and enter new social networks in a host society. The host society presents its own difficulties, and migrants may go through stages of loneliness and alienation (Kuo 1976). All migrants need to learn new norms and values or to reintegrate their old ones with those of the host society. And while the change in living conditions may bestow added value (mostly in terms of economic benefit), the immigration process also involves multiple losses, including loss of familiarity with the physical, social, and cultural environments, as well as loss of language, social support systems, identity, belief system, and socioeconomic status (Berger 2004). Even though the level of stress may diminish depending on "the specific meaning attributed to change in terms of the individual's life and goals" (Roskies, Iida-Miranda, and Strobel 1975,

18) or increase depending on vulnerability to the adverse impact of immigration based on self-esteem, racial identity, and self-efficacy (Lazarus and Opton 1966; Lazarus 1971; Padilla, Alvarez, and Lindholm 1986), the problem of physical and psychological rootlessness confronts every immigrant. Carlos Sluzki (1979) has noted that this physical and psychological rootlessness is a direct result of separation from people, things, or places of attachment, as well as from the imposition of a new set of values and customs by host societies onto immigrants.

In a recent work, Guillermina Jasso and colleagues (2005) focused on the immigration process's impact on health by examining both the pre- and postmigration health status of immigrants; they asked, What is the immigrant's health trajectory over the course of immigration? Jasso et al. traced the health of immigrants long before their arrival in the United States and noted certain demographic factors and the effects of prolonged exposure to stressful events. They reported increased risks of hypertension, leading to a likelihood of blood clots and greater risk of obesity and type II diabetes. Such stress also compromises the human immune system by either slowing it down or stimulating it. Jasso et al. (2005) proposed that specific moments in the migration process affect the health of migrants, including making the decision to migrate, applying for a visa (visa stress), and arriving in the United States. Visa stress is experienced differently for individuals, depending on their status. The health trajectory of migrants proposed by Jasso et al. (2005)—visa stress, migration stress, and stress due to U.S. exposure—therefore accounts for the various kinds of categorical experiences and stresses associated with migration. Jasso et al. (2005) also identified gender differences and they found that visa stress appears to affect women more than men.

Upon arrival in the United States, many African immigrants will not talk about having just one "home" and struggle to retain "many homes," including their place of birth and the new place of settlement. These homes capture many facets of their family and community that include history, language, and identity. To a certain extent, this is a way to manage their new immigrant status. Although few can afford to return regularly to their families and countries, many keep in contact and attempt to maintain strong ties with their families and countries of origin, either through regular communication or through monthly remittances. It is not uncommon for many African immigrants to provide not only material help for extended family members at home but also psychological and emotional support. And for African immigrants, the journey to the United States also involves coming to terms with a certain sense of the lingering effects of colonial domination by European countries as they realize that to succeed economically, they must relocate (Kamya 2005; McCulloch 1995).

The concepts of social isolation, culture shock, cultural change, and goal-striving stress describe the changes encountered by African immigrants in the migration process. These ideas have been used in early attempts to organize the study of cross-cultural transitions and understand the relationship between migration and mental well-being. A common theme running through these processes is that the adverse factors in migration induce a certain vulnerability to stress in immigrants (Mezey 1960; Kuo 1976; Smither and Rodriguez-Giegling 1982). Additionally, some theorists have proposed that several developmental phases, or stages, of the migration process help describe the experience. Two such theories are Sluzki's (1979) five phases and Alan Richardson's (1967) three stages of migration.

According to Wen Kuo (1976), social isolation involves physical separation from one's homeland and one's orienting set of mutual rights, obligations, and networks of social interaction. These experiences all contribute to "strong feelings of loneliness, alienation and desocialization, low self-esteem, and inability to cultivate or sustain social relationships" (Kuo 1976, 297). Furthermore, grief and bereavement may also serve as blocks to coping with and adjusting to the demands of a new environment (Moos 1976; Taft 1977; Arredondo-Dowd 1981; Schneller 1981). E. Gartly Jaco (1954) also documented the negative impact of social isolation. In a study of an area in Austin, which had the highest rates of schizophrenia, Jaco found that the same residents suffered a greater degree of social isolation. Social isolation was measured by such indices as knowledge of neighbor, number of friends, and memberships in fraternal organizations.

The concept of social isolation suggests that limited contact and communication with the larger society is associated with greater stress in the performance of social roles. For immigrants, changes in social roles and role expectations are frequently cited as stressors that might directly or indirectly contribute to the onset of mental illness (Richardson 1967; Kuo 1976; Taft 1977). M. P. Naditch and R. F. Morrissey (1976) have suggested that ambiguity and conflicts regarding changes in roles create stress among immigrants.

As studies of immigrant groups have shown, social isolation may be moderated by membership in associations that may provide social support for new immigrants. John Arthur (2000) reports that African immigrants are able to support one another through such immigrant organizations. Many African immigrants tend to settle near fellow Africans. While this caucusing gives many Africans the strength to work together and enables the continuation of ethnic or national cultures, it also alienates many Africans from the host culture with which they must constantly negotiate for their survival. Still, such resettlements heighten immigrants' visibility and reduce their vulnerability to the discrimination and oppression they may confront as they seek to enter mainstream culture. Often, immigrants rely on informal services and seek solutions to their problems from among their own people in their place of settlement.

The experience of culture shock among African immigrants is part of the process of adjusting and contending with the cultural divide among races. While this "shock" may be moderated by prior knowledge of their country of settlement, it is important to note that the vast store of knowledge possessed by these immigrants may be in the form of stereotypes of people and places. Originally coined by Kalvero Oberg, the term *culture shock* suggests that immigrants undergo strain, a sense of loss, and feelings of deprivation, rejection, role confusion, surprise, anxiety, disgust, indignation, and impotence as they adjust to their new status. Oberg (1960) defined it as a state "precipitated by the anxiety that results from losing all our familiar signs and symbols of social intercourse" (177). Oberg's research built on earlier research by Oscar Handlin (1951) and Shmuel Eisenstadt (1955).

Cultural change focuses on the disrupting effect of the migration process on the psychological orientation of the immigrant undergoing acculturation. The immigrant is said to adopt new core cultural values, "which involves a fundamental disruption of and shift in the cognitive, affective and evaluative modes of behavior which were patterned by the immigrant's native culture" (Kuo 1976, 298). As immigrants enter a new culture, their cultural orientation is challenged by competing values of the new culture, resulting sometimes in family disorganization and affecting family members' personalities. African immigrants may experience this change not only in their dealings with the majority group but with native black Americans, who may not necessarily identify with these new immigrants despite a shared racial type. Africans, like other immigrants, experience a deep sense of loss of their culture, not only for themselves but also for their children. Parents lament their inability to communicate with their children as they could in their home countries and are pained when their Americanized children fail to learn their language. Prolonged separation from family members can create gaps in shared family histories. Family members become strangers to each other, leading to major strains and disappointments. For many, losing contact with loved ones can negatively affect connections within families. Most frightening of all is the fear of deportation for those who have arrived illegally (Kamya 2005).

Many immigrants experience stress as they strive toward achieving goals. Goal-striving stress points to immigrants' unique problem of unfulfilled aspiration. Newly arrived immigrants hold a "reasonable level of aspiration while they strive hard for achievement" (Kuo 1976, 298). An immigrant experiences difficulty in achieving upward mobility. These difficulties produce what is termed *goal-striving stress*, which is related to the failure to achieve or maintain one's own or the host society's standards. Young African immigrants, especially, are often consumed by the need to succeed. They will take on jobs and work long hours, even in the face of medical or mental crises, simply because the need to succeed overrides other concerns. Women will often take subservient positions at the expense of their mental health. Goal achievement is constrained by status at the time of entry, the duration of stay, and eventual attainment of full residency status. As they wait to achieve residency status, many African immigrants experience a cuts off from mainstream opportunities, including access to services. Their official or unofficial status often carries with it major limitations, be it student status, work status, visitor or refugee/asylum status, or undocumented immigrant status.

Sluzki's (1979) five phases provide another perspective on the demands of the process of migration. The first preparatory stage is triggered by concrete behaviors or events that define a clear commitment to migrate. For African immigrants, these events have ranged from wars to seeking educational or economic opportunities. During this time, according to Sluzki (1979), the family develops rules about roles and functions with regard to migration. For many African immigrants, however, the migration often starts out with one person before families are reunited.

The second phase involves the act of migration, which is often unique to each family. Although some people will cut ties with home cultures, many will plan on temporary moves and will maintain some ties with their original homes. The third stage, the period of overcompensation, is described as one of heightened task-oriented efficiency, often facilitated by an increased dichotomy between instrumental and affective roles among family members. The fourth stage, the period of decompensation, is one in which most of the immigrants first seek treatment. The immigrant's main task in reshaping a new reality is twofold: (1) to maintain continuity and identity, and (2) to maximize compatibility with the new environment. Sluzki (1979) has noted that the successful outcome of this fourth period will be marked by immigrants' ability to mourn their loss and to integrate both old and new rules, models, and values into their new realities.

The fifth stage, intergenerational phenomena, refers to any delays or maladaptation inherited by the second-generation after migration, when clashes between generations highlight conflicts in norms and values between the new culture and the culture of origin. The prologue to migration is a crucial stage to consider as it points to the voluntariness or involuntariness of the decision to migrate. The act and mode of migration may occur individually or in small or large groups and may be sanctioned or not sanctioned. In some cases, entire families deliberate on which member of the family must emigrate.

Sluzki's periods of overcompensation and decompensation and transgenerational phenomena parallel Richardson's (1967) stages of satisfaction, identification, and acculturation. Satisfaction is defined by a dual reaction to the host culture: elation, which is described as consisting of pleasant experiences and favorable attitudes toward the host culture, and depression, which is described as a lowered satisfaction level consisting of negative experiences and a critical attitude toward the host culture. In this model, an initial feeling of elation is followed by depression, which is then followed by a return to satisfaction.

The second stage, identification, is marked by the individual's change in group identity. As the immigrant acquires a sense of belonging and moves away from feelings related to "social isolation," he or she begins to develop identification with the host culture. Identification refers to a subjective feeling of membership, that is, "coming to feel more like a typical member of one's host group" (Richardson 1967, 14). The third stage, acculturation, refers to one's degree of involvement with the host culture and adoption of the norms of the host culture.

The foregoing highlight the many factors that converge in the cross-cultural transition process to affect the well-being and lifestyle of African immigrants as they make their homes in the United States. The emergent themes of stress and coping are important because they encapsulate (1) the myriad of demands the migratory process makes on the immigrant and the stressor events involved in the change that migration brings, and (2) how immigrants cope with these stresses and stressor events. In the following section, the discussion focuses on the concepts of stress and acculturation, the argument being that acculturation makes stressful demands on immigrants that ultimately affect their mental health. A discussion of coping, self-esteem, and hardiness is then presented to illustrate the specific coping mechanisms used in managing the stressors of immigration.

STRESS AND ACCULTURATION

The concept of stress was used by endocrinologist Hans Selye, who applied the term to extreme disturbances, traumatic shock, and shock from burns and loss of blood. A survey of the stress literature shows that some theorists have written about stress as an internal phenomenon (Selye 1974), as an external phenomenon (Grinker and Spiegel 1945), and as a transactional phenomenon that occurs within the person-environment relationship (Lazarus 1971). The study of the concept of stress has, however, gained research currency not only in psychology but in physiology, as well as in sociology and anthropology (Dohrenwend and Dohrenwend 1974; Lazarus 1971; Selye 1976). As a phenomenon yielded by one's social circumstance, stress may be conceived of as a distress or discomfort experienced in daily life events, and these daily life changes are often accompanied by loss and grief (cf. Mena, Padilla, and Maldonado 1986). Richard Lazarus and Edward Opton (1966) outlined three central issues in understanding stress: (1) the conditions and processes that determine when stress reactions will be produced and when they will not, (2) coping with stress and factors influencing the choice of coping process, and (3) the patterns of reaction that define the presence of the stress processes. In general, immigrants carry the burden of stress with them into host societies and do experience greater psychological stress than nonimmigrants (Dyal and Dyal 1981) as they grapple with personal loss, grief, urgencies, and crises as a result of changes associated with immigration (Sluzki 1979; Arredondo-Dowd 1981). The process of immigration stimulates mixed and varied responses as immigrants learn to adjust to different situations. Some immigrants will adjust and cope successfully with the stresses related to immigration. Thomas Holmes and Richard Rahe (1967), who developed the Social Readjustment Scale, argued that stress accompanies the burden of making behavioral changes associated with the intensity of change experienced by an individual.

The concept of stress permeates the literature on migration and informs us particularly about how adaptation to the new host culture or acculturation involves changes for individuals that include physical, biological, cultural, and psychological dimensions. As a sociocultural phenomenon, the acculturation process begins as a "result of contact and interaction between two or more autonomous cultural groups" (Mena, Padilla, and Maldonado 1986). Acculturation is also a bilevel adjustment process in which an individual acquires, or fails to acquire, the customs of the host culture while retaining, or failing to retain, the norms of the native culture (Martinez and Mendoza 1984). Jaco (1954) also described this adjustment process as a two-stage developmental process marked by desocialization from old norms and values and resocialization into a new environment and adoption of those norms and values. Berry (1980) posits contact, conflict, and adaptation as three typical stages during acculturation. The nature, extent, duration, and purpose of the contact affect the magnitude of the acculturation. Conflict occurs as individuals are more or less willing to adjust their cultural values and customs. The task of adjusting one's cultural norms and values is a delicate one and may involve assimilation, integration, separation, and marginalization as immigrants attempt to adjust to their new status (Berry and Annis 1974). Assimilation refers to the process of relinquishing original cultural identity and moving into the larger society. Integration refers to the maintenance of cultural values and integrity, as well as a movement toward participation in the dominant society. Separation refers to the self-imposed withdrawal from the dominant society, and when imposed by a dominant group, separation becomes a form of segregation. Sometimes, an individual may opt for separation as a way to maintain his or her own self-esteem. Marginalization refers to the nonidentification with either one's own or the dominant culture. These ideas of adaptation and acculturation are consonant with Milton Gordon's (1964) writings on assimilation (see chapter 1).

The demands and the task of negotiating and adapting to American culture involve changes in interpersonal relationships and role expectations. For immigrants, many role changes and conflicts have to be negotiated in order to achieve a certain level of comfort or satisfaction in the new home. Amado Padilla (1980) has called these demands, due to the process of acculturation, "acculturative stress."

Berry et al. (1987) maintain that acculturative stress (which may include physical, psychological, and social aspects) negatively affects the health status of an individual. They proposed that the acculturation-stress relationship depends on a number of moderating factors, including the nature of the larger society, the type of acculturating group, the mode of acculturation, and the acculturating individual's demographic, social, and psychological characteristics. The nature of the larger society, as a moderating factor, refers to the host culture's attention to cultural diversity as a multicultural ideology, or a host culture's attention to conformity to one cultural standard as an assimilationist ideology. H. B. Murphy (1965) argued, and provided evidence to support the hypothesis, that immigrants in pluralistic societies experience fewer mental-health problems than those in assimilationist societies.

The modifying aspect related to the type of the acculturating group is also important. Variations exist in the degree of voluntariness, movement, and permanence of contact. Those who choose voluntarily to immigrate may experience less difficulty than those with little choice since the attitude toward contact and change may be more positive.

Similarly, those without permanent social supports may experience more mental-health problems than those more permanently settled and established.

The demographic, social, and psychological characteristics of the acculturating individual can modify the relationship between acculturation and stress. Some individuals possess a variety of coping strategies that may predispose them to successful acculturation, while others are unable to cope successfully. These factors include, among others, education, age, gender, cognitive style, prior intercultural experiences, and contact experiences. These moderating factors between acculturative stress and mental-health outcomes are similar to those espoused by Lazarus (1984) when he argued that personality variables that work to ensure adaptation and reduce psychological distress include appraisals, self-esteem, racial identity, and self-efficacy. Lazarus has also maintained that coping strategies include emotional, cognitive, and problem-solving abilities, as well as social supports and social networks.

Francisco Mena, Amado Padilla, and Margarita Maldonado (1986) investigated acculturative stress and specific coping strategies among immigrants and later-generation college students. Their findings indicate that an individual's age at the time of immigration is associated with different types of coping strategies. Individuals in their study who immigrated before age twelve usually coped with stress by talking to others about their problems. These individuals also had an extensive social network. In contrast, individuals who migrated after age twelve coped with stress by taking an active and planned individualistic approach; they also usually had smaller social networks. In another study, Padilla, Monica Alvarez, and Kathryn Lindholm (1986) investigated the effect of generational status on stress and several personality factors; their results confirm earlier studies showing that immigrants who migrate after the age of twelve experienced more acculturative stress than those who migrate before age twelve.

In a comparative study of acculturative stress, Berry et al. (1987) found that higher education is a consistent predictor of low stress across all groups. The subjects of their study included immigrants, refugees, native peoples, ethnic groups, and sojourners. This study also revealed lower levels of stress among those individuals with greater contact experiences.

COPING WITH THE STRESS OF MIGRATION

How do African immigrants cope with the stress of the cross-cultural transition? Do immigrants go through phases of coping regardless of their status at the time of entry into the United States? In this section, I examine ways African immigrants cope with entry into a new culture and, ultimately, how coping dovetails with utilization patterns of services.

Because the immigration experience is often accompanied by varying levels of acculturative stress, immigrants attempt to cope with the demands of this experience in a variety of ways. Coping has, by definition, always been related to the concept of stress. Coping always implies a referent, namely, what one must cope with under specific circumstances. The concept of coping developed out of the psychological concepts of defense and threat. Lazarus and Opton (1966) state that threat is the key variable in the psychological-stress analysis. Threat is the psychological phenomenon that influences coping in stressful situations.

The early formulations of coping in the 1900s emphasized the concepts of threat and defense. Threat was viewed almost entirely as an internal rather than an environmental phenomenon, and defense mechanisms were viewed as internal protective emotional strategies rather than behavioral coping strategies.

Anna Freud (1946), Karl Menninger (1954), and George Vaillant (1977) each defined coping as a functioning of the ego. In her description, Freud (1946) analyzed various defense mechanisms. Menninger (1954) arranged coping endeavors on a continuum from least to most pathological and ranked them according to the level of internal disorganization they indicate. Vaillant (1977) grouped defenses into four levels, including psychotic mechanisms, immature mechanisms, neurotic mechanisms, and mature mechanisms. These formulations, however, fail to account for adaptive coping behaviors that respond to environmental demands. Instead, they emphasize pathological defensive responses to internal threats. Lazarus and Susan Folkman (1984) have pointed out four limitations to these approaches, some of which have emerged because of operational measures of coping. The four central issues are (1) treatment of coping as a structural trait or style, (2) failure to distinguish coping from automatized adaptive behavior, (3) confusion of coping with adaptational outcome so that the definition and description of a coping process hinges on the adaptational outcome it yields, and (4) the equation of coping with mastery.

In their work, Elizabeth Kubler-Ross (1969) and Colin Parkes (1972) have investigated the normative rules that explain how people cope with environmental and internal demands. Their research on the normative responses to stressful events such as death (Kubler-Ross 1969) and bereavement (Parkes 1972) has yielded a stage theory of coping underlining how coping often changes with time. However, the stage-normative approach often deemphasizes, or fails to account for, individual differences. The approach also confounds the process of coping with its outcome. Another framework used to study the process of coping is the behavioral approach. Behaviorists interpret all psychological phenomena in behavioral terms. The behaviorists have tended to view coping behavior as an adaptive or nonadaptive response to a stressful stimulus. The behavioral theorists have emphasized the environmental demands (stressors) and the action-oriented processes (coping behaviors) that deal with them. Because of the strong emphasis on behavior, behaviorists will admit that the coping behavior of an individual depends on the particular threat variables within the environment and the individual's coping history. However, the behavioral approach to coping has limitations. It emphasizes the coping situation to the exclusion of the individual's personal and contextual variables. Lazarus (1971) termed individual differences the "mediators" of reactions to stressful situations.

In their review of coping, Lazarus and Folkman (1984) pointed out that measures of coping traits and styles underestimate both the complexity and the variability of ways people actually cope, and this has been the case with African immigrants. Coping implies effort, and many coping behaviors "are originally effortful and hence reflect coping, but become automatized through learning processes" (Lazarus and Folkman 1984, 140). These authors also underline the fact that coping must be viewed as efforts to manage stressful demands regardless of outcome, not as mastery over the environment. Lazarus and Folkman emphasized a contextual approach to understanding any coping strategy and define effective coping as "that which allows the person to tolerate, minimize, accept, or ignore what cannot be mastered" (140). By emphasizing the fact that coping involved constantly changing cognitive and behavioral efforts to manage events, Lazarus and Folkman provide a cognitive-phenomenological approach as an alternative to traditional ideas about coping.

This cognitive-phenomenological coping framework addresses certain limitations. First, it is process oriented. Second, the definition seeks to distinguish between coping and automatized adaptive behavior by limiting coping to conditions of psychological stress. Third, coping is defined as efforts made to manage a situation. These efforts include anything a person does or thinks, thereby addressing the problem of confounding coping with outcome. It also makes coping both intrapsychic and action oriented. Fourth, the use of the word "manage" avoids equating coping with mastery. To "manage" can include to master, tolerate, reduce, minimize, avoid, and accept the stressful conditions, as well as to master the environment. Hence, coping involves all efforts to manage, regardless of outcome, which, for most immigrants, also includes the manner in which health services are utilized.

The importance of personal resources in coping is clear; these resources include health and energy, one's existential and personal beliefs, general beliefs about control, commitments (which have a motivational property that can help sustain coping), problem-solving skills, social support, and material resources. Belief systems about an individual's transactions with the environment may also affect one's coping. Beliefs about one's occupation, education, relationships, quality of life, relocation, and death may affect the way an immigrant appraises the difficulties and changes involved in immigration. Similarly, such beliefs do affect appraisal of health care and utilization patterns. Religious beliefs and spiritual well-being may also strongly affect an individual's appraisal of threat when faced with relocation or any threatening life event.

For many African immigrants, Afrocentric values—existential, religious, and spiritual beliefs (Dixon 1976; Jones 1986; Mbiti 1970)—serve as significant coping resources in their lives and, not surprisingly, in their health care utilization as well.

The fact that many African immigrants come to the United States with a belief in the presence of a supreme being or spiritual being underscores their own sense of contingency and belonging to a world beyond themselves. It is not uncommon for these spiritual beings to be invoked in times of difficulty. Many African immigrants will hold the belief of the presence of a superior power in times of stress. African immigrants seek balance through harmony not only with individuals but also with the outside world and nature. Life is perceived as occurring within a larger context governed by a supreme being or by spiritual beings, all of whom control and provide harmony in the lives of individuals, the community, and nature. These values have implications in terms of barriers to help seeking for African immigrants in the United States.

The African worldview reflects an overwhelming interrelationship between the personal and collective worlds. Generally, the self is perceived as part of the community. This community identity is reflected in several proverbs, such as "I am because we are." Most African immigrants continue to live this experience as part of a larger community, and the community for them includes both living and dead members (Mbiti 1970). The will to survive is lived out most intimately in their sense of endurance. Endurance is a form of allowing nature to take its course in humble obedience to a supreme being or spiritual beings, as well as in great defiance of life's adversities.

These coping strategies are "the characteristics or ongoing behaviors that enable individuals to handle stressors more effectively, experience fewer . . . symptoms upon exposure to a stressor, or recover faster from exposure" (Zeidner and Hammer 1990, 693; see also Hammer and Marting 1985).

Other determinants of coping are the constraints that mitigate the use of resources. Linked with one's personal beliefs are personal constraints that include internalized cultural values and beliefs that proscribe certain ways of behaving. There are also environmental constraints that include competing demands for the same resources and agencies or institutions that thwart coping efforts. One's efforts to exercise control are also a way of coping. The discourse on coping has been informed by several recent studies examining the postmigration coping experiences of refugees as they adjust to and cope with the experience of a collective trauma (Fuertes 2004; Goodman 2004; Keyes and Kane 2004). These studies on adaptation and resilience have expanded our understanding of the refugee experience as an adaptive process. At the same time, these studies are limited to the postmigration period, ignoring coping strategies that precede migration (cf. Jasso et al. 2005).

Self-Esteem

Self-esteem is a key mediating variable in coping with stress. Leonard Pearlin and Carmi Schooler (1978) raise the question, Does an efficacious handling of stress depend on what people do or on what people are? They found that personality characteristics indicative of psychological resources, are "the most helpful in sustaining people facing strains arising out of conditions over which they may have little direct control" (Pearlin and Schooler 1978, 13). Self-esteem, or the extent to which a person feels good about, likes, and respects him- or herself, has been shown to aid one's ability to cope with stress.

The importance of self-esteem to one's functioning has been a subject of discussion by early and contemporary theorists. Leading contributors have included Stanley Coopersmith (1967), George Mead (1934), and Mark Rosenberg (1965). These early theorists argued that one's self-esteem comprises various components related to one's subjective experiences and appraisals from others. Others, like Harry Sullivan and Erich Fromm, emphasized the interaction of unconscious, preconscious, and conscious activity within the self as influencing one's experience of self-esteem. Sullivan (1953) proposed that the developmental origins of one's self-esteem arise out of a child's learning and internalizations from childhood, based on a child's experiences of "good me, bad me, and not me." Carl Rogers (1951) has theorized that positive self-esteem depends on a supportive, empathic overall environment, an environment that gives one the sense of being important and valued. Fromm (1955) stated that self-esteem is directly related to one's capacity to experience love. Edith Jacobson (1964) also emphasized the importance of love in producing self-esteem. D. W. Winnicott (1965) used the term *good enough mothering* to portray a mother's support toward an infant, which provides the necessary basis for a positive self-image.

Coopersmith (1967) has done perhaps the most widely known research on self-esteem (cf. Coopersmith Self-Esteem Inventory). Noting that the term *self-esteem* is vague and subject to manifold interpretations, he defined self-esteem as "a personal judgment of worthiness that is expressed in the attitudes the individual holds towards himself [*sic*]" (Coopersmith 1967, 5).

Based on this definition and research, Coopersmith maintains that self-esteem is a set of attitudes and beliefs that a person brings with him- or herself when facing the world. It includes beliefs as to whether he or she can expect success or failure, how much effort should be put forth, whether failure at a task will hurt, and whether he or she will become more capable as a result of different experiences. Self-esteem provides a mental set that prepares the person to respond according to expectations of success, acceptance, and personal strength. Coopersmith observed that feelings of significance enhance one's self-esteem, while feelings of powerlessness diminish it. Based on the Coopersmith Self-Esteem Inventory, a study conducted by Padilla, Y. Wagatsuma, and Lindholm (1985) found that self-esteem is a personality dimension associated with a person's capacity to respond to a stressful environment; they further noted that although self-esteem is considered a stable personality dimension that remains constant under various situations, it may be affected by migration and acculturation. Indeed, studies in race and race relations show, too, that self-esteem is constantly challenged by intergroup interactions.

Other researchers have argued that one's level of self-esteem may be seen as a coping strategy or resource or as enhancing one's coping ability. Blair Wheaton (1983) has stated that self-esteem lowers stress and increases problem-solving ability. K. B. Chan (1977) has also argued that "an individual becomes vulnerable to negative maladaptive stress reactions by virtue of seeing himself [*sic*] being of low self-esteem, and of high anxiety proneness, powerless and helpless, and externally oriented and unable to cope" (97). In the case of African immigrants, the experience of racism in America will have the effect of lowering self-esteem and increasing anxiety as they confront issues of invisibility, inequality, and racial identity (Franklin 1999; Bryce-Laporte 1972; Hardy and Lazloffy 1998). This suggests that the coping mechanisms of black Africans might be compromised when compared to other immigrant groups who are not racially typed as black.

Hardiness

Suzanne Kobasa (1979) has proposed the concept of hardiness as a personality characteristic that serves as a resource in resisting the negative effect of stress. She developed the concept of hardiness from existentialist philosophy, which looks at the best way to confront, utilize, and shape a life that is always changing and therefore, always stressful. Thus, the goal of existence is to create personal meaning through decision making, action, and confronting new possibilities and challenges. The argument is that hardiness consists of commitment, control, and challenge. Hardiness, therefore, refers to one's ability to handle and manage problems or difficulties. It emphasizes viewing hardships and new life experiences as challenges. It also underlines a sense of internal control rather than feeling one is a victim of circumstances. Many African immigrants would embrace this emphasis on life experiences as challenges. Indeed, Kobasa's formulations offer an alternate examination of coping mechanisms and extend, for example, the resources available to native black Americans and immigrants who may experience racism.

Kobasa (1979) looked specifically at inherent personality characteristics that differentiate some individuals from others and concluded that some people have a personality structure that allows them to experience high degrees of stress without experiencing illness. She describes this personality characteristic as hardiness because she believes that it implies an active, rather than a passive, reactive response to stress. Her review of the research demonstrates that the characteristics of control, commitment, and challenge are advantageous qualities in dealing with stress. The hardiness model is based on three hypotheses: (1) people experiencing stress, who have a greater sense of control over what occurs in their lives, will remain healthier than those who feel powerless in the face of external stressors; (2) people experiencing stress, who feel committed to the various areas of their lives, will remain healthier than those who feel alienated; and (3) people experiencing stress, who view change as a challenge, will remain healthier than those who view change as a threat. Hardy people, therefore, possess these three basic characteristics, commitment, control, and challenge, which were found to have several consequences for constructive behavior.

Kobasa (1979) concluded, using instruments she developed to measure commitment, control, and challenge, that personality may directly affect one's ability to stay healthy and that the hardy individual articulates a sense of meaningfulness to life events and has an internal locus of control. The belief that they can control or influence their life events allows hardy people to exercise greater control over their courses of action, to develop greater coping skills, and to develop "the ability to interpret, appraise and incorporate various sorts of stressful events into an ongoing life plan" (Kobasa 1979, 3). Also, hardy people's ability to feel deeply involved with or committed to their life activities minimizes their feeling of alienation, giving them a sense of purpose, and supports their internal balance or confidence. Finally, their anticipation of change as an exciting challenge enables hardy persons to explore their environments and to seek support resources to cope with stress.

Other researchers have demonstrated that a hardy personality may serve as a buffer to moderate the potentially harmful effects of stressful life events (Lambert and Lambert 1987; Holahan and Moos 1985) and that hardiness probably works in concert with other psychological variables (Kobasa, Maddi, and Pucetti 1982). While the original study on hardiness used an all-male sample, it has been shown that the concept is generalizable to women as well (Kobasa et al. 1985). Other studies have shown that hardiness is a significant predictor of psychological well-being among women (Lambert and Lambert 1987).

The studies conducted by Kobasa and her colleagues led them to assert that a hardy personality uses cognition, affect, and action to transform a stressful situation. It has been hypothesized that the constellation of commitment, control, and challenge moderates the effects of stress by altering the perception of the event from one of disaster to one of challenge and by instituting positive coping. Kuo and Tsai Yung-Mei (1986) explored the effect of hardiness and social networking on the mental health of immigrants and concluded that "the hardy person's ability to plan for the future, to take risks, to feel confident in personal ability, and to tolerate uncertainty seems to coincide with the requirements for successful adaptation" (138).

CONCLUSION

The consensus in the literature on adjustment and coping is that immigrant adaptation and acculturation occur over time. Ilana Redstone and Douglas Massey (2004) put it succinctly when they write that "where theories differ is with respect to the nature and pace of adjustment, not its occurrence. As foreigners accumulate time in the host country and learn its language, social conventions, and cultural practices, behaviors and outcomes are altered in systematic ways" (721). This assimilationist approach, however, ignores the complexity of experiences that immigrants go through. Indeed, the question remains as to how much newer experiences help to rework older experiences in people's lives. As Alejandro Portes and Rubén Rumbaut (2001) point out, immigrants' identities are continually being molded as they accumulate more years in their land of settlement, come into contact with and compete with natives, and encounter prejudice and discrimination.

African immigrants come from a variety of contexts; therefore, no one narrative can capture the myriad of immigrant experiences. For many African immigrants seeking mental health services, delayed positive outcomes from psychotropic medications lead to questions of efficacy (i.e., depression, anxiety if not cured right away), creating a self-fulfilling prophecy about the effectiveness of these services. At the same time, many African immigrants will not admit to being depressed or affected by the difficulties of migration, and if they are indeed depressed, they will work hard to get out of the depression. Since many African immigrants will not admit to being depressed, few will seek treatment for depression. Similarly, immediate negative side effects of psychotropic drugs increase ambivalence toward mental health interventions (e.g., dry mouth, headaches, stomach aches, low sexual energy, all of which become too high a cost in exchange for symptom relief).

In terms of accessing health services, African immigrants struggle as they negotiate the complex web of American society and learn about the health-care system. The immigrant experience becomes more bearable if health practitioners also educate themselves about the various customs, cultures, and values that affect their clients. To do so, they must develop a listening stance that acknowledges the complexities of the narratives of African immigrants. These practitioners must be prepared to learn and to challenge themselves when treating immigrants from different ethnic backgrounds. They should listen carefully to values regarding the importance of kinship, gender, generational roles, class, politics, spirituality, work, and leisure (Kamya 2005). This is especially important because there may be cultural variations among seemingly homogenous racial groups that affect health behaviors and beliefs. The psychocultural orientation of African immigrants needs to be taken into account. Therefore, a holistic approach is crucial in attending to African immigrants. A holistic picture must not only look at African immigrants in their presentation but must address all contexts of the African immigrant's life.

Government agencies and educational institutions ought to commit themselves to training culturally competent practitioners. The training ought to focus not only on the recruitment but also the retention of Africans in the helping professions. A commitment to examine best practices for African immigrants and to measure program effectiveness is essential to the viability and sustainability of these programs. Education and curricula must offer depth in the exploration of cultural competency. Such a commitment to cultural competency must address issues of health in its complexity from the Africans' worldviews. Helping professionals need to explore various concepts, such as healing, wholeness, self, community, and God. Providing culturally sensitive health services is the key strategy for addressing the stress of migration and helping these immigrants maintain health in their new homes.

One issue uncovered by the writing of this chapter is the paucity of data on African immigrants. More research is needed on how African immigrants cope with stresses related to migration. We lack important information about the stressors during critical moments in the journey of these African immigrants, as well as knowledge about their coping strategies at specific points in dealing with chronic challenges or short-lived experiences during migration.

REFERENCES

Akhtar, Salman. 1999. *Immigration and Identity: Turmoil, Treatment and Transformation.* Northvale, NJ: Jason Aronson.

Apraku, Kofi. 1991. *African Emigres in the United States*. Westport, CT: Praeger.

Arredondo-Dowd, Patricia. 1981. "Personal Loss and Grief as a Result of Migration." *Personnel and Guidance Journal* 59: 376–78.

Arthur, John. 2000. *Invisible Sojourners: African Immigrant Diaspora in the United States*. Westport, CT: Praeger.

Berger, Roni. 2004. *Immigrant Women Tell Their Stories*. New York: Haworth Press.

Berry, John W. 1980. "Acculturation and Adaptation." In *Acculturation: Theory, Models and Some New Findings*, ed. Amado M. Padilla, 9–25. Boulder, CO: Westview Press.

Berry, John W., and Robert Annis. 1974. "Acculturative Stress: The Role of Ecology, Culture, and Differentiation." *Journal of Cross-Culture Psychology* 5: 382–406.

Berry, John W., Uichol Kim, Thomas Minde, and Doris Mok. 1987. "Comparative Studies of Acculturative Stress." *International Migration Review* 21, no. 3 (autumn): 491–511.

Bryce-Laporte, Roy S. 1972. "Black Immigrants: The Experience of Invisibility and Inequality." *Journal of Black Studies* 3, no. 1: 29–56.

Cervantes, Richard C., and Felipe G. Castro. 1985. "Stress, Coping, and Mexican American Mental Health: A Systematic Review." *Hispanic Journal of Behavioral Science* 7: 1–73.

Chan, K. B. 1977. "Individual Differences in Reactions to Stress and Their Personality and Situational Determinants: Some Implications for Community Mental Health." *Social Science and Medicine* 11: 89–103.

Coll, Cynthia G., and Katherine Magnuson. 1997. "The Psychological Experience of Immigration: A Developmental Perspective." In *Immigration and the Family: Research and Policy on U.S. Immigrants*, ed. Alan Booth, Ann C. Crouter, and Nancy Landale, 91–131. Hillsdale, NJ: Lawrence Erlbaum Associates.

Coopersmith, Stanley. 1967. *The Antecedents of Self-Esteem*. Palo Alto, CA: Consulting Psychologists Press.

———. 1990. *Self-Esteem Inventories*. Palo Alto, CA: Consulting Psychologists Press.

Dixon, V. J. 1976. "World Views and Research Methodology." In *African Philosophy: Assumptions and Paradigms for Research on Black Persons*, ed. L. King, Vernon Dixon, and W. Nobles, 38–51. Los Angeles: Fannon Research and Development Center.

Djamba, Yanyi K. 1999. "African Immigrants in the United States: A Socio-Demographic Profile in Comparison to Native Blacks." *Journal of Asian and African Studies* 34, no. 2: 210–15.

Dohrenwend, Barbara Snell, and Bruce P. Dohrenwend. 1974. *Stressful Life Events: Their Nature and Effects*. New York: Wiley.

Drachman, Diane, and Angela Shen Ryan. 1991. "Immigrants and Refugees." In *Handbook of Social Work Practice with Vulnerable Populations*, ed. Alex Gitterman, 618–46. New York: Columbia University Press.

Dyal, J. A., and R. Y. Dyal. 1981. "Acculturation, Stress and Coping." *International Journal of Intercultural Relations* 5: 301–28.

Eisenstadt, Shmuel N. 1955. *The Absorption of Immigrants*. Glencoe, IL: Free Press.

Franklin, Anderson. 1999. "Invisibility Syndrome and Racial Identity Development in Psychotherapy and Counseling African American Men." *Counseling Psychologist* 27, no. 6: 761–93

Freud, Anna. 1946. *War and Children*. New York: Medical War Books.

Fromm, Erich. 1955. *The Sane Society*. New York: Rinehart and Company.

Fuertes, Al B. 2004. "In Their Own Words: Contextualizing the Discourse of (War) Trauma and Healing." *Conflict Resolution Quarterly* 21, no. 4: 491–501.

Garza-Guerrero, César. 1974. "Culture Shock: Its Mourning and the Vicissitudes of Identity." *Journal of the American Psychoanalytic Association* 22: 408–29.

Glassman, Urania, and Louise Skolnik. 1984. "The Role of Social Group Work in Refugee Resettlement." *Social Work with Groups* 7: 45–62.

Goodman, Janice H. 2004. "Coping with Trauma and Hardship among Unaccompanied Refugee Youths from Sudan." *Qualitative Health Research* 14, no. 9: 1176–96.

Gordon, Milton M. 1964. *Assimilation in American Life: The Role of Race, Religion and National Origins.* New York: Oxford University Press.

Grinker, Roy R., and John P. Spiegel. 1945. *Men under Stress.* New York: McGraw-Hill.

Hammer, Allen, and Susan Marting. 1985. *Manual for Coping Resources Inventory.* Palo Alto, CA: Consulting Psychologists Press.

Handlin, Oscar. 1951. *The Uprooted.* New York: Grosset and Dunlop Publishers.

Hardy, Kenneth, and Tracy Lazloffy. 1998. "The Dynamics of a Pro-Racist Ideology: Implications for Family Therapists." In *Re-Visioning Family Therapy: Race, Culture and Gender in Clinical Practice,* ed. Monica McGoldrick, 118–28. New York: Guilford Publications.

Holahan, Charles J., and Rudolf H. Moos. 1985. "Life Stress and Health: Personality, Coping, and Family Support in Stress Resistance." *Journal of Personality and Social Psychology* 49, no. 3: 739–47.

Holmes, Thomas H., and Richard H. Rahe. 1967. "The Social Readjustment Rating Scale." *Journal of Psychosomatic Research* 11: 213–18.

Jaco, E. Gartly. 1954. "The Social Isolation Hypothesis and Schizophrenia." *American Sociological Review* 19: 567–77.

Jacobson, Edith. 1964. *The Self and the Object World.* New York: International Universities Press.

Jasso, Guillermina, Douglas S. Massey, Mark R. Rosenzweig, and James P. Smith. 2005. "Immigration, Health, and New York City: Early Results Based on the U.S. New Immigrant Cohort of 2003." *Federal Reserve Bank of New York Economic Policy Review* (December): 127–51.

Jones, James M. 1986. "Racism: A Cultural Analysis of the Problems." In *Prejudice, Discrimination and Racism,* ed. John F. Dovidio and Samuel Gaertner, 279–314. Orlando, FL: Academic Press.

Kamya, Hugo. 1997. "African Immigrants in the United States: The Challenge for Research and Practice." *Social Work* 42: 154–65.

———. 2005. "African Immigrant Families." In *Ethnicity and Family Therapy,* ed. Monica McGoldrick, Joe Giordano, and Nydia Garcia-Preto, 101–16. 3rd ed. New York: Guilford Press.

Kamya, Hugo, and David Trimble. 2002. "Response to Injury: Toward Ethical Construction of the Other." *Journal of Systemic Therapies* 21, no. 3: 19–29.

Keyes, Emily F., and Catherine F. Kane. 2004. "Belonging and Adapting: Mental Health of Bosnian Refugees Living in the United States." *Issues in Mental Health Nursing* 25, no. 8: 809–31.

Kobasa, Suzanne. 1979. "Stressful Life Events, Personality, and Health: An Inquiry into Hardiness." *Journal of Personality and Social Psychology* 37, no. 1: 1–11.

Kobasa, Suzanne, Salvatore Maddi, and M. Pucetti. 1982. "Personality and Exercise as Buffers in the Stress-Illness Relationship." *Journal of Behavioral Medicine* 5, no. 4: 391–403.

Kobasa, Suzanne, Salvatore Maddi, M. Pucetti, and M. Zola. 1985. "Effectiveness of Hardiness, Exercise and Social Support as Resources against Illness." *Journal of Psychosomatic Research* 29, no. 5: 525–33.

Kubler-Ross, Elizabeth. 1969. *On Death and Dying.* New York: Macmillan.

Kuo, Wen. 1976. "Theories of Migration and Mental Health: An Empirical Testing on Chinese-Americans." *Social Science and Medicine* 10: 297–306.

Kuo, Wen, and Yung-Mei Tsai. 1986. "Social Networking, Hardiness and Immigrant's Mental Health." *Journal of Health and Social Behavior* 27, no. 2: 133–49.

Lambert, C. E., and V. A. Lambert. 1987. "Hardiness: Its Development and Relevance to Nursing." *Image: Journal of Nursing Scholarship* 19, no. 2: 92–95.

Lazarus, Richard S. 1971. "The Concepts of Stress and Disease." In *Society, Stress and Disease*, ed. L. Levi, 53–58. New York: Oxford University Press.

———. 1984. "Puzzles in the Study of Daily Hassles." *Journal of Behavioral Medicine* 7: 375–89.

Lazarus, Richard S., and Susan Folkman. 1984. *Stress, Appraisal, and Coping*. New York: Springer.

Lazarus, Richard S., and Edward M. Opton. 1966. "The Use of Motion Picture Films in the Study of Psychological Stress: A Summary of Theoretical Formulations and Experimental Findings." In *Anxiety and Behavior*, ed. C. D. Spielberger. New York: Academic Press.

Martinez, Joe L., and Richard H. Mendoza, eds. 1984. *Chicano Psychology*. New York: Academic Press.

Mbiti, John S. 1970. *African Religions and Philosophy*. New York: Doubleday.

McCulloch, Jock. 1995. *Colonial Psychiatry and the African Mind*. Cambridge: Cambridge University Press.

McEwen, Bruce, and Elizabeth N. Lasley. 2002. *The End of Stress as We Know It*. Washington DC: Joseph Henry Press.

McGoldrick, Monica, and Joe Giordano. 1996. "Overview: Ethnicity and Family Therapy." In *Ethnicity and Family Therapy*, ed. Monica McGoldrick, Joe Giordano, and John K. Pearce, 1–30. 2nd ed. New York: Guilford Press.

Mead, George H. 1934. *Mind, Self and Society*. Chicago: University of Chicago Press.

Mena, Francisco J., Amado M. Padilla, and Margarita Maldonado. 1986. "Acculturative Stress and Specific Coping Strategies among Immigrant and Later Generation College Students." *Hispanic Journal of Behavioral Sciences* 9: 207–25.

Menninger, Karl. 1954. "Regulatory Devices of the Ego under Major Stress." *International Journal of Psychoanalysis* 35: 412–20.

Mezey, A. G. 1960. "Psychiatric Aspects of Human Migrations." *International Journal of Social Psychiatry* 5: 245–65.

Moos, Rudolf H., ed. 1976. *Human Adaptation*. Lexington, MA: D.C. Heath and Company.

Murphy, H. B. 1965. "Migration and Mental Health Disorders." In *Mobility and Mental Health*, ed. Mildred Kantor, 221–49. Springfield, MA: Charles C. Thomas Publishers.

Naditch, M. P., and R. F. Morrissey. 1976. "Role Stress, Personality, and Psychopathology in a Group of Immigrant Adolescents." *Journal of Abnormal Psychology* 85, no. 1: 113–18.

Oberg, Kalvero. 1960. "Cultural Shock—Adjustment to New Cultural Environments." *Practical Anthropology* 7: 177–82.

Padilla, Amado M., ed. 1980. *Acculturation: Theory, Models and Some New Findings*. Boulder, CO: Westview Press.

Padilla, Amado M., Monica Alvarez, and Kathryn Lindholm. 1986. "Generational Status and Personality Factors as Predictors of Stress in Students." *Hispanic Journal of Behavioral Sciences* 8: 275–88.

Padilla, Amado M., Y. Wagatsuma, and Kathryn Lindholm. 1985. "Acculturation and Personality as Predictors of Stress in Japanese and Japanese-Americans." *Journal of Social Psychology* 125: 295–305.

Parkes, Colin. 1972. *Bereavement*. New York: International Universities Press.

Pearlin, Leonard I., and Carmi Schooler. 1978. "The Structure of Coping." *Journal of Health and Social Behavior* 19: 2–21.

Portes, Alejandro, and Rubén G. Rumbaut. 2001. *The Story of the Immigrant Second Generation*. Berkeley: University of California Press.

Redstone, Ilana, and Douglas S. Massey. 2004. "Coming to Stay: An Analysis of the U.S. Census Question on Immigrants' Year of Arrival." *Demography* 41, no. 4: 721–38.

Richardson, Alan. 1967. "Theory and a Method for the Psychological Study of Assimilation." *International Migration Review* 2: 3–30.

Rogers, Carl. 1951. *Client-Centered Therapy*. Boston: Houghton Mifflin Company.

Rosenberg, Mark. 1965. *Society and the Adolescent Self Image*. Princeton, NJ: Princeton University Press.

Roskies, E., M. Iida-Miranda, and M. G. Strobel. 1975. "Life Changes as Predictors of Illness in Immigrants." *Journal of Psychosomatic Research* 19: 235–40.

Schneller, Debra P. 1981. "The Immigrant's Challenge: Mourning the Loss of Homeland and Adapting to the New World." *Smith College Studies in Social Work*: 95–125.

Selye, Hans. 1974. *Stress without Distress*. New York: J. B. Lippincott Company.

——. 1976. *The Stress of Life*. New York: McGraw-Hill.

Shuval, Judith T. 1993. "Migration and Stress." In *Handbook of Stress: Theoretical and Clinical Aspects*, ed. Leo Goldberger and Shlomo Breznitz, 641–57. New York: Free Press.

Sluzki, Carlos. 1979. Migration and Family Conflict. *Family Process* 18, no. 4: 379–90.

Smither, Robert, and Marta Rodriguez-Giegling. 1982. "Personality, Demographics, and Acculturation of Vietnamese and Nicaraguan Refugees to the United States." *International Journal of Psychology* 17: 19–25.

Stewart, Edward C. 1986. "The Survival Stage of Intercultural Communication." *International Christian University Bulletin* 1: 109–21.

Sullivan, Harry S. 1953. *The Interpersonal Theory of Psychiatry*. New York: W. W. Norton Company.

Taft, Ronald. 1977. "Coping with Unfamiliar Cultures." In *Studies in Cross-Cultural Psychology*, ed. Neil Warren, 121–53. London: Academic Press.

Takyi, Baffour. 2002. "The Making of the Second Diaspora: On the Recent African American Immigrant Community in the United States of America." *Western Journal of Black Studies* 26: 32–44.

Vaillant, George E. 1977. *Adaptation to Life*. Boston: Little, Brown and Company.

Wheaton, Blair. 1983. "Stress, Personal Coping Resources, and Psychiatric Symptoms: An Investigation of Interactive Models." *Journal of Health and Social Behavior* 24: 208–29.

Winnicott, D. W. 1965. *The Maturational Processes and the Facilitating Environment*. Madison, CT: International Universities Press.

Zeidner, M., and Allen Hammer. 1990. "Life Events and Coping Resources as Predictors of Stress Symptoms in Adolescents." *Personal Individual Differences* 11, no. 7: 693–703.

Selected Data from the
New Immigrant Survey

The New Immigrant Survey (NIS) is a multicohort, prospective-retrospective panel study of new immigrants to the United States. The first full cohort (NIS-2003) sampled immigrants from May to November 2003. The sampling frame consists of newly arrived immigrants. It is the first survey of this kind to provide a wide range of data on immigrants in the United States.

The baseline adult (eighteen years of age or older) survey was conducted from June 2003 to June 2004 and included a nationally representative sample of adult immigrants admitted to legal permanent residence during a specified period based on electronic administrative records compiled for new immigrants by the U.S. government (through the then Immigration and Naturalization Service, or INS). Geographic sampling design includes all top eighty-five metropolitan statistical areas (MSAs) and all top thirty-eight counties. A random sample of ten MSAs and fifteen county pairs was selected. Interviews were conducted in respondents' preferred languages. Survey content includes demographic and family background, health measures, social variables, economic items, and housing environment. The response rate was 68.6 percent.

The NIS was supported by several federal agencies and is a collaborative project of RAND, Princeton University, New York University, and Yale University. The data were collected by the National Opinion Research Center at the University of Chicago.

The tables presented here provide information on current marital status, number of jobs held, number of years of schooling completed, whether respondents own the place where they live, self-rating of health condition, respondents' health before coming to the United States, religious service attendance in the United States, whether respondents have ever felt sad about the immigration process, and whether they intend to live in the United States for the rest of their lives. We excluded information from the broad category of "Latin America and Caribbean" because of the preponderance of data on people who do not consider themselves black. We do not make inferences from these data.

Cell sizes for some of the frequency distributions are small. Where the frequency count is less than ten (<10), data are represented by a dash (–). Percentages and frequency counts are both reported.

Table A.1. Sample Size of Adult Survey

Country/Region of Birth	
Sub-Saharan Africa (excluding Nigeria and Ethiopia)	392
Nigeria	172
Ethiopia	199
Jamaica	116
Haiti	152
Dominican Republic	166

Table A.2. Current Marital Status

Country/Region of Birth	Married	Living Together, Not Married	Separated/ Divorced or Widowed	Never Married
Sub-Saharan Africa (excluding Nigeria and Ethiopia)	59.9% 235	2.6% 10	9.9% 39	27.6% 108
Nigeria	48.8% 84	—	11.6% 20	38.9% 67
Ethiopia	47.2% 94	—	—	47.2% 94
Jamaica	44.8% 52	—	—	50.9% 59
Haiti	38.2% 58	—	13.2% 20	44.7% 68
Dominican Republic	38.5% 64	6.6% 11	12.7% 21	42.2% 70

Compare discussion in chapter 4.

Table A.3.   Current Employment: Number of Jobs Held

Country/Region of Birth	One	Two or More
Sub-Saharan Africa (excluding Nigeria and Ethiopia)	89.6% 190	10.4% 22
Nigeria	86.6% 71	13.4% 11
Ethiopia	90% 90	10% 10
Jamaica	91.1% 51	—
Haiti	92.1% 58	—
Dominican Republic	100% 87	—

Compare discussion in chapter 5.

Table A.4.   Number of Years of Schooling Completed

Country/Region of Birth	1 to 12	13 to 16	17+
Sub-Saharan Africa (excluding Nigeria and Ethiopia)	29.9% 117	38.3% 150	27.3% 107
Nigeria	23.8% 41	42.4% 73	29.6% 51
Ethiopia	48.8% 97	41.2% 82	8.1% 16
Jamaica	58.6% 68	28.5% 33	12.1% 33
Haiti	44.7% 68	28.9% 44	9.9% 15
Dominican Republic	71.7% 119	15.1% 25	8.4% 14

Compare information in chapters 2 and 5.

Table A.5.   Ownership of Residence*

Country/Region of Birth	
Sub-Saharan Africa (excluding Nigeria and Ethiopia)	12.3% 39
Nigeria	13.5% 19
Ethiopia	—
Jamaica	16.3% 16
Haiti	9.3% 13
Dominican-Republic	—

*Item nonresponse is high for a corollary variable: real estate ownership outside of the United States. Item nonresponse is also high for money transfers. Compare discussion in chapter 2.

Table A.6.   Self-Rating of Health Condition

Country/Region of Birth	Excellent or Very Good	Good	Fair or Poor
Sub-Saharan Africa (excluding Nigeria and Ethiopia)	76.5% 300	18.4% 72	5.1% 20
Nigeria	84.9% 146	11.6% 20	—
Ethiopia	80.4% 160	18.1% 36	—
Jamaica	72.4% 84	18.9% 22	8.6% 10
Haiti	54.6% 83	26.9% 41	17.1% 26
Dominican Republic	64.5% 107	22.3% 37	12.6% 21

Compare discussion in chapter 9.

Table A.7.   Health before Coming to United States

Country/Region of Birth	Better	Same	Worse
Sub-Saharan Africa (excluding Nigeria and Ethiopia)	22.4% 85	71.2% 270	6.3% 24
Nigeria	17.5% 29	76.5% 127	—
Ethiopia	11.6% 23	83.4% 166	5% 10
Jamaica	16.1% 18	76.8% 86	—
Haiti	25.7% 39	64.5% 98	8.6% 13
Dominican Republic	18.5% 29	77.1% 121	—

Compare discussion in chapter 9.

Table A.8.   Attendance of Religious Services in United States

Country/Region of Birth	
Sub-Saharan Africa (excluding Nigeria and Ethiopia)	34.8% 132
Nigeria	12.7% 21
Ethiopia	15.6% 31
Jamaica	38.4% 43
Haiti	18.5% 28
Dominican Republic	44.6% 70

Compare discussion in chapter 6.

Table A.9.   Experience of Sadness about Immigration Process

Country/Region of Birth	Yes	No
Sub-Saharan Africa (excluding Nigeria and Ethiopia)	15.6% 59	84.4% 320
Nigeria	19.3% 33	80.1% 133
Ethiopia	22.6% 45	77.4% 154
Jamaica	19.6% 22	79.6% 89
Haiti	11.9% 18	87.4% 132
Dominican Republic	21.7% 34	78.3% 123

Table A.10.   Intention to Live in United States for Rest of Life

Country/Region of Birth	Yes	No	Don't Know
Sub-Saharan Africa (excluding Nigeria and Ethiopia)	75.0% 144	12.5% 24	12.5% 24
Nigeria	73.8% 62	15.5% 13	—
Ethiopia	84.5% 98	11.2% 13	—
Jamaica	78.6% 44	—	17.9% 10
Haiti	67.1% 49	17.8% 13	13.7% 10
Dominican Republic	81.3% 65	—	—

About the Authors

Joe R. Feagin was the ninety-first president of the American Sociological Association. His presidential address was entitled "Social Justice and Sociology in the 21st Century." He is currently Ella C. McFadden Professor of Liberal Arts at Texas A&M University. Among his forty-eight books are the following recent ones: (with Clairece Feagin) *Racial and Ethnic Relations*, 7th ed. (2003); (with Kenneth Bolton) *Black in Blue: Black Police Officers in White Departments* (2004); *Systemic Racism* (2006); *Social Problems: A Power-Conflict Perspective*, 6th ed. (2006).

Solomon Getahun is an assistant professor of history at Central Michigan University. He was Fulbright Fellow in 2002–2003. His publications include *History of the City of Gondar* (2005) and a monograph titled *The History of Ethiopian Immigrants and Refugees in America, 1900–2000, Patterns of Migration, Survival, and Adjustment* in The New Americans: Recent Immigration and American Society Series (2006).

Lewis R. Gordon is the Laura Carnell University Professor of Philosophy and director of the Institute for the Study of Race and Social Thought and the Center for Afro-Jewish Studies at Temple University. He is also an ongoing visiting professor of government and philosophy at the University of the West Indies at Mona, Jamaica, and president of the Caribbean Philosophical Association. He is the author of several books; recent works include *Disciplinary Decadence: Living Thought in Trying Times* (2006) and *An Introduction to Africana Philosophy* (2006).

Regine O. Jackson is an assistant professor of American studies at Emory University. She has been a fellow at Harvard University's DuBois Institute, the Salzburg Seminar, and Boston University's Institute on Race and Social Division, and she has been an Open Society Institute Visiting Scholar at Vilnius University in Lithuania. Her work has been published in the *Journal of Haitian Studies*, *African American Research Perspectives*, and *Wadabagei: A Journal of the Caribbean and Its Diaspora*. She is currently completing her first book, entitled *No Longer Invisible: Haitian Immigrants in the "New" Boston.*

Hugo Kamya is an associate professor of clinical practice at Simmons College School of Social Work. He was previously associate professor and chair of the clinical program at Boston College Graduate School of Social Work. He has worked extensively with Sudanese and other African refuges and immigrants and is frequently called as an expert witness in refugee asylum cases. His research publications have appeared in *Social Work*, *Journal of Systemic Therapies*, and the edited volume *Ethnicity and Family Therapy*, 3rd ed. (2005). His clinical practice is in Arlington, Massachusetts.

Ana S. Q. Liberato is a visiting assistant professor in women's studies at the University of Florida. Her areas of interest include social stratification, globalization, transnationalism, and political attitudes and behavior. Her current research also explores the relationship between memory and political attitudes, as well as racial identity among Dominican and Caribbean immigrants in the United States.

John R. Logan is a professor of sociology and director of the initiative on spatial structures in the social sciences at Brown University. Until summer 2004, he was a distinguished professor of sociology at the University at Albany, State University of New York, as well as director of the Lewis Mumford Center for Comparative Urban and Regional Research. His books include *Beyond the City Limits: Urban Policy and Economic Restructuring in Comparative Perspective* (1990) and *The New Chinese City: Globalization and Market Reform* (2002).

Harriette Pipes McAdoo is University Distinguished Professor at Michigan State University, Department of Family and Child Ecology. She was a professor at Howard University in the School of Social Work and a visiting lecturer at Smith College, the University of Washington, and the University of Minnesota. Her books include *Family Ethnicity: Strength in Diversity,* 2nd ed. (1999) and *Black Children: Social, Educational, and Parental Environments,* 2nd ed. (2002).

Yoku Shaw-Taylor is a research scientist at the National Opinion Research Center at the University of Chicago. He has taught at the University of Maryland, George Washington University, Goucher College, and the University of Baltimore. His research publications include a monograph titled *Measurement of Community Health: The Social Health Index* (1999) and studies in *Teaching Sociology, Journal of African Development, Health Affairs,* and *Cities: The International Journal of Urban Policy and Planning.*

Yanick St. Jean is a visiting assistant professor of sociology at the University of Wisconsin, Eau Claire. Beginning in September 2006, she will be a Fulbright Scholar at the L'Université Catholique de l'Afrique de l'Ouest, located in Cotonou, Benin, in West Africa. She has taught at the University of Nevada and University of Wisconsin, Parkside. She coauthored, with Joe R. Feagin, the book *Double Burden: Black Women and Everyday Racism* (1998).

Steven A. Tuch is a professor of sociology at George Washington University. He has published widely on racial attitudes. His books include (coedited with Jack Martin) *Racial Attitudes in the 1990s: Continuity and Change* (1997) and (with Ronald Weitzer) *Race* and *Policing in America: Conflict and Reform* (2006).

Sinead Younge is a postdoctoral fellow at the Emory School of Public Health's Department of Behavioral Science and Health Education. Her research publications have appeared in *Journal of African American Studies, Journal of Adolescence,* and *Race and Society.*